Modern Critical Views

Edward Albee
African-American
 Poets Volume I
American and
 Canadian Women
 Poets, 1930–present
American Women
 Poets, 1650–1950
Maya Angelou
Asian-American
 Writers
Margaret Atwood
Jane Austen
James Baldwin
Samuel Beckett
Saul Bellow
The Bible
William Blake
Jorge Luis Borges
Ray Bradbury
The Brontës
Gwendolyn Brooks
Elizabeth Barrett
 Browning
Robert Browning
Italo Calvino
Albert Camus
Lewis Carroll
Willa Cather
Cervantes
Geoffrey Chaucer
Anton Chekhov
Kate Chopin
Agatha Christie
Samuel Taylor
 Coleridge
Joseph Conrad
Contemporary Poets
Stephen Crane
Dante
Daniel Defoe
Charles Dickens
Emily Dickinson

John Donne and the
 17th-Century Poets
Fyodor Dostoevsky
W.E.B. Du Bois
George Eliot
T. S. Eliot
Ralph Ellison
Ralph Waldo Emerson
William Faulkner
F. Scott Fitzgerald
Sigmund Freud
Robert Frost
George Gordon, Lord
 Byron
Graham Greene
Thomas Hardy
Nathaniel Hawthorne
Ernest Hemingway
Hispanic-American
 Writers
Homer
Langston Hughes
Zora Neale Hurston
Henrik Ibsen
John Irving
Henry James
James Joyce
Franz Kafka
John Keats
Jamaica Kincaid
Stephen King
Rudyard Kipling
D. H. Lawrence
Ursula K. Le Guin
Sinclair Lewis
Bernard Malamud
Christopher Marlowe
Gabriel García
 Márquez
Cormac McCarthy
Carson McCullers
Herman Melville
Molière

Arthur Miller
John Milton
Molière
Toni Morrison
Native-American
 Writers
Joyce Carol Oates
Flannery O'Connor
Eugene O'Neill
George Orwell
Octavio Paz
Sylvia Plath
Edgar Allan Poe
Katherine Anne
 Porter
J. D. Salinger
Jean-Paul Sartre
William Shakespeare:
 Histories and
 Poems
William Shakespeare:
 Romances
William Shakespeare:
 The Comedies
William Shakespeare:
 The Tragedies
George Bernard Shaw
Mary Wollstonecraft
 Shelley
Percy Bysshe Shelley
Alexander
 Solzhenitsyn
Sophocles
John Steinbeck
Tom Stoppard
Jonathan Swift
Amy Tan
Alfred, Lord Tennyson
Henry David Thoreau
J. R. R. Tolkien
Leo Tolstoy
Mark Twain
John Updike

Modern Critical Views

Modern Critical Views

CORMAC McCARTHY

Edited and with an introduction by
Harold Bloom
Sterling Professor of the Humanities
Yale University

CHELSEA HOUSE PUBLISHERS
Philadelphia

©2002 by Chelsea House Publishers, a subsidiary of
Haights Cross Communications.

Introduction © 2001 by Harold Bloom.

Printed and bound in the United States of America

10 9 8 7 6 5 4 3 2

Library of Congress Cataloging-in-Publication Data

Cormac McCarthy / edited and with an introduction by Harold Bloom.
      p. cm. – (Modern critical views)
   Includes bibliographical references and index.
   ISBN 0-7910-6333-X (alk. paper)
   1.McCarthy, Cormac, 1933---Criticism and interpretation. 2. Mexican-American
Border Region--In literature. 3. Southern States--In literature. 4. Tennessee, East--In
literature. I. Bloom, Harold. II. Series.

PS3563.C337 Z624 2001
813'.54--dc21
                                                            2001053682

contributing editor: Pamela Loos

http://www.chelseahouse.com

Contents

Editor's Note

My Introduction centers upon Judge Holden, the frightening prophet of War Everlasting in Cormac McCarthy's masterwork, *Blood Meridian*.

John M. Grammer, who regards the superb *Suttree* as McCarthy's best novel, reads in it an ultimate nihilism, akin to Beckett's.

Blood Meridian returns in Leo Daughery's intense essay, where Judge Holden is viewed as a Gnostic Archon, a ruler of the *kenoma* or cosmological emptiness in which we dwell.

Vereen Bell, commenting upon John Grady Cole, in the admirable *All the Pretty Horses*, sees McCarthy's protagonist as a visionary quester, riding on in search of his own country, while Edwin T. Arnold reminds us of McCarthy's pervasive mysticism.

To Wade Hall, McCarthy is one of the "serious comedians"— Aristophanes, Dante, Faulkner—whose human comedy is life-affirming, after which Tim Parrish presents a very different vision, shared by McCarthy with the fierce Flannery O'Connor, in which the American spirit and the American God alike seek one another with exuberant violence.

We return to *All the Pretty Horses* in Sara L. Spurgeon's dark essay, in which John Grady Cole is judged as sharing in the blindness of the "sacred cowboy myth," while Barcley Owens finds in John Grady's fate, in *Cities of the Plain*, an American version of the tragic hero.

Dianne C. Luce, returning us to the early McCarthy, discovers a continuity in the quest of his protagonists to get beyond the historicized past to a truth perhaps open to transcendence, after which Charles Bailey finds John Grady Cole in *Cities of the Plain* to be more pathetic than tragic.

The metaphor of "burden crossings" in the trilogy is interpreted by Mark Busby as an exaltation of storytelling itself as a kind of "nihilistic optimism." In this volume's final essay, Grace Kim brings us back to Judge Holden, shrewdly doubting his claim to divinity, since he destroys "all potential successors or heirs." To uncover in Holden his own deep anxiety in regard to the Kid (kid, in McCarthy's spelling) is another reminder that *Blood Meridian* is endless to meditation, a novel worthy of comparison to *Moby-Dick* and to Faulkner at his strongest in *As I Lay Dying* and *Light in August*.

Introduction

*B*lood *Meridian* (1985) seems to me the authentic American apocalyptic novel, more relevant even in 2000 than it was fifteen years ago. The fulfilled renown of *Moby-Dick* and of *As I Lay Dying* is augmented by *Blood Meridian*, since Cormac McCarthy is the worthy disciple both of Melville and of Faulkner. I venture that no other living American novelist, not even Pynchon, has given us a book as strong and memorable as *Blood Meridian*, much as I appreciate Don DeLillo's *Underworld*, Philip Roth's *Zuckerman Bound, Sabbath's Theater,* and *American Pastoral,* and Pynchon's *Gravity's Rainbow* and *Mason & Dixon*. McCarthy himself, in his recent Border trilogy, commencing with the superb *All the Pretty Horses,* has not matched *Blood Meridian,* but it is the ultimate Western, not to be surpassed.

My concern being the reader, I will begin by confessing that my first two attempts to read through *Blood Meridian* failed, because I flinched from the overwhelming carnage that McCarthy portrays. The violence begins on the novel's second page, when the fifteen-year-old Kid is shot in the back and just below the heart, and continues almost with no respite until the end, thirty years later, when Judge Holden, the most frightening figure in all of American literature, murders the Kid in an outhouse. So appalling are the continuous massacres and mutilations of *Blood Meridian* that one could be reading a United Nations report on the horrors of Kosovo in 1999.

Nevertheless, I urge the reader to persevere, because *Blood Meridian* is a canonical imaginative achievement, both an American and a universal tragedy of blood. Judge Holden is a villain worthy of Shakespeare, Iago-like and demoniac, a theoretician of war everlasting. And the book's magnificence—its language, landscape, persons, conceptions—at last

From *How to Read and Why*. ©2000 by Harold Bloom.

transcends the violence, and convert goriness into terrifying art, an art comparable to Melville's and to Faulkner's. When I teach the book, many of my students resist it initially (as I did, and as some of my friends continue to do). Television saturates us with actual as well as imagined violence, and I turn away, either in shock or in disgust. But I cannot turn away from *Blood Meridian*, now that I know how to read it, and why it has to be read. None of its carnage is gratuitous or redundant; it belonged to the Mexico-Texas borderlands in 1849–50, which is where and when most of the novel is set. I suppose one could call *Blood Meridian* a "historical novel," since it chronicles the actual expedition of the Glanton gang, a murderous paramilitary force sent out both by Mexican and Texan authorities to murder and scalp as many Indians as possible. Yet it does not have the aura of historical fiction, since what it depicts seethes on, in the United States, and nearly everywhere else, as we enter the third millennium. Judge Holden, the prophet of war, is unlikely to be without honor in our years to come.

Even as you learn to endure the slaughter McCarthy describes, you become accustomed to the book's high style, again as overtly Shakespearean as it is Faulknerian. There are passages of Melvillean-Faulknerian baroque richness and intensity in *The Crying of Lot 49*, and elsewhere in Pynchon, but we can never be sure that they are not parodistic. The prose of *Blood Meridian* soars, yet with its own economy, and its dialogue is always persuasive, particularly when the uncanny Judge Holden speaks:

> The judge placed his hands on the ground. He looked at his inquisitor. This is my claim, he said. And yet everywhere upon it are pockets of autonomous life. Autonomous. In order for it to be mine nothing must be permitted to occur upon it save by my dispensation.
>
> Toadvine sat with his boots crossed before the fire. No man can acquaint himself with everything on this earth, he said.
>
> The judge tilted his great head. The man who believes that the secrets of this world are forever hidden lives in mystery and fear. Superstition will drag him down. The rain will erode the deeds of his life. But that man who sets himself the task of singling out the thread of order from the tapestry will by the decision alone have taken charge of the world and it is only by such taking charge that he will effect a way to dictate the terms of his own fate.

Judge Holden is the spiritual leader of Glanton's filibusters, and McCarthy persuasively gives the self-styled judge a mythic status, appropriate for a deep Machiavelli whose "thread of order" recalls Iago's magic web, in which Othello, Desdemona, and Cassio are caught. Though all of the more colorful and murderous raiders are vividly characterized for us, the killing-machine Glanton with the others, the novel turns always upon its two central figures, Judge Holden and the Kid. We first meet the Judge on page 6: an enormous man, bald as a stone, no trace of a beard, and eyes without either brows or lashes. A seven-foot-tall albino almost seems to have come from some other world, and we learn to wonder about the Judge, who never sleeps, dances and fiddles with extraordinary art and energy, rapes and murders little children of both sexes, and who says that he will never die. By the book's close, I have come to believe that the Judge is immortal. And yet the Judge, while both more and less than human, is as individuated as Iago or Macbeth, and is quite at home in the Texan-Mexican borderlands where we watch him operate in 1849–50, and then find him again in 1878, not a day older after twenty-eight years, though the Kid, a sixteen-year-old at the start of Glanton's foray, is forty-five when murdered by the Judge at the end.

McCarthy subtly shows us the long, slow development of the Kid from another mindless scalper of Indians to the courageous confronter of the Judge in their final debate in a saloon. But though the Kid's moral maturation is heartening, his personality remains largely a cipher, as anonymous as his lack of a name. The three glories of the book are the Judge, the landscape, and (dreadful to say this) the slaughters, which are aesthetically distanced by McCarthy in a number of complex ways.

What is the reader to make of the Judge? He is immortal as principle, as War Everlasting, but is he a person, or something other? McCarthy will not tell us, which is all the better, since the ambiguity is most stimulating. Melville's Captain Ahab, though a Promethean demigod, is necessarily mortal, and perishes with the *Pequod* and all its crew, except for Ishmael. After he has killed the Kid, *Blood Meridian*'s Ishmael, Judge Holden is the last survivor of Glanton's scalping crusade. Destroying the Native-American nations of the Southwest is hardly analogous to the hunt to slay Moby-Dick, and yet McCarthy gives us some curious parallels between the two quests. The most striking is between Melville's chapter 19, where a ragged prophet, who calls himself Elijah, warns Ishmael and Queequeg against sailing on the *Pequod*, and McCarthy's chapter 4, where "an old disordered Mennonite" warns the Kid and his comrades not to join Captain Worth's filibuster, a disaster that preludes the greater catastrophe of Glanton's campaign.

McCarthy's invocation of *Moby-Dick*, while impressive and suggestive, in itself does not do much to illuminate Judge Holden for us. Ahab has his preternatural aspects, including his harpooner Fedellah and Parsee whaleboat crew, and the captain's conversion to their Zoroastrian faith. Elijah tells Ishmael touches of other Ahabian mysteries: a three-day trance off Cape Horn, slaying a Spaniard in front of a presumably Catholic altar in Santa, and a wholly enigmatic spitting into a "silver calabash." Yet all these are transparencies compared to the enigmas of Judge Holden, who seems to judge the entire earth, and whose name suggests a holding, presumably of sway over all he encounters. And yet, the Judge, unlike Ahab, is not wholly fictive; like Glanton, he is a historic filibuster or freebooter. McCarthy tells us most in the Kid's dream visions of Judge Holden, towards the close of the novel:

> In that sleep and in sleep to follow the judge did visit. Who would come other? A great shambling mutant, silent and serene. Whatever his antecedents, he was something wholly other than their sum, nor was there system by which to divide him back into his origins for he would not go. Whoever would seek out his history through what unraveling of loins and ledgerbooks must stand at last darkened and dumb at the shore of a void without terminus or origin and whatever science he might bring to bear upon the dusty primal matter blowing down out of the millennia will discover no trace of ultimate atavistic egg by which to reckon his commencing.

I think that McCarthy is warning his reader that the Judge is Moby-Dick rather than Ahab. As another white enigma, the albino Judge, like the albino whale, cannot be slain. Melville, a professed Gnostic, who believed that some "anarch hand or cosmic blunder" had divided us into two fallen sexes, gives us a Manichean quester in Ahab. McCarthy gives Judge Holden the powers and purposes of the bad angels or demiurges that the Gnostics called archons, but he tells us not to make such an identification (as the critic Leo Daugherty eloquently has). Any "system," including the Gnostic one, will not divide the Judge back into his origins. The "ultimate atavistic egg" will not be found. What can the reader do with the haunting and terrifying Judge?

Let us begin by saying that Judge Holden, though his gladsome prophecy of eternal war is authentically universal, is first and foremost a Western American, no matter how cosmopolitan his background (he speaks all languages, knows all arts and sciences, and can perform magical, shamanistic metamorphoses). The Texan-Mexican border is a superb place for a war-god like the Judge to be. He carries a rifle, mounted in silver, with its name inscribed under the checkpiece: *Et In Arcadia Ego*. In the American Arcadia, death is also always there, incarnated in the Judge's weapon, which never misses. If the American pastoral tradition essentially is the Western film, then the Judge incarnates that tradition, though he would require a director light-years beyond the late Sam Peckinpah, whose *The Wild Bunch* portrays mildness itself when compared to Glanton's paramilitaries. I resort though, as before, to Iago, who transfers war from the camp and the field to every other locale, is a pyromaniac setting everything and everyone ablaze with the flame of battle. The Judge might be Iago before *Othello* begins, when the war god Othello was still worshipped by his "honest" color officer, his ancient or ensign. The Judge speaks with an authority that chills me even as Iago leaves me terrified:

> This is the nature of war, whose stake is at once the game and the authority and the justification. Seen so, war is the truest form of divination. It is the testing of one's will and the will of another within that larger will which because it binds them is therefore forced to select. War is the ultimate game because war is at last a forcing of the unity of existence.

If McCarthy does not want us to regard the Judge as a Gnostic archon or supernatural being, the reader may still feel that it hardly seems sufficient to designate Holden as a nineteenth-century Western American Iago. Since *Blood Meridian*, like the much longer *Moby-Dick*, is more prose epic than novel, the Glanton foray can seem a post-Homeric quest, where the various heroes (or thugs) have a disguised god among them, which appears to be the Judge's Herculean role. The Glanton gang passes into a sinister aesthetic glory at the close of chapter 13, when they progress from murdering and scalping Indians to butchering the Mexicans who have hired them:

> They entered the city haggard and filthy and reeking with the blood of the citizenry for whose protection they had contracted. The scalps of the slain villagers were strung from the windows of the governor's house and the partisans were paid out of the all but exhausted coffers and the Sociedad was disbanded and the bounty rescinded. Within a week of their quitting the city there would be a price of eight thousand pesos posted for Glanton's head.

I break into this passage, partly to observe that from this point on the filibusters pursue the way down and out to an apocalyptic conclusion, but also to urge the reader to hear, and admire, the sublime sentence that follows directly, because we are at the visionary center of *Blood Meridian*.

> They rode out on the north road as would parties bound for El
> Paso but before they were even quite out of sight of the city they
> had turned their tragic mounts to the west and they rode
> infatuate and half fond toward the red demise of that day, toward
> the evening lands and the distant pandemonium of the sun.

Since Cormac McCarthy's language, like Melville's and Faulkner's, frequently is deliberately archaic, the *meridian* of the title probably means the zenith or noon position of the sun in the sky. Glanton, the Judge, the Kid, and their fellows are not described as "tragic"—their long-suffering horses are—and they are "infatuate" and half-mad ("fond") because they have broken away from any semblance of order. McCarthy knows, as does the reader, that an "order" urging the destruction of the entire Native American population of the Southwest is an obscene idea of order, but he wants the reader to know also that the Glanton gang is now aware that they are unsponsored and free to run totally amok. The sentence I have just quoted has a morally ambiguous greatness to it, but that *is* the greatness of *Blood Meridian*, and indeed of Homer and of Shakespeare. McCarthy so contextualizes the sentence that the amazing contrast between its high gestures and he murderous thugs who evoke the splendor is not ironic but tragic. The tragedy is ours, as readers, and not the Glanton gang's, since we are not going to mourn their demise except for the Kid's, and even there our reaction will be equivocal.

My passion for *Blood Meridian* is so fierce that I want to go on expounding it, but the courageous reader should now be (I hope) pretty well into the main movement of the book. I will confine myself here to the final encounter between the preternatural Judge Holden and the Kid, who had broken with the insane crusade twenty-eight years before, and now at middle age must confront the ageless Judge. Their dialogue is the finest achievement in this book of augmenting wonders, and may move the reader as nothing else in *Blood Meridian* does. I reread it perpetually and cannot persuade myself that I have come to the end of it.

The Judge and the Kid drink together, after the avenging Judge tells the Kid that this night his soul will be demanded of him. Knowing he is no match for the Judge, the Kid nevertheless defies Holden, with laconic replies playing against the Judge's rolling grandiloquence. After demanding to know where their slain comrades are, the Judge asks: "And where is the fiddler and where the dance?"

> I guess you can tell me.
> I tell you this. As war becomes dishonored and its nobility called into question those honorable men who recognize the sanctity of blood will become excluded from the dance, which is the warrior's right, and thereby will the dance become a false dance and the dancers false dancers. And yet there will be one there always who is a true dancer and can you guess who that might be?
> You aint nothin.

To have known Judge Holden, to have seen him in full operation, and to tell him that he is nothing, is heroic. "You speak truer than you know," the Judge replies, and two pages later murders the Kid, most horribly. *Blood Meridian*, except for a one-paragraph epilogue, ends with the Judge triumphantly dancing and fiddling at once, and proclaiming that he never sleeps and he will never die. But McCarthy does not let Judge Holden have the last word.

The strangest passage in *Blood Meridian*, the epilogue is set at dawn, where a nameless man progresses over a plain by means of holes that he makes in the rocky ground. Employing a two-handled implement, the man strikes "the fire out of the rock which God has put there." Around the man are wanderers searching for bones, and he continues to strike fire in the holes, and then they move on. And that is all.

The subtitle of *Blood Meridian* is *The Evening Redness in the West*, which belongs to the Judge, last survivor of the Glanton gang. Perhaps all that the reader can surmise with some certainty is that the man striking fire in the rock at dawn is an opposing figure in regard to the evening redness in the West. The Judge never sleeps, and perhaps will never die, but a new Prometheus may be rising to go up against him.

JOHN M. GRAMMER

A Thing Against Which Time Will Not Prevail: Pastoral and History in Cormac McCarthy's South

Early on in *Suttree*, Cormac McCarthy's best novel, Cornelius Suttree—drunken and disaffected scion of an old southern family—visits the ruins of that family's plantation house. He wanders around, eyeing the "tall fluted columns," the smashed chandelier, the ruined plaster, "the wallpaper hanging in great deciduous fronds" and an old "Keep Out" sign, which "[s]omeone must have turned . . . around because it posted the outer world." While thus exploring he recalls a scene from childhood: he and an old man have watched a racehorse run on a track; the old man gestures with his stopwatch and declares that they have seen a wonder, "a thing against which time would not prevail." Something to remember, he means, but young Suttree, already given to morbid speculation, thinks only of mortality and time's inevitable way with all of us: he "had already begun to sicken at the slow seeping of life." Thus defined as a tension between the permanence of memory and the power of time, the misunderstanding between them remains unresolved, at least until Suttree, now grown but no less obsessed with death, revisits the scene in his own ritual of memory and raises the issue again. His efforts to resolve it will be, essentially, the subject matter of his novel.

The plantation scene is notable for being one of the most flagrantly "southern" moments in McCarthy's work. Southern writing, from the antebellum period onward, has been full of ruined old houses, symbolizing

From the *Southern Quarterly* 30, no. 4 (Summer 1992): 19–30. ©1992 by the University of Southern Mississippi.

the failure of southern order to preserve itself against time. One is a bit surprised to encounter such a symbol in McCarthy's work: he is a writer who studiously avoids cliches, for one thing, and a writer who—except perhaps for his allegedly Faulknerian prose style—seems to have very little to do with southern literary tradition. We will search his novels in vain for the great theme of "the past in the present," for the burden of southern history, for (excepting *The Orchard Keeper*) the conflict between tradition and modernity. And we will be hard pressed to wring from them the sort of humanistic content which, for all his gothicism, finally emerges from Faulkner's; it is hard to imagine McCarthy on some platform in Stockholm, assuring us that man will survive and prevail. "If this is the South," John Ditsky has said of McCarthy's characteristic landscape, "it is the South perceived by Vladimir and Estragon."

Indeed one may be startled to discover, in one of McCarthy's notoriously inscrutable novels, not just "southern" symbols but any intelligible symbols at all. They suggest after all the presence of *theme* in a body of work which, as Vereen Bell has cogently argued, is essentially anti-thematic. What one takes from McCarthy's novels, Bell has taught us, is a "hyperrealistic" rendering of the physical world in all its dense, vivid specificity—and particularly the power of that world to upend whatever conceptual grids are imposed on it. To begin discovering themes and symbols in McCarthy's work is to risk the very delusive logocentrism that the novels themselves are meant to expose.

And yet there it is, a ruined mansion which might have been lifted from the pages of any southern pastoral lament since, say, George Tucker's *The Valley of Shenandoah* (1824). I have the feeling that McCarthy employs this symbol, and the cluster of thematic associations it evokes, quite deliberately, and that in doing so he is (among other things) asserting a particular sort of relationship to the southern literary tradition. And he is introducing a theme, though one so closely related to Bell's "anti-thematic" reading of McCarthy that distinguishing them will take some time.

We ought to begin by defining the tradition in question, which will require a bit of cultural history, some familiar, some perhaps less so. If in general terms the ruined mansion in *Suttree* represents the southern past, more specifically it refers to the failure of the pastoral dream with which the South has identified itself since the settlement of Virginia. This was a dream, essentially, of an escape from history. As Lewis Simpson has shown in *The Dispossessed Garden*, the South has from the very first represented itself as a refuge from all the ills to which European culture was heir—from politics, commerce, corruption, war and, ultimately, from time itself. The plantation, a quite deliberate symbolization of that dream of escape, was designed precisely as "a thing against which time would not prevail." It was indeed "posted"—it attempted to warn the outer world, the realm of time and change, to keep out. But the message was double, containing as well a warning to the plantation to attempt no entry into history, but rather to cling—hopelessly, it turned out—to the promise of changeless order offered by the pastoral realm.

Simpson, far and away our best guide to the pastoral impulse in the South, has characterized that impulse as a version of "gnosticism," as Eric Voegelin has glossed the term: a denial of history which becomes, at last, a denial of being; a desire to remake man and his world according to utopian theory. Recent research in the field of political philosophy sheds still more light on the phenomenon: J.G.A. Pocock, writing brilliantly about "the Atlantic Republican Tradition," has instructed us that republican cultures— of which the South, at least since Jefferson's day, has been a quintessential example—are characterized by their imprisonment within a "Machiavellian moment": the moment when the republic, conceived as a civic order created in defiance of history, begins to recognize its mortality. The response, almost invariably, is an attempt to theorize some social transformation which will effect an escape from history; the pastoral myth of the plantation has served this purpose admirably. The South, guided by pastoral and republican imperatives, has persistently attempted to portray itself as a region somehow outside of time and change, a permanent refuge of order in a chaotic world.

I think that we will discover in McCarthy's southern fiction a profoundly serious interrogation of this oldest cultural impulse of southern history. This is to say that McCarthy participates in the South's second-oldest intellectual tradition, that of the anti-pastoral. In common with, for example, William Byrd (who sought to expose the naive pastoral daydream of "Lubberland") and Robert Beverley (who discovered similar delusions among the early settlers of Virginia), McCarthy wants to question the old southern dream of escape from history. Like the humorists of the Old Southwest, the southern writers whom he most resembles, he would remind us of the wildness at the heart of nature, despite pastoral efforts to domesticate it, of the flux at the heart of experience, despite our attempts to stand athwart history, yelling stop: "Nothing ever stops moving," Suttree learns at the end of his novel. I believe McCarthy, like many modern southern writers, has been fascinated throughout his career with this characteristically southern delusion, the pastoral will to create a timeless order.

At one point in *The Orchard Keeper*, McCarthy's first published novel, Arthur Ownby offers this wistful reflection:

> If I was a younger man . . . I would move to them mountains.
> I would find me a clearwater branch and build me a log house
> with a fireplace. And my bees would make black mountain honey.
> And I wouldn't care for no man.

For those who have learned to read McCarthy with an eye peeled for
the buried literary allusion, this passage will set off alarms. Arthur's statement
paraphrases the first stanza of "The Lake Isle of Innisfree," a poem which,
with its own echoes of *Walden*, is already a kind of foster-child of the
American pastoral myth:

> I will arise and go now, and go to Innisfree,
> And a small cabin build there, of clay and wattles made:
> Nine bean rows will I have there, a hive for the honey-bee,
> And live alone in the bee-loud glade.

This allusion, put in the mouth of the admirable "Uncle Ather," is well
chosen, and it hints at McCarthy's own powerful attraction to the pastoral
impulse. One is not altogether surprised to discover this affinity, for it is a
commonplace that antipastoral writing is a version of the pastoral, usually
issuing from some disappointed or embittered engagement with the old
pastoral dream. *The Orchard Keeper* is a more or less straightforward, elegiac
celebration of a vanishing pastoral realm; the book is in the tradition of
Virgil's *Eclogues*, Goldsmith's *Deserted Village* and the Agrarians's *I'll Take My
Stand*. Unlike most of McCarthy's work in this vein, the novel offers a
positive image of pastoral order, an image which we may employ as a kind of
touchstone when reading McCarthy's later and bleaker examinations of the
pastoral impulse.

Like many works in this tradition, *The Orchard Keeper* centers upon the
fortunes not of a single protagonist but of a community—here, of a primitive
community clinging tenaciously to existence in the mountains east of
Knoxville, Tennessee:

> a dozen jerrybuilt shacks strewn about the valley in unlikely
> places, squatting over their gullied purlieus like great brooding
> animals rigid with constipation, and yet endowed with an air
> transient and happenstantial as if set there by the recession of
> floodwaters. Even the speed with which they were constructed
> could not outdistance the decay for which they held such affinity.
> Gangrenous molds took to the foundations before the roofs were
> fairly nailed down.

Passages like this one lead Vereen Bell to read *The Orchard Keeper* as asserting the insubstantiality of human communities, their helplessness before encroaching wildness. I think that is only half the story, for the community of Red Branch, though perpetually in the advanced stages of decomposition, somehow does keep renewing itself; it has evidently maintained its armed truce with nature for a long time. I think that the great virtue of this community, as McCarthy presents it, is precisely that it has worked out such a truce, one which involves both tenacity and flexibility, an acceptance of the flux at the heart of things. Instead of trying to stand outside of time, Red Branch has somehow learned to swim comfortably in its currents.

The purest expression of this knowledge is the social center of Red Branch, a saloon known as the Green Fly Inn, built so as to hang precariously over a deep hollow, buffetted by the winds:

> [T]he inn-goers trod floors that waltzed drunkenly beneath them, surged and buckled with huge groans. At times the whole building would career madly to one side as though headlong into collapse. The drinkers would pause, liquid tilting in their glasses, the structure would shudder violently, a broom would fall, a bottle, and the inn would slowly right itself and assume once more its normal reeling equipoise. The drinkers would raise their glasses, talk would begin again. Remarks alluding to the eccentricities of the inn were made only outside the building. To them the inn was animate as any old ship to her crew and it bred an atmosphere such as few could boast, a solidarity due largely to its very precariousness.

The interdependence of "solidarity" and "precariousness" is an essential idea for McCarthy; for him it seems that the only sort of permanence ultimately available to us is one based upon an intense awareness of impermanence; life is possible only in a continual and more or less cordial dialogue with death.

The main characters in *The Orchard Keeper* seem to have learned the lesson well. Thus Marion Sylder is violent enough to kill the murderous hitchhiker who attacks him, but humane enough to play the part of father to his victim's son. Arthur Ownby, an old man terrified of death, is able to domesticate that fear by ritualistically tending the corpse of that victim, which he has discovered in the woods. The dead man's son John Wesley Rattner, a boy deeply attracted to the dangerous wilderness around him, disciplines that attraction by learning woodcraft from his two elders;

Trapping the Fur Bearers of North America, a book given him by Uncle Ather, becomes the bible of his homemade creed. That the three characters are unaware of the fact which really unites them—their shared connection to the dead Kenneth Rattner—emphasizes the communal and traditional nature of their relationships: they behave as they do not out of any sense of personal obligation, obedient to some Lockean social contract, but because their inherited modes of being instruct them to do so. The community of which these three are representative citizens seems quite real to me, and able to go on indefinitely keeping up its end of the tug of war with nature.

As in the *Eclogues* and nearly everything else in the tradition of elegiac pastoral, the more serious threat to this world comes from the other direction, from the city and what McCarthy will later call its "gnostic" impulses—impulses to impose stability, order and reason upon the fluid reality of existence at Red Branch. The central dilemmas of the story all concern the efforts of Red Branch and its representative citizens—Arthur, Marion and John Wesley—to resist these gnostic impulses and preserve something of their old-fashioned existence. Thus Arthur finds himself threatened not only by wildness and death (symbolized by the "painters" that haunt his dreams) but also by a mysterious government tank which has intruded upon the wilderness, and then by the lawmen who come to arrest him for damaging it. Marion Sylder must contend not only with Kenneth Rattner but also with the constable who seeks to end his bootlegging business and jail him. And John Wesley is confronted not only by the wild hound which peers in at him from the wilderness, but by the constable who bullies him, the government office which pays a bounty for the corpses of red tail hawks and his mother's insane demand that he avenge his father's death. This last threat typifies them all, for Mildred Rattner, invoking an essentially literary cliche in order to rationalize the unexplained disappearance of her husband, is trying to impose on the situation precisely the sort of totalizing closure which Red Branch preserves itself by resisting. She wants, in effect, to involve her son in a plotted narrative, an involvement which he rightly shuns. Like the lawmen, social workers and engineers who threaten Red Branch, she is ruled by the gnostic desire to remake a terrifyingly fluid reality by imposing stable order upon it.

Red Branch is thus poised between two threats, and it is this latter, "civilized" one which ultimately dooms the community. Uncle Ather ends his days in an insane asylum, harrassed by a social worker who "talk[s] like a God-damned yankee" and apparently makes his living by asking foolish questions. Marion is likewise jailed for bootlegging and then beaten up by the constable; in marked contrast to Mrs. Rattner, he dissuades John Wesley from taking vengeance on the lawman. John Wesley himself elects to leave

Red Branch, dear as it has been for him; its value for him has been eliminated upon the arrest of his friends. The book ends tragically, that is to say, but affirmatively; we might think of it as an elegy for an older sort of pastoral community, nobly resisting but finally defeated by the gnostic will to deny history.

McCarthy's subsequent books depict a later stage in pastoral history, one in which the pastoral realm—terrified of mortality but lacking, say, Uncle Ather's means of facing that fear—surrenders to those gnostic impulses and defines itself a refuge from time. Certainly that is the case with *Outer Dark*, the author's second novel. Here the pastoral flight from history and its consequences are suggested quite vividly in an early scene, a description of the band of murderers who harry the community in which the main action occurs:

> *They entered the lot at a slow jog, the peaceful and ruminative stock coming erect, watchful, shifting with eyes sidled as they passed, the three of them paying no heed, seeming blind with purpose, passing through an ether of smartweed and stale ammonia steaming from the sunbleared chickenrun and on through the open doors of the barn and almost instantly out the other side marvelously armed with crude agrarian weapons, spade and brush-hook, emerging in an explosion of guineafowl and one screaming sow, unaltered in gait demeanor or speed, parodic figures transported live and intact and violent out of a proletarian mural and set mobile upon the empty fields, advancing against the twilight, the droning bees and windtilted clover.*

These menacing riders, armed with farming tools, are of course figures of time, reapers who move through the novel, leaving a trail of violent death behind them; the farm tools they carry will indeed become weapons as their spree commences. Thus they embody the deadly threat which history poses to the pastoral realm. And yet they are themselves pastoral figures, or at least parodic versions of such figures, bearing spades and brush hooks through a barnyard, frightening the stock. Whatever threat they represent, that is, emerges in some sense from the pastoral realm they scourge; they are that community's nightmare, the seed of destruction which lurks within the pastoral dream.

I believe that the novel as a whole bears out this reading. Its main action concerns a brother and sister, Culla and Rinthy Holme, their incestuous relationship and the surrealistically horrible consequences of this time. Culla abandons the baby they produce in the woods; the baby is then taken by a mad tinker; Rinthy goes aimlessly in search of it; Culla goes in pursuit of

Rinthy, finds himself continually accused of crimes large and small, pursued by lawmen and lynch mobs, often obliged to flee for his life, and at last, disturbingly, welcomed as a brother by the band of murderers: "Well, I see ye didn't have no trouble finding us," one says as Culla stumbles into their camp. The landscape through which they wander is full of robbed graves, mangled corpses, hanged men and a herd of Gadarene swine, transplanted directly from the New Testament. *Outer Dark*, like much of McCarthy's work, seems positively turgid with moral import, and yet it is difficult to say just what the moral issues involved might be. "It is almost as if these two poor souls, the brother and sister both, had let loose all the demons in the world by the fact of their formation," says John Ditsky. Just so; yet why should this be? How is it that incest calls forth such dire retribution? And whence, in McCarthy's apparently godless universe, does this retribution come?

In answering these questions we might begin by taking account of an oddity which many readers of the novel have noticed, the vagueness of its temporal setting sometime before the advent of the internal combustion engine, one gathers; beyond that it is difficult to say. The vagueness is appropriate, for *Outer Dark* concerns a pastoral community which has taken its retreat from history to pathological and eventually criminal lengths. It is a community outside of time; thus its citizens continually seem lost in time. At one point Culla travels to town, trying to purchase groceries, and needs to be told by the irate storekeeper that it is Sunday; somehow his isolated existence has not been subject to the calendar. "We still christians here," this same merchant growls, claiming membership in an apparently endangered remnant, left behind by history. A bit later, a family which has helped Rinthy are likened to "stone figures quarried from the architecture of an older time." In fact the book's temporal setting is not only vague but contradictory: the band of marauders seem a kind of Murrell gang, figures from the antebellum days of frontier settlement; how can they coexist with a world equipped with coolboxes for "dope," storebought meat and bread, and so on? The temporal setting is strange and surreal, emphasizing the novel's general sense of displacement in time.

Some have taken the book's temporal vagueness to suggest that specific historical references are insignificant, that the tale is in some sense timeless and universal. I think nearly the opposite is true; *Outer Dark* refers not to a vaguely defined moment but a fairly specific one—a Machiavellian moment, in Pocock's phrase: the moment when a community organized as a refuge from history is forced to confront it. And it is, therefore, about that confrontation, about time's revenge on a community which has attempted to deny its power: retribution, in this novel obsessed with retribution, comes not from God but from history.

We are given a number of clues that the community, even apart from the depredations of the murderers, is beginning to fall apart. Custom, neighborliness, even simple communication are nearly gone, replaced by fear, suspicion, estrangement. We encounter a woman who has made a lovely quilt, but complains of having to undertake this traditionally communal creation alone: "It's tedious to piece one for one person by herself." Having made the quilt, she can think of nothing to do with it but sell it for three dollars. Rinthy, whose wanderings cannot have taken her very far from home, repeatedly meets neighbors who can't quite place her: I *ought* to know you, people keep saying to her. "They ain't a soul in this world but what is a stranger to me," she says at one point; it is a statement nearly any character in the book might make. Culla, trying to buy cheese and crackers in the local store, finds it nearly impossible to make the grocer understand how much he wants of each. Culla finds himself met with senseless suspicion and hostility everywhere he goes: he is pursued by a lynch mob, which for no apparent reason suspects him of robbing graves; later he is arrested on a flimsy charge of trespassing and set to work on "the Squire's" farm; when his sentence is up Culla asks to stay on, for room and board, and is turned away. A group of hog drovers, whose herd has stampeded and been lost, randomly assign the blame to Culla and prepare to lynch him. The whole social atmosphere of *Outer Dark* is one of near-total estrangement; we are shown a community, presumably once unified and solid, now shattered to atoms; such cohesion as remains becomes a destructive centripetal force.

The central event of the novel—which, like the adultery in *The Scarlet Letter*, occurs before the novel begins—is the clearest expression of this condition. Incest conventionally represents a social order which, in its anxiety to avoid contact with the corrupting outer world, ends by collapsing inward on itself—such an order as was dreamed by the pastoral visionaries of the South. Culla and Rinthy, that is, are the representative figures, in a sense the first citizens, of their dying pastoral world: one reason, perhaps, why everyone believes they know Rinthy, and why everyone, including the band of killers whose path he inadvertently follows, seems to suspect Culla of some dire crime. Rinthy's aimless and hopeless quest for her child, the entire plot of her half of the novel, is an attempt to redeem the pastoral order. The powerfully maternal Rinthy, hunting her "chap" and lactating helplessly, is of course a figure of great natural fecundity, the earth-as-mother who lies at the heart of the pastoral myth. Bell has pointed out that Rinthy is McCarthy's version of Lena Grove, Faulkner's footloose embodiment of the maternal (and pastoral, as her name implies) life force. But Rinthy is a dark and hopeless version of Lena, just as *Outer Dark*—the very title suggests it—is a dark and hopeless version of *Light in August*. In Faulkner's work Lena's untouchable will to life balances Joe Christmas's death wish; but in this doomed pastoral community the death wish is nearly universal, and Rinthy's sad effort to redeem it is manifestly futile. Here the avengers, apparently summoned up by the community's, and particularly Culla and Rinthy's sins, end by killing their child and, perhaps more heartlessly, sparing the incestuous parents. The novel is a kind of *Paradise Lost*, but it ends with the sinful pair wandering hopelessly and separately through the ruins of their fallen garden—with all the world before them, perhaps, but not the faintest hint of providential guidance.

Child of God, McCarthy's third novel, is the one which most explicitly raises the issue of the pastoral, and particularly of the republican or Jeffersonian version of it which has dominated the southern imagination. This concern is revealed with astonishing clarity in the first scene, which depicts the sale at auction of Lester Ballard's farm, forfeited for nonpayment of taxes. As the sale progresses, Lester appears—a "[s]mall man, ill-shaven, now holding a rifle"—and quixotically attempts to interrupt the proceedings. "I want you to get your goddamn ass off my property," he says. "And take these fools with ye." The auctioneer tries and fails to reason with him, and at last the dispossessed farmer is clubbed over the head with an axe and carried off by the high sheriff of Sevier County. "Lester Ballard never could hold his head right after that," explains an anonymous witness.

That judgment, as we see when Lester takes up his mad career as murderer and necrophiliac, turns out to be a considerable understatement. Thus we need to see just what is at stake in this early scene, somehow the beginning of Lester's descent into madness. Consider for instance the small detail of Lester's rifle. He is virtually never without it in the novel, the weapon apparently serving him as a powerful totem of some sort. He acquired it as a boy, we learn, and by now his skills with it are the stuff of local legend: "He could by god shoot it," one neighbor recalls. "Hit anything he could see." Early on Lester demonstrates this proficiency by winning several stuffed animals at a shooting gallery; later, taking up his career as a killer, he puts it to deadlier use.

What does the rifle mean to Lester? For one thing it identifies him as an anachronism, left behind by history: a Daniel Boone with only stuffed animals to shoot for. But there is more to it than that; in the mythology of the pastoral republic, with which *Child of God* is suffused, weapons like Lester's rifle carry enormous symbolic value. An armed man, prepared to defend the country and his own liberty and property, was for our ancestors the ideal republican citizen, the foundation of stable order: an idea which will seem most familiar to us, perhaps, as it is enshrined in the Second Amendment to the Constitution.

And so when Lester appears, rifle in hand, prepared to defend his property against the agents of tyrannical power (or so he perceives the situation), he is claiming a role for himself in one of the central dramas in the pastoral republican mythology. Raymond Williams has noted that almost invariably in pastoral literature "the contrast . . . is between the pleasures of rural settlement and the threat of loss and eviction." The theme goes back all the way to Virgil's first *Eclogue*, but acquires additional force in America, where property-holding has been an important component of civic virtue, a guarantee of personal and social stability. The scene in which the yeoman farmer loses his property is the one which pastoral republics dread—the moment when death enters their world. It is Lester's personal Machiavellian moment. The sheriff and the auctioneer, with their talk of law, taxes and investment potential, are figures of modernity, of time; Lester casts himself as a reactionary, still hoping to resist the tides of history.

The scene is indeed the beginning of Lester's descent into madness—a madness which carries out, in horrifying ways, the essential impulses of the threatened pastoral republic. For, deprived of his land, he must now reconstitute the order which it represents. He begins, harmlessly enough, by trying to re-establish some conventional domestic arrangement: by setting up housekeeping in an abandoned cabin, and by paying court to several potential spouses, each more indifferent than the last. But finally, frustrated in these attempts, he begins killing women and collecting their corpses as lovers, eventually accumulating quite a supply in a remote cave. This gesture, as other readers have noted, is Lester's mad protest against history itself, against the passing of time. Among his corpses, there is a timeless order, immunity to change: the descriptions of them faintly echo the scene in *Outer Dark* in which rural folk sit like "stone figures quarried from the architecture of an older time." Here the figures really are motionless, outside of time. Lester's cave—which is discovered, with almost allegorical appropriateness, when a plowman's mules fall into it through a sinkhole—is the ultimate, deranged expression of the pastoral will to deny history.

McCarthy is fairly clear about Lester's gnostic version of the pastoral impulse: "Given charge," he explains, "Ballard would have made things more orderly in the woods and in men's souls." In *Suttree*, the last of his southern novels, he shows us the logical end of this gnostic dreaming: the destructive urban landscape of Knoxville, where Lester Ballard's wish to "make things more orderly" has been realized with a vengeance. Cornelius Suttree's family, former inhabitants of the ruined mansion, have made a remarkably smooth transition from the old "plantation" version of the dream of changeless order to a new one, approved by the chamber of commerce. "If it is life that you feel you are missing," Suttree's father has instructed him, "I can tell you where to find it. In the law courts, in business, in government." But Suttree has turned his back on that dream of order and, trying to discover some more authentic existence, now lives in the slum neighborhood of McAnally Flats, amid what his father calls "a dumbshow composed of the helpless and the impotent." Here, living on a houseboat and fishing for a living, Suttree seems to divide his time about equally between a succession of mad prophets, from whom he seeks revelation, and the derelicts of the neighborhood, in whose company he pursues the temporary oblivion of drunkenness and the permanent one of death. Yet what he finds in this most optimistic of McCarthy's novels is neither deliverance nor death but a new awareness of the nature of life, of the solidarity which arises from precariousness.

Of the many literary allusions in McCarthy's work, one of the most important comes in the naming (really the nicknaming) of his protagonist in *Suttree*. "Sut," his Knoxville friends call him: instantly we are reminded of another famous East Tennesseean in our literature, George Washington Harris's Sut Lovingood. But at first the allusion seems a strange one, for Harris's Sut is an illiterate, anti-intellectual creature of instinct; he sums up his own epistemology by explaining that "plannin and studdyin"

> . . . am ginerly no count. All pends, et las' on what yu dus an' how
> yu kerries yursef *at the moment ove ackshun*. Sarcumstances turn
> about pow'ful fas', an all yu kin du is tu think jis' es fas es they kin
> turn, an' jis' as they turn, an' ef yu du this, I'm durn'd ef yu don't
> git out sumhow.

Now Cornelius Suttree, as everyone has noticed, is unique among McCarthy's protagonists in being reflective and articulate; he has been to college, is known to his friends as a smart fellow and is presumably more able than most when it comes to planning and studying. But he seems to have deliberately suppressed these gifts, out of a growing awareness of what his spiritual ancestors at the Green Fly Inn (and his literary ones in the pages of George Washington Harris) have always known about the interdependence of solidarity and precariousness. He learns to accept what the rest of Knoxville, barring McAnally Flats, is engaged in denying: the flux at the heart of existence, to which we must simply adjust ourselves. In McCarthy's world planning and studying never *are* any use; to resort to them is to slip into the gnostic fallacy of the southern pastoral dream in all its versions.

This notion is made plainest, perhaps, in the presentation of Suttree's friend Gene Harrogate, certainly the most memorable character in the book. We realize as soon as we meet him that Harrogate represents a particularly virulent strain of naive pastoralism: if modern environmentalists are "tree huggers," if Faulkner's Ike Snopes falls in love with a cow, then McCarthy goes them all one better in his comic presentation of the "moonlight melonmounter," whose erotic encounters in the garden patch land him in the workhouse with Suttree. Upon his release the former "country mouse" re-christens himself "city rat" and travels to Knoxville, full of schemes for success. He learns that the city, fearing an outbreak of rabies, will pay a bounty for dead bats, so he devises a method for poisoning the creatures and delivers an enormous sackful to the Health Department; he is astonished when his foolproof plan fails. He follows the caverns which lie under Knoxville until he reckons he is just beneath a bank vault, then sets off a charge of dynamite; again he is astonished to find himself almost blown up, then nearly drowned in the wash from the sewer main he has breached and finally lost in the caves for days. Prospering for a time with an ambitious plan to steal coins from half the pay phones in town, Harrogate is chased into hiding by the notoriously implacable "telephone heat"; at last, in desperation, he attempts a robbery and is arrested. In his very crudeness and naivete Harrogate is an ideal expression of the ethic which governs contemporary Knoxville—and more broadly, of the "gnostic" error of attempting to manage the wildness of existence by means of planning and studying. We might think of him as a sort of benign Lester Ballard, considerably less alarming but sharing not only unconventional sexual habits but, what underlies those habits, a pastoral desire to impose order on a chaotic world.

Such efforts, *Suttree* suggests, are deluded and destructive. Suttree does not fully recognize this at first: he seems to be seeking, haphazardly, his own sort of release from flux. He first ventured into McAnally, apparently, in search of a martyr's revenge on a meaningless world:

> I spoke with bitterness about my life and I said that I would take my own part against the slander of oblivion and against the monstrous facelessness of it and that I would stand a stone in the very void where all would read my name.

Suttree is at first determined to extract some sort of stable meaning from life, seeking either religious revelation or death. Later, perhaps despairing of these alternatives, he attempts his own sad versions of ordinary middle-class stability: with the parody of domestic bliss he achieves with the whore Joyce, or with his halfhearted effort to make a fortune in mussel shells with the doomed Reese and his family. But of course all these efforts come to naught, ending in comic disappointment or bloody tragedy: each time he returns to his houseboat on the river.

The river is, to put it mildly, a symbol: of life, since it gives Suttree the fish which sustain him, and of death—in the opening scene the bloated body of a suicide is grappled from its depths—and ultimately (as for Heraclitus) of the mysterious flux at the heart of existence, of everything that Knoxville attempts to deny. Suttree gets his share of clues about its significance: one of the preachers he meets, at a baptism in the river, warns him that the sprinkling he received as an infant in church is insufficient: "It wont take if you dont get total nursin. That old sprinklin business wont get it, buddy boy." Indeed it won't; a line from Conrad comes to mind: "The way is to the destructive element submit yourself, and with the exertions of your hands and feet in the water make the deep, deep sea keep you up." Sut Lovingood would agree, and his namesake learns to at last: Suttree's salvation, such as it is, comes when at last he recognizes this truth. Following a nearly fatal bout with typhoid fever, accompanied by a series of visionary hallucinations, Suttree is able to tell what he has learned: God, he explains to the priest who has come to administer last rites, "is not a thing. Nothing ever stops moving."

And so Suttree mustn't stop moving either; for movement, action, participation in the flux at the heart of experience, is the only alternative to destruction. Disabuse yourself of your gnostic delusions, promised Sut Lovingood, forego plannin' and studyin' and the effort to impose order on experience, and "I'm durn'd ef yu don't git out somehow." And his namesake does get out somehow, leaving Knoxville just one step ahead of the "huntsman," death, which has pursued him throughout the novel. Death is of course a major presence in *Suttree*, essentially bracketing its main action: "Who's dead?" Suttree asks his friend J-Bone early in the novel—an appropriate question in his violent world, and one which needs to be asked repeatedly. By the end, as the hero takes his leave from Knoxville, we have at least a negative answer: "Shit," says one of his McAnally friends, "Old Suttree aint dead." This is the nearest thing to affirmation we will find in McCarthy's grim works. He's not dead yet; like the denizens of Red Branch in *The Orchard Keeper*, and unlike most of the author's other protagonists, Suttree manages, for a while longer at least, to keep up his end of the dialogue with death. This is all the deliverance that is available in McCarthy's world: deliverance from the pastoral delusions which have plagued his region—those represented by the ruined mansion, and also those represented by the expressway being built over the ruins of McAnally Flats as he takes his leave, the work of "[g]nostic workmen who would have down this shabby shapeshow that masks the higher world of form." To be saved is to continue swimming in the currents of time; the only cessation, as Lester Ballard knew, is death.

LEO DAUGHERTY

Gravers False and True: Blood Meridian as Gnostic Tragedy

I want to argue that gnostic thought is central to Cormac McCarthy's *Blood Meridian*. I will go about this by discussing four of its characters—the judge, the kid, the graver and the mysterious man of the epilogue—and the particular sort of world they inhabit. I am aware at the outset of the difficulties involved in establishing a relationship between any two things (in this case *Blood Meridian* and Gnostic thought) when some readers may have a working knowledge of only one of them (in this case, I hope, the novel). While it is impossible to provide more than an introductory sketch of Gnosticism here, I believe that its dualistic core can be simply and briefly shown, and that it can then be understood well enough to make clear its connections with McCarthy's book.

I. The Gnostics

No one knows exactly how or when Gnosticism originated, but it is generally agreed that it came about as yet another answer to the question, How is it that the world is experienced as so very evil and that so many people's central response to it is alienation? The Gnostic answer took two basic forms, the Syrian-Egyptian and the Iranian, the latter of which

From the *Southern Quarterly* 30, no. 4 (Summer 1992): 122–33. ©1992 by the University of Southern Mississippi.

probably stemmed from Zoroastrianism and found its principal exponent in
Mani (215–277 AD). Because *Blood Meridian* exemplifies the latter, I will use
it almost exclusively here.

In the beginning, there was a "pleroma," a condition of perfection and
thus of literal plentitude, in the divine realm. This realm was made up of God
and the lesser divinities, themselves called aeons. Then, somehow, this unity
was sundered, either from within or without. In the Iranian version it was
riven from without, by some sort of opposing "dark force." (This
presupposes, as Hans Jonas has noted, some yet more primal dualism.) In the
words of one scholar of this (Manichean) version: "All existing things derive
from one of these two: the infinite light of spiritual goodness or the
bottomless darkness of evil matter, coexistent and totally opposed to each
other." A state of affairs ensued which is termed the "crisis in the pleroma,"
one result of which was the "falling" or "sinking" of some of the aeons,
including (in Mani's system) "primal man." Of these, some became the
archons (lords), who took charge of the various lower realms. The
characteristics most typically found in them are judgment and jealousy, and
their "creative" energies are spent in satisfying their "ambition, vanity, and
just for dominion."

One of the archons' works was the creation of the world. A second was
the creation of man, who would contain some of the original divine
substance. Their motive for making human beings is unclear, but Jonas
argues convincingly that it was either simple envy and ambition, or the more
calculating "[motive] of entrapping divine substance in their lower world by
the lure of a seemingly congenial receptacle [the body] that will then become
its most secure bond"). As Robert Grant has noted, "The Gnostic, like the
Platonist, regarded his body as a tomb." To him, it is *this*, then, that is *imago
Dei* of Genesis, and in Manicheanism the *imago* is that of the original fallen
"primal man." Yet the spirit within humans is not from the archons. Rather,
it is from the great original god of the pleroma, and it is imprisoned *in*
humans *by* the archons—in Mani's version through a violent victory of the
archons over the real, good god of the pleroma—and the result, on the earth,
is obviously a state of affairs in which the good and the light are eternally
trapped inside the evil and the dark.

The spirit imprisoned within matter is called *pneuma*—the "spark of the
alien divine," in the familiar Gnostic phrase—and its presence naturally
causes some humans to *feel* alienated, although they are for the most part
comatose. The spirit within is, however, capable of learning, and the
alienation it feels is its clue that there is indeed something to be learned. In
the various Gnostic systems, knowledge is the key to extrication. It is thus a
central task of the archons to prevent the human acquisition of liberational

knowledge at all costs. To this end, they have established *heimarmene*—Fate—which is, in Jonas's words, a "tyrannical world rule [which] is. . .morally the law of *justice*, as exemplified in the Mosaic law."

Humans are comprised of flesh, soul and spirit. Of these, the first two are from the archons and the third is from the original, good god. This god has nothing to do with the world the archons made, and is in fact as alien to it as the spirit of humankind. But he feels something akin to incompleteness, and he is thus moved to "call his spirit home." He does this by means of messengers, who go into the world with the "call of revelation." This revelation is the "facts of the case"—the knowledge necessary to enable humans to overcome the world and return to their true home with him. God's revelational messenger "penetrates the barriers of the [lower spheres, including the world], outwits the archons, awakens the spirit from its earthly slumber, and imparts to it has saving knowledge from without." These salvational Gnostic envoys—those in possession of *gnosis*—called (and still call) themselves "pneumatics." Their work necessarily entails assuming "the lot of incarnation and cosmic exile"; moreover, in Mani's system, the revelator is "in a sense identical with those he calls—the once-lost part of his divine self—[thus giving rise] to the moving idea of the 'saved savior' (*salvator salvandus*)."

Manichean Gnosticism is easily confused with nihilism, as the latter is commonly understood. The reason is that the Gnostic god, being totally not of this world, generates no *nomos*, no law, for either nature or human activity. The law, instead, is the law of the archons, and justice is theirs as well. And so is vengeance—the "vengeance that is mine." God's only activity with respect to matter is his attempt, via his suffering-servant pneumatic messengers, to rescue the spirit within humans—the truth of them—*out* of matter. So, while Jonas is right in arguing that Gnostic "acosmism" makes for the worldly *appearance* of nihilism, the mere fact that the Gnostic god has a rescuing function makes Gnosticism and nihilism differ importantly. In Gnosticism, because of this difference, there is conflict and drama. Its human drama takes place within and is a microcosm of its larger cosmic drama which spirit against matter, light against darkness and the alien god (and the alien pneumatic spirit within sleeping humankind) against the archons. It is precisely a war. For humans, it is war against the archons' *heimarmene*, but this is merely part of the larger war in which the fate of the original god is the primal stake. Mani taught that the cosmic drama amounts to "a war with changing fortunes [in which] the divine fate, of which man's fate is a part and the world an unwilled byproduct, is explained in terms of . . . captivity and liberation . . ." And in his teachings, the primal man, the "knightly male figure, the warrior, assumes the role of the exposed and suffering part of divinity."

With respect to this warrior-knight, Wilhelm Bousset, who was perhaps the most esteemed nineteenth-century authority on Gnosticism, held that he represents god in the form of a hero

> who makes war on, and is partly vanquished by darkness. He descends into the darkness of the material world, and in so doing begins the great drama of the world's development. From [god] are derived those portions of light existing and held prisoner in this lower world. And as he has raised himself again out of the material world, or has been set free. . . . so shall also the members of the primal man, the portions of light still imprisoned in matter, be set free.

The practicing Gnostics naturally saw themselves as such heroes, as such messengers of god or "primal men." And in this fact, Bousset concludes, is to be found the obvious meaning of the primal man figure in some Gnostic strains, including Mani's for it provides a simple (and self-serving) answer to the question, "How did the portions of light to be found in the lower world, among which certainly belong the souls of [us] Gnostics, enter into it?"

So, whereas most thoughtful people have looked at the world they lived in and asked, How did evil get into it?, the Gnostics looked at the world and asked, How did *good* get into it? This was of course a very sensible question, and remains so. After all, the Satan of Roman Catholicism, the Orthodox Church and the Protestant Reformation is a strikingly domesticated, manageable, partitioned-off personification of evil as the Gnostics saw evil. They saw it as something so big that "evil" is not really an applicable term—because too small. For them, evil was simply everything that *is* with the exception of the bits of spirit emprisoned here. And what they saw is what we see in the world of *Blood Meridian*.

II. The Archon and His World

Early in *Blood Meridian*, the reader comes upon this passage: "The survivors. . . slept with their alien hearts beating in the sand like pilgrims exhausted upon the face of the planet Anareta, clutched to a namelessness wheeling in the night." Anareta was believed in the Renaissance to be "the planet which destroys life," and "violent deaths are caused" when the "malifics" have agents in "the anaretic place" (OED entry, "anareta"). Because McCarthy has not placed a comma after "pilgrims," it is likely that his simile includes the entire remainder of the phrase; yet it is easily possible to read the passage *as if* a comma were present, thus producing the reading: *this* is Anareta. Either way, the implication is clearly that our own Earth is Anaretic.

And in *Blood Meridian* the Earth is the judge's.

Even so, on our own evil planet judge Holden's power is not yet complete, since his will is not yet fulfilled in its passion for total domination. He is working, as he implies to Toadvine, to become a full "suzerain"—one who "rules even where there are other rulers," whose authority "countermands local judgments." Yet this was also necessarily true of the Gnostic archons, just as it was true of the Old Testament Yahweh, whom they saw as evil. And, like those archons, Holden also possesses all the other characteristics of Yahweh as the Gnostics saw him: he is jealous, he is vengeful, he is wrathful, he is powerful and—most centrally—he possesses, and is possessed by, a will. And he is enraged by any existence or any act outside that will. At point, he places his hands on the ground, looks at Toadvine, and speaks:

> This is my claim, he said. And yet everywhere upon it are pockets of autonomous life. Autonomous. In order for it to be mine nothing must be permitted to occur upon it save by my dispensation.

In Holden, the stressed archonic element is of course *judgment*. Yet, like Yahweh, he judges things simply according to the binary criterion of their being inside or outside his will. In one of the passages most crucial to an adequate understanding of *Blood Meridian*, he tells David Brown, "Every child knows that play is nobler than work," that "men are born for games" and that "all games aspire to the condition of war for here that which is wagered swallows up game, player, all." We are reminded here of the novel's epigraph from Jacob Boehme: "It is not to be thought that the life of darkness is sunk in misery and lost as if in sorrowing. There is no sorrowing. For sorrow is a thing that is swallowed up in death, and death and dying are the very life of the darkness." Indeed, *war is the ultimate cause of unity*, involving as it does the "testing of one's will and the will of another within larger will [i.e., war itself] which because it binds them is therefore forced to select. War is the ultimate game because war is at last a forcing of the unity of existence. War is god."

And it is the warrior judge's work to achieve dominion—to be the realized territorial archon of *this* Anaretic planet—through becoming the totalizing victor in all conflicts, real and perceptual, involving his will. The corollary is to show no mercy to those others whose wills have them to be outside one's own: as Holden tells the kid late in the novel, "There's a flawed place in the fabric of your heart. . . . You alone reserved in your soul some corner of clemency for the heathen." And because the kid *has* shown them mercy, the judge must *not* show *him* and does not. Ultimately, a person serves the god of war, as Holden tells Tobin, in order to be "no godserver but god himself."

III. The Name of the Gun

The Earth is the judge's, and, when he names his gun, the judge makes ironic comment upon the fact that not only is the earth his, but also that it is an anti-pastoral, anti-Arcadian world.

The gun's name is *Et in Arcadia Ego*.

This is a familiar late Renaissance proverb, dating back at least to Schidoni (*c.* 1600). It was a commonplace memorial inscription for tombs and representations of tombs, it was scrawled as graffiti under pictures of skulls, and it was conventionally employed by painters such as Poussin and Reynolds as a verbal/visual icon. It means, "Even in Arcadia there am I [Death]." The more interesting, least sentimentalizing pastoral poets had stressed this all along, of course, and had accordingly positioned death prominently in their Arcadias—Marguerite of Navarre in her *Heptameron*, as well as Shakespeare in *Love's Labors Lost*, for example, and most importantly Sidney in the seminal *Arcadia*.

Blood Meridian centers upon what can be reasonably thought of as a fraternity of male shepherds who kill the sheep entrusted to them. One of the shepherds is the kid, who feels the "spark of the alien divine" within him through the call of what seems to be conscience. He thus "awakens" a bit, attaining in the process a will outside the will of his murdering shepherdic subculture and the archon who runs it. The kid reminds us here of Huckleberry Finn, who in the crucial act of saving his friend Jim from slaveholder justice, similarly defies the will of a pernicious subculture, but who is judged only by his own cultural conscience, saying to himself at the novel's turning point, "All right, then, I'll go to hell." Both these boys are a little bit awakened by the spark of the divine, and both extend acts of fraternal mercy when they are "not supposed to." In the Mark Twain world, Huck gets away with it; in the McCarthy word, the kid is killed by the judge for it in an outhouse. The kid has "awakened," but he is not progressed sufficiently in wisdom much beyond mere awakening and thus has no chance at survival, much less at the victory of Gnostic liberation.

Even so, it would be gross understatement to call *Blood Meridian* a "pastoral tragedy," or even to term it "anti-pastoral." The point of the gun's name is not that because of its appearance in the landscape, or by synechdoche the judge's appearance, death has been introduced into an idyllic Arcadia: the entire novel makes clear (primarily through the judge, who continuously emphasizes the point in his preachments) that the human world is, and has always been, a world of killing. This is surely the point of the book's third epigraph, a quote provided by McCarthy from a 1982 news release: "Clark, who led last year's expedition to the Afar region of northern Ethiopia, and UC Berkeley colleague Tim D. White, also said that a re-examination of a 300,000-year-old fossil skull found in the same region earlier shows evidence of having been scalped." Rather, I would argue that the name suggests the judge's awareness of, and his enthusiastic endorsement of, the reality that the world has been a place of murder ever since the first victorious taking of a human life by another human. The judge's name *Et in Arcadia Ego* stands not for his gun and not himself, but rather for murderous humankind on this very real killing planet.

Blood Meridian is a study of power relations within what, to the habituated expectations of our "received culture," ought by all rights to have been a pastoral setting. But McCarthy's long-meditated observations, coupled with his reading of the relevant southwestern history, have led him to other conclusion, and he extrapolates from what he knows of the Glanton gang's exploits make a narrative about a world-program seemingly set up by something like a gnostic grand demiurge and enjoyed by him as proprietor, with earthly power being that of judgment sprung from will (the judge's judgment, the judge's will, both perhaps signifying the author's as-above-so-below—and *vice-versa*—notions), untempered by mercy and wisdom: this is Yahweh's programmatic power (as the Gnostics saw it), exercised by his archonic overseer. A good "alien" god exists somewhere, as is always the case in Gnosticism, and he is the god of the epilogue who put the fire in the earth and part of himself in the souls of humans, including the kid—to which we will return. But: with respect to these southwestern doings on this southwestern set, so what?

IV. The False Graver

Midway through *Blood Meridian* the kid asks Tobin, the ex-priest, the obvious and paramount question about Judge Holden: "What's he a judge of?" The ex-priest cautions the kid to be quiet: "Hush now. The man will hear ye."

The question goes unanswered for a long time, and when it finally *is* answered—in the kid's feverish dream—it comes in a passage which is at once the most difficult in the book and yet absolutely necessary to understanding it adequately:

The judge smiled. The fool was no longer there but another man and this other man he [the kid] could never see in his entirety but he seemed an artisan and a worker in metal. The judge enshadowed him where he crouched at his trade but he was a coldforger who worked with hammer and die, perhaps under some indictment and an exile from men's fires, hammering out like his own conjectural destiny all through the night of his becoming some coinage for a dawn that would not be. It is this false moneyer with his gravers and burins who seeks favor with the judge and he is at contriving from cold slag brute in the crucible a face that will pass, an image that will render this residual specie [the judge, as explained in the previous paragraph] current in the markets where men barter. Of this is the judge judge and the night does not end.

On first reading, the passage seems impenetrably perverse. It is clearly outside the judge's will for the forger to succeed in contriving a face that will pass, an image that will render this residual specie current in the markets where men barter, whereas it appears to us as more likely that this *would* be the judge's will. And it is clearly outside his will for the night to end, for the dawn to come, and this too has to strike us as odd, since the dawn being spoken of is one in which the engraver's counterfeit coin, which he quite reasonably believes the judge wishes him to succeed at producing, would "pass"—with the judge thereby presumably profiting. But the judge keeps judging its likeness of him inadequate. The reason is that the judge doesn't want a victory based on any currency (even his own counterfeit currency) in any "marketplace." The point is that he is a warrior—one who wants only war and the continuous night of war—in *opposition* not only to "true coinage" but to *any* coinage involving him. The "markets where men barter" exist, of course, but the judge believes them derivative, not primary—derivative of the war culture, which is the true culture upon which the markets (themselves only arenas for decadent symbolic war *games*) depend. (This view is presented in small in the brief picture of the "sutler" presented early in the novel. A sutler is a peddlar to an army, following along behind it, in McCarthy's image, like any debased and predatory camp-follower: a predator upon predators.)

Yet it is to the judge's advantage to foster the delusion that he wishes to create a new civilizational order, because this is a goal toward which he can encourage people to work at their various professions and trades—people like this graver. "Of this is the judge judge and the night does not end." Yes: because if he ever judges his own likeness "passable," thus allowing the transformation of war (which for him is god, as we know) into the merely symbolic, "civilized" competition of money-based conflict, he loses, there being little or no blood, and therefore no ultimately unifying victory, in symbolic warfare.

Another way of saying the same thing is that, just as the ascetic Gnostics thought it the wisest course not to "play the game" of the creator and his archons, so this archon will not play the (to him, "safe") money-changing game of marketplace humans as a means to defeating, dominating and destroying them. For him, *all* human coinage is counterfeit, and any victories won with it would just be meaningless counterfeit victories—solving, settling and signifying nothing.

It is helpful here to remember an earlier passage in which the judge debates a "Tennessean named Webster." In that passage the judge makes the familiar argument that many people in many cultures intuitively know that accurate portraiture "chain[s] the man to his own likeness," thus weakening him and perhaps killing him. The judge himself obsessively draws likenesses from nature, he says, in order to "expunge them from the memory of man." Webster counters that "no man can put all the world in a book," no matter what his goals for trying to do so might be—"No more than everything drawed in a book is so." "My book or some other book," answers the judge: "Whether in my book or not, every man is tabernacled in every other and he in exchange and so on in an endless complexity of being and witness to the uttermost edge of the world." The word to notice here is *exchange*. The judge refuses to be tabernacled in any other man. He refuses to be part of the exchange system.

What is the judge judge of? He is judge of all attempts—including those of patronage-seekers—to place him *within* that system, and he thus judges all attempts inadequate. It is not merely that he positions himself outside all tabernacles filled with "money-changers"; rather, it is that he positions himself outside all temples, period—to stand beyond that "outermost edge of the world" of which he speaks to Webster.

V. The Man of the Epilogue

In the dawn there is a man progressing over the plain by means of holes which he is making in the ground. He uses an implement with two handles and he chucks it into hole and he enkindles the stone in the hole with his steel hole by hole striking the fire out of the rock which God has put there. On the plain behind him are the wanderers in search of bones and those who do not search and they move haltingly in the light like

mechanisms whose movements are monitored with escapement and
pallet so that they appear restrained by a prudence or reflectiveness
which has no inner reality and they cross in their progress one by one
that track of holes that runs to the rim of the visible ground and which
seems less the pursuit of some continuance that the verification of a
principle, a validation of a sequence and causality as if each round and
perfect hole owed its existence to the one before it there on that prairie
upon which are the bones and the gatherers of bones and those who do
not gather. He strikes fire in the hole and draws out his steel. Then they
all move on again.

When I first read *Blood Meridian*, I took walking, digging, fire-striking
man of its epilogue as somehow standing for the judge as some manner of
(Nietzschean? evil Promethean?) culture-making force, with the mass of
humanity blindly following along after him in a line—an interpretation
which a little "close reading" shortly caused me to abandon. My attempts at
reinterpreting it—with the help of others—then led to my first glimpses of
what I am arguing here to be the novel's Gnostic, and perhaps even
specifically Manichean, features. I now believe that *Blood Meridian*
exemplifies the rare coupling of Gnostic "ideology" with the "affect" of
Hellenistic tragedy by means of its depiction of how power works in the
making and erasing of culture, and of what the human condition amounts to
when a person opposes that power and thence gets introduced to fate.

The epilogue pictures a brutal contrast between a man who is very
much alive and a host of other people who are effectively (or perhaps even
actually) dead, and the picture it paints is one based directly on the sort of
machine of which the watch or clock is the most familiar example. This is
what the words "escapement" and "pallet" refer to. And the idea is that the
alive digger and the dead wanderers are all *moving* in the way that such a
machine moves. The wanderers move "haltingly" because they are "cogs in
the wheel," it is suggested, groping forward in tick-tock fashion, just as the
digger goes forward in the pursuit of his continuance in tick-tock fashion
himself (digging and walking, digging and walking), even though *they* have
no holes to dig or fire to strike. The idea appears to be that the vast majority
of people, moving one by one through space (and presumably time), cross
this track, this "evidence," of fire struck out of the earth, but that these
people go neither backward to try to trace its source nor forward to follow
its lead. They just stumble over it—and either fail to notice it at all or
experience a dull moment of bemusement or puzzlement because of it. (And,
as we are talking about a writer and his book here—and an uncommonly
erudite writer at that—it is worth noting that the other prominent use of the

escapement device is in the typewriter, where, activated by the struck keys, it controls the horizontal movement of the carriage.)

The natural question to ask is, What is the connection between the man of the epilogue and the main narrative body of *Blood Meridian*? To this I have two answers. The first is a fairly obvious corrective to my initial feeling that the man somehow represents the judge, while the second is a reflection upon the significance of the first for studies of McCarthy. The first is that the man provides a "structural" element which is absolutely necessary to the novel's Gnostic world-view, but which is nowhere to be found in the characters who figure in its primary story: he is the revealer or "revelator" of the divine, working to free spirit from matter—the pneumatic (albeit corporeal) messenger, in possession of *gnosis*, who is in service to the good "alien god." This reading is, I think, clearly supported (if not indeed mandated) by the imagery of his striking and freeing bits of fire, imprisoned in the earth, which come from God; by the fact of his solitary, ascetic and superior nature and work (set in clear opposition to other people's nature and work, themselves the "sleepers" of Manichean thought); and by the Gnostic context provided by the novel proper, which not only implies his existence but mandates his eventual appearance. The "continuance" of which the digging man is in "pursuit" is the ongoing work of making his way back to the good, alien god—and of freeing and revealing imprisoned bits of holy fire in the evil world of the archons and all their sleeping inmates as he goes.

My second answer is more provisional. Even so, it will likely strike a good many readers as curious, irrelevant, outright wrong or all of the above. I think McCarthy may be showing us in the epilogue, in parable form, his reading of himself as writer—particularly in opposition to others. I think he goes so far as to make of himself a "presence" at the end—he has always been, after all, something of a Stendhalian editorialist as a narrator—affirming among other things that he is a particular, rare sort of "supply-side" producer of very serious stories: a solitary obsessive who, in his alienation from this Anareta world, this killing planet, and in his fidelity to the real god, has a "can do no other" (because Called) *purpose*, and who cares not a whit for the "market." ("Selling a book is the job of the publisher," the reclusive author said in the mid-1980s, in response to questions about his unwillingness to do the usual interviews and promotional work.) If there were a "god of this world," such a sense of artistic purpose might be usefully termed *mithectic*, with the artist doing his part to help his god out—to make the sun come up for the tribe by sitting and facing east every morning, for example, because it has been given to him as his calling to do this as the work of his life. But when there is *no* "god of this world," the artist-as-solitary obsessive is truly solitary and thus truly obsessive throughout his sentence here.

If this is so, then McCarthy has carried the romantic conception of the artist-as-creator/progenitor (itself derived from strains in the Italian Renaissance, in part Neoplatonist) to a new apotheosis based on an opposing premise. In McCarthy, the idea of the world-creating artist retains much of the romantic one—particularly its notion of the *stance* of the artist on earth—but everything is changed by virtue of the fact that *this* artist reflects and serves neither the Old Testament Yahweh nor some other good god of this world. Rather, he is inextricably bound to, and reflective of, the good "alien god" who did not make the world, is not in charge of it and is no part of it—except for the "spark of original divinity" residing in people, waiting to be awakened (by the Call) and then nurtured to the most of those persons' capacities. I think this has been a logical step for artists since Nietzsche—whom McCarthy has certainly read and read well—although Nietzsche, no Gnostic, would not have approved of the theology. And if I am right, it would actually be an understatement to call McCarthy an "elitist" for having taken it, because he has actually gone about as far as Nietzsche himself went while he still had a grip—and that was a ways.

All of which is just to say: The man in the epilogue, as he moves over the landscape digging holes and striking his God's fire in them, is the exact antithesis of the false "graver" of the kid's dream who seeks the judge's favor through a different sort of line-drawing. And just as the judge (although unbeknownst to the graver) does not want to "pass" in the civilized world, but wants only war, victory and then more war in the unending night of fallen matter, so the man of the epilogue cares nothing for playing and winning in the judge's world (for to win is to lose there just as much as to lose is to lose), but wants only the "pursuit of his continuance" in the service of what he takes to be the good and right way to go. Neither the man nor the judge will enter the exchange system.

VI. Gnostic Tragedy and Enchantment

Finally, how could it be so exhilarating and so obviously good for us to read such an excessive, doom-obsessed, bone-chilling, novel of blood? How could such a thing be so oddly exuberant and elicit such a pleasurable response? The answer, I think, directly demonstrates how, on the level of what we used to so embarrassedly call the "human condition," Gnosticism is not really so far from Hellenism (to which it has often been opposed) after all. I think *Blood Meridian* elicits the same human responses as Greek tragedy, the reason being that its archon, Holden, plays the same role as the original untamed Fates (in *The Oresteia*, most notably), who judge and avenge, or who sometimes just do whatever they want. In the Western tradition, they have been steadily domesticated—from Fates to Eumenides to Fortune to Chance to Lady Luck. But if Fates stay Fates, then the just-doing-one's-best, divine-spark, protagonist has got to lose, through no fault of his or her own, and it has always been bizarrely energizing, bracing, "cathartic" and joy-producing to feel the delirious pity and fear when the protagonist takes his or her heroic bloodbath at the end—to read it and weep.

Students of Gnosticism agree that its version of Fate (*heimarmene*) is central to its system, and scholars of literature know that it is not that unusual to find writers working with Gnostic materials. Yet I know of no writers in English save McCarthy who have seen the potential for human tragedy in those materials when Fate is placed front and center—as it must be if Gnosticism is to be Gnosticism—and who have then proceeded to make the tragedy. (This is why *Blood Meridian* is so much more powerful in its effect than either other Gnostic narratives or mere pastoral tragedies.) And, while it could be argued that the kid is no "tragic hero," it seems clear enough that some tragic heroes do not really fill any formulaic bill, most notably Antigone; all that's needed is a dumb kid possessed of a spark of the divine who's outside the will of some Yahweh or other and meets his or her fate at said nemesis' hands at the end. The *peculiar* thing, really, is that it strikes us Americans in the 1990s as so outlandishly shocking to find one of our writing countrymen not only refusing to water down the tragic vision, but embracing it with open arms.

McCarthy's greatness lies most centrally and most obviously in the fact that, in "progressing over the plain," he has become our finest living tragedian. And part of genuine tragic enchantment is the unrepressed gaity which both results from and then informs cosmic alienation in the greatest tragedians and their characters. In 1604 London, a long forgotten storyteller known only as "An.Sc., Gentleman," implied that the secret of *Hamlet*'s fineness is that in Shakespeare "the comedian rides when the tragedian stands on tiptoe." There are precious few writers of whom one could say this, but one can say it of the writer of *Blood Meridian*. In major consequence of his mastery of the high tragedian's art, Cormac McCarthy has become the best and most indispensable writer of English-language narrative in the second half of the century.

VEREEN BELL

"Between the Wish and the Thing the World Lies Waiting"

Cormac McCarthy's most sympathetic characters wish to live only in the mode of description—the less narrative the better—but the God that rules their world—an editor, clearly—likes stories and, either for his own amusement or to test them, he imposes plots upon them. Take this case of John Grady Cole, in *All the Pretty Horses*. The plot for him begins before he is born and with someone else's kin:

> It runs in the family, said Blevins. My grandaddy was killed in a minebucket in West Virginia it run down in the hole a hunnerd and eighty feet to get him it couldnt even wait for him to get to the top. They had to wet down the bucket to cool it fore they could get him out of it, him and two other men. It fried em like bacon. My daddy's older brother was blowed out of a derrick in the Batson Field in the year nineteen and four, cable rig with a wood derrick but the lightnin got him anyways and him not nineteen year old. Great uncle on my mother's side—mother's side, I said—got killed on a horse and it never singed a hair on that horse and it killed him graveyard dead they had to cut his belt off him where it welded the buckle shut and I got a cousin aint but four years oldern me was struck down in his own yard

From the *Southern Review* 28, no. 4 (October 1992): 920–27. ©1992 by the Louisiana State University.

comin from the barn and it paralyzed him all down side and
melted the fillins in his teeth and soldered his jaw shut.

From thirteen-year-old Jimmy Blevins's fear of lightning—and from his not
being afraid of anything else—otherwise inconceivably evil consequences for
John Grady and his friend Lacey Rawlins ensue. Blevins, who has taken up
with them on their ride into Mexico, loses his horse and his gun one night
when he frantically dismounts and takes shelter in an arroyo during a
thunderstorm. When against their better judgment the older boys help him
repossess the horse in the next village—and later because Blevins goes back
to repossess his gun as well—persecution and misfortune hound them as they
ride on, seeking the good life that home in Texas no longer offers them.
Worst of all, they are discredited and exiled from the ancient place of the
good life, the Hacienda de Nuestra Señora de la Purísima Concepción, that
they believe they have found.

These circumstances, which the boys endure stoically and resourcefully,
are generated not only by the plot that comes upon them out of nowhere but
by their own generous impulses and honorable conduct. John Grady is asked
at a point later in the story if he does not fear God and he says, "I got no
reason to be afraid of God. I've even got a bone or two to pick with him." A
kindly café proprietor says to him later "that it was good that God kept the
truths of life from the young as they were starting out or else they'd have no
heart to start out at all." This turns out to be the real point: whether John
Grady can endure such gratuitous tribulation with his hardheaded boy's
idealism intact. By the time he makes his way back to Texas—on
Thanksgiving Day—he has good reason to fear the God of such plots; but he
is also sobered and stronger, so he does not. He also now knows what the
main question is even if takes the form of an answer.

> He remembered Alejandra and the sadness he'd first seen in the
> slope of her shoulders which he'd presumed to understand and of
> which he knew nothing and he felt a loneliness he'd not known
> since he was a child and he felt wholly alien to the world
> although he loved it still. He thought that in the beauty of the
> world were hid a secret. He thought the world's heart beat at
> some terrible cost and that the world's pain and its beauty moved
> in a relationship of diverging equity and that in this headlong
> deficit the blood of multitudes might ultimately be exacted for
> the vision of a single flower.

The word *being* still means something in McCarthy's writing—after all
this time since Heidegger—and his finest and simplest characters set their

bearings by it in a way that determines their lives. It is greater than God Himself, and it is sacred. It is also elusive and perhaps illusory, and human beings are wholly incidental to it, if not its nemesis. McCarthy's nature exists wholly on its own, indifferent to human purpose or desire; his vivid, austere landscapes seem mysteriously to be gazing at us rather than the reverse. In this novel even horses, in some sweetly comic way, reflect upon the issue. When the boys, drunk off a canteenful of a Mexican moonshine called sotol, become sick and commence vomiting:

> The browsing horses jerked their heads up. It was no sound they'd ever heard before. In the gray twilight those retchings seemed to echo like the calls of some rude provisional species loosed upon that waste. Something imperfect and malformed lodged in the heart of being. A thing smirking deep in the eyes of grace itself like a gorgon in an autumn pool.

At best, human understanding and language can mediate being only imperfectly and, in action, only intuitively and in dreams or through the feeble agency of objective correlatives.

This is why McCarthy's narratives always seem to verge upon, without ever moving wholly over into, allegory: everything is potentially meaningful (even puking). It is also why the photorealistic details of processes or landscape and the substance and speech of ordinary human life ("The waitress brought their dinner, thick china lunchplates with steak and gravy and potatoes and beans. 'I'll get you alls bread'") are enveloped in an aura of stylization and romance. The aforementioned Alejandra Rocha y Villareal, for instance, with whom John Grady falls hopelessly in love as only a boy of seventeen can, is barely represented and, at that, only through John Grady's eyes; and yet she and her thwarted romance with John Grady are credible because of that special dimension of desire she inhabits which not only John Grady's infatuation but the novel itself creates. On the surface this central episode of the novel seems quite conventional, but its conventionality is animated by McCarthy's writing, which makes it new, and by the larger purpose that gives it value. The scene in which the two part for the last time is like a thousand others in film and literature and yet somehow redefines the genre. For John Grady it is like this: "He saw very clearly how all his life led only to this moment and all after led nowhere at all. He felt something cold and soulless enter him like another being and he imagined that it smiled malignly and he had no reason to believe that it would ever leave." And we believe him because we have been there before, in real life and in other fiction—not, precisely speaking, in love for the first time, but where love reaches. Love's having failed will change John Grady's reality, as the war and now cancer have changed his father's.

The deepest continuity with life in this novel is through horses:

> His father rode sitting forward slightly in the saddle, holding the reins in one hand about two inches above he saddlehorn. So thin and frail, lost in his clothes. Looking over the country with those sunken eyes as if the world out there had been altered or made suspect by what he'd seen of its elsewhere. As if he might never see it right again. Or worse did see it right at last. See it as it had always been, would forever be. The boy who rode on slightly before him sat a horse not only as if he'd been born to it which he was but as if were he begot by malice or mischance into some queer land where horses never were he would have found them anyway. Would have known that there was something missing for the world to be right or he right in it and would have set forth to wonder wherever it was needed for as long as it took until he came upon one and he would have known that was what he sought and it would have been.

What John Grady is said to love in horses is what, when he finds it there, he loves in men, "the blood and the heat of the blood that ran them. All his reverence and all his fondness and all the leanings of his life were for the ardenthearted and they would always be so and never be otherwise." The deepest offense in this story is to steal another's horse, and much of the novel's action is devoted to the obsession with recovering those that have been stolen and restoring them to their rightful owners, for such a theft is not simply a crime but the desecration of a type of invisible bond with the powers of the earth. When John Grady has dreams he dreams of horses, and those dreams are of sacred order:

> That night he dreamt of horses in a field on a high plain where the spring rains had brought up the grass and the wildflowers out of the ground and the flowers red and blue and yellow far as the eye could see and in the dream he was among the horses running and in the dream he himself could run with the horses and they coursed the young mares and fillies over the plain where their rich bay and their rich chestnut colors shone in the sun and the young colts ran with their dams and trampled down the flowers in a haze of pollen that hung in the sun like powdered gold and they ran he and the horses out along the high mesas where the

ground resounded under their running hooves and they flowed
and changed and ran and their manes and tails blew off of them
like spume and there was nothing else at all in that high world
and they moved all of them in a response that was like a music
among them and they were none of them afraid horse nor colt
nor mare and they ran in that resonance which is the world itself
and which cannot be spoken but only praised.

McCarthy's symbols are never less than artfully naive, and their
simplicity allows the reader to bear in mind that though this is a boy's story—
in a richer but similarly ironic way that *Huckleberry Finn* is—it is deeply
serious about the uncomplicated, romantic values that the boy's point of view
keeps before us. We are not encouraged by the slightest inflection of the style
to look upon John Grady and his friends with amusement or condescension.
John Grady's youthfulness, and its associated idealism, is a correlative in
itself—less a point of view than a private *episteme*, and one that refuses to be
diminished. It is challenged persuasively both by experience and by a
compelling history lesson in which John Grady is set straight by Alejandra's
protective great-aunt; but it is never quite undone and we are not meant to
think that is should be.

The Dueña Alfonsa, Alejandra's great-aunt, is friendly toward and
admires John Grady, but in the end she opposes him as a suitor for her niece
not because he is of the wrong class or nationality or because he is penniless
but, in effect, because his luck is bad—or more precisely because he has not
been hardened in the ways that would give him more control over his—and
by extension Alejandra's—destiny. The old woman's agenda is pragmatic and
revolutionary and—allowing for the culture she speaks through and
against—resolutely feminist:

Society is very important in Mexico. Where women do not even
have the vote. In Mexico they are mad for society and for politics
and very bad at both. My family are considered gachupines here,
but the madness of the Spaniard is not so different from the
madness of the Creole. The political tragedy in Spain was
rehearsed in full dress twenty years earlier on Mexican soil. For
those with eyes to see. Nothing was the same and yet everything.
In the Spaniard's heart is a great yearning for freedom, but only
his own. A great love of truth and honor in all its forms, but not
in its substance. And a deep conviction that nothing can be
proven except that it be made to bleed. Virgins, bulls, men.
Finally God himself.

Her own history encapsulates the horror and pathos of Mexico's history and because of that—because her story is a version of her culture's story—she has learned that the greatest tragedy is the cowardice of self-betrayal, and that self-betrayal occurs when one permits oneself to be diverted from the truth:

> It may be that the life I desire for her no longer exists, yet I know what she does not. That there is nothing to lose. In January I will be seventy-three years old. I have known a great many people in that time and few of them led lives that were satisfactory to them. I Would like for my grandniece to have the opportunity to make a very different marriage from the one which her society is bent upon demanding of her. I wont accept a conventional marriage for her. Again, I know what she cannot. That there is nothing to lose. I dont known what sort of world she will live in and I have no fixed opinions concerning how she should live in it. I only know that if she does not come to value what is true above what is useful it will make little difference whether she lives at all. And by true I do not mean what is righteous but merely what is so.

In this respect, for the old woman, no matter how courageous and honorable he might be otherwise, John Grady is dangerously unfinished. "In the end," she says, "we all come to be cured of our sentiments. Those whom life does not cure death will. The world is quite ruthless in selecting between the dream and the reality, even when we will not. Between the wish and the thing the world lies waiting." This long Conradian monologue is presented through dramatic writing as chilling and as resonant as anything McCarthy has yet achieved.

The Dueña Alfonsa's position in John Grady's story brings to the foreground its profoundest irony. The ruling desire of McCarthy's strongest characters, from Arthur Ownby in *The Orchard Keeper* to Cornelius Suttree in *Suttree*, is to live in some place that is not yet touched by the complications of the modern world, where it is possible to be one with the earth and to live in a genuine human communion. In practice this means that they want not so much to reverse history as to transcend it. It is no coincidence that when Cornelius Suttree is leaving Tennessee for the last time he stands above a roadbed where the new Knoxville expressway system is being built, connecting to the interstate system that will cause towns to die and cities to become indistinguishable. It is also no coincidence that he sees himself momentarily reflected and reclaimed in the blue eyes of a boy who has climbed the embankment of offer him water from a tin dipper.

John Grady Cole is Arthur Ownby in another time at a different age and also that reflection of himself younger that Suttree is permitted to see. Until now, in 1949, his grandfather's 18,000-acre cattle ranch has insulated him from history, but now that it is to be sold from around him, he can see the future coming. "People don't feel safe no more," his father says to him. "We're like the Comanches was two hundred years ago. We don't know what's goin to show up here come daylight. We don't even know what color they'll be." The father has given up, but John Grady is not waiting around to find out, and this is why he and Rawlins set out on horseback—how else? — meaning, without thinking or saying it in so many words, to move back in history by riding south. The great irony, as Señorita Alfonsa's story underscores, is that some kind of history is everywhere. The boys are too young to understand this yet (and many novelists and poets who should know better still don't): that there is no human place outside of time, and where human places are there are also the constructs and institutional artifacts of history. The fleas come with the dog. John Grady and Rawlins escape for a time the dissociating effects of the technology and capital of the new American order, but what they get from their adopted ancient culture is an attractive but totalitarian hierarchy—the autocratic rule of families, at best, and at worst, of brute power instead of law. In Enlightenment terms, a dignified ancient culture is also, inescapably, a primitive one.

It is not difficult at all to lapse into thinking of this story as taking place in the nineteenth century, or even earlier. The occasional battered truck and an especially ominous plane are surrealistically incongruous. John Grady and Rawlins bring an uncomplicated if wary democratic spirit into this old world which the system is unwilling to accommodate—itself stranded between past and future. What promises to be a dialectic turns out to be unproductive. What the outcome might have been imagined to be is, in the end, beside the point, for as the Dueña Alfonsa says, in history there are no control groups—there is nothing but what happens—and he own paradigmatic reading of history is grounded in the authentic tragedy of Francisco Madero's rise and fall—a story for her for all time of what results when intellectual idealism and political reality collide.

The story of Madero (his brother had been a suitor of Señorita Alfonsa's) seems to be a paradigm for McCarthy as well. There can be no doubt by now that McCarthy is a genuine—if somehow secular—mystic. This novel along with Blood Meridian shows him to be also a serious student of history, and that he reads history's lessons clearheadedly without the slightest chance of projecting politically correct or utopian back-formations upon it. His project is like Conrad's Marlow's, to continue to be able to believe in a numinous value at the heart of existence while remaining wholly without reassurance about this project from the realities of political life. Nor are there any practical hopes that what we can imagine in our moments of concentrated intuition has any chance at all of flourishing in the institutions—using the term advisedly—of men. In his writing, too, McCarthy must therefore always wrestle with the deconstructive angel, seeking to represent in mere words the "resonance . . . like music . . . which is the world itself" while knowing full well that language and music cannot be the same and that to try to represent this presence through a medium which is hopelessly grounded in material nature is to fail, and that to fail in this dedicated way is to enact, yet again—a human fractal—the whole problem in itself of being in the world.

So as a writer McCarthy's story is exactly the same as John Grady Cole's, except in a different time. John Grady in turn is clearly intended to be a saint of this project, and humorous and ordinary as he is at one level, he is inhumanly demanding at another, both of the world and of himself. When he reconnoiters with Rawlins back in Texas for the last time, his friend tries halfheartedly to talk him into staying on, maybe going to work on the oil rigs where the money's good. This is still good country," he says. "Yeah. I know it is," John Grady says. "But it ain't my country." "What is your country," says Rawlins. "I don't know," John Grady says. "I don't know where it is. I don't know what happens to country." So he rides on out, as each unaccommodated visionary must inevitably do. Riding on in McCarthy's world gets to be a habit. His characters remain both medieval and irredeemably American.

On the other hand almost all of the foregoing is both reductive and redundant, for this time around a McCarthy novel speaks lucidly and eloquently for itself. *All the Pretty Horses* is being described as more accessible than his other novels, and that is certainly the case. And that being the case no doubt accounts for its position (as of this writing) on the *New York Times* bestseller list. Probably this novel has already sold more copies than all of McCarthy's previous novels combined. The editors at Random House who stuck by him during the lean years deserve knighthood. Now that Random House/Knopf sees that they have a promotable book, they are promoting it and McCarthy. This has required him to emerge briefly from hiding and, not surprisingly, he has conducted himself with a dignity one could wish upon other authors. The faint of heart will be pleased to discover, too, that in *All the Pretty Horses* the overpowering ratio of evil to good that we have come to expect from McCarthy's fiction has been pretty much reversed. This may bode well for the next two volumes of what is being represented as a trilogy. On the other hand it is the very essence of tragedy that, as the Dueña Alfonsa expresses it, "the world is quite ruthless in selecting between the dream and the reality, even when we will not." The God who loves plots works in mysterious ways, and He stays busy. So we shall see.

EDWIN T. ARNOLD

The Mosaic of McCarthy's Fiction

With the exception of *The Orchard Keeper*, which I read immediately after *Outer Dark* in 1968, I have had the opportunity to follow the career of Cormac McCarthy, book by book, as each was published. McCarthy, it seemed to me as I read, was constantly reinventing himself with each new work, telling a new story in a new style and daring the reader to guess what next, or what before. McCarthy's fiction has now begun to take a shape, to reveal its major themes and concerns and influences so that we can start to perceive both the intertextuality of the works—the way they relate or react to, reflect, respond, grow from, and speak against other works, traditions, cultural assumptions, historical surroundings—and the intratextuality of the books—the interconnectedness and cross-fertilization of the stories and images of the stories themselves—and we can thus begin to apprehend the larger construct of McCarthy's art.

Texts, of course, have lives outside of their publication dates, and the impulse or gestation of a book sometimes cuts across the beginning and completion of many another. (McCarthy was writing *Suttree* [1979], for example, during the time he published both *The Orchard Keeper* [1965] and *Outer Dark* [1968], it appears.) The "mosaic" of my title comes, of course, from Julia Kristeva's contention that any text is a construction of other "quotations"; and although McCarthy's mosaic can and does include authors,

From *Sacred Violence: A Reader's Companion to Cormac McCarthy*. ©1995 by Texas Western Press.

histories, folklore, common knowledge, and so forth (as John Sepich has conclusively shown, for example, in *Notes on "Blood Meridian"*), I want to concentrate exclusively on the intratextuality of McCarthy's own works. Like Faulkner's Yoknapatawpha and non-Yoknapatawpha novels, McCarthy's novels now seem to be dividing themselves into his "southern" and "western" books, and there are many readers who know one but not the other, or who know one book, *All the Pretty Horses*, but not those which came before. Yet, again like Faulkner's, these books speak one to another whatever their setting and, with each response, deepen and expand and give shape to McCarthy's overall artistic vision.

The most obvious example (to me) of one McCarthy novel's interacting with another is *All the Pretty Horses* as response to *Blood Meridian*. If *Pretty Horses* is, as advertised, the first volume of a proposed *Border Trilogy*, *Blood Meridian* must surely stand as prologue to the work. The titles themselves, one a lovely refrain from a child's lullaby and the other a stark image of man's capacity for carnage, establish two opposing views of human experience. But the elegiac *Horses* does contain moments of brutality, just as *Blood Meridian* provides moments of unexpected grace and beauty, and, taken together, they present, I think, two variations of the same text, the same narrative elements considered from different perspectives. Both have as protagonist a sixteen-year-old "kid"—anonymous, unnamed in one book and given name, background, and family history in the other. The two boys are separated by a hundred years: the "kid" is born in 1833 and joins John Joel Glanton's gang in 1849; John Grady Cole is born in 1934 and goes to Mexico on his own excursions in 1949. *Blood Meridian* ends with a mysterious epilogue in which one man is "progressing" across the desert plain, digging holes for the fences to come. The "track of holes" forms a path leading "to the rim of the visible ground," and a group of people follow, "less the pursuit of some continuance than the verification of a principal, a validation of sequence and causality as if each round and perfect hole owed its existence to the one before it there on that prairie." Just as the fence will impose an appearance of order on the open territory, so the movement of the people seems to be toward some future time beyond the horizon, the "rim of the visible ground." On the first page *All the Pretty Horses*, John Grady Cole steps outside his house: "Dark and cold and no wind and a thin gray reef beginning along the eastern rim of the world," McCarthy writes. "He walked out on the prairie and stood holding his hat like some supplicant to the darkness over them all and he stood there for a long time." A train passes in the dark, and its headlight "came boring out of the east like some ribald satellite of the coming sun" and illuminates "the endless fenceline down the dead straight right of way and sucking it back again wire and post mile on mile into the darkness. . . ." Later

John Grady rides west from his house to the nearby old Comanche road, "and the sun sat blood red and elliptic under the reefs of bloodred cloud before him." There he witnesses "a dream of the past where the painted ponies and the riders of that lost nation came down out of the north with their faces chalked and their long hair plaited and each armed for wars which was their life and the women and children and women with children at their breasts all of them pledged in blood and redeemable in blood only." Thus, the ending of *Blood Meridian* looks forward, the beginning of *Pretty Horses* looks backward, and they meet at a point where text joins text.

McCarthy loves the idea of dark twinship ("The candleflame and the image of the candleflame caught in the pierglass" reads the first sentence of *All the Pretty Horses*), and it seems clear to me that John Grady Cole and the kid are such twins, a century apart and each a product of his experience and learning but brothers nonetheless. If the kid is "pledged in blood," John Grady is "redeemable in blood," and, reversing the circumstances, each could live the other's life.

But these books are, as I've suggested, only the most obvious of the interconnections. To go back to the beginning, *The Orchard Keeper*, the first novel, begins with its own rather ambiguous italicized prologue in which three men cut down a tree and find running through it "the twisted wrought-iron, the mangled fragment of [a] fence": "Growed all up in that tree," one says, reversing the natural process so that the iron fence has done the growing into the tree, rather than the tree around the fence. The scene is then dropped until the very end of the book, when the boy, John Wesley Rattner, visits his mother's grave. "The workers had gone, leaving behind their wood-dust and chips, the white face of the stump pooling the last light out of the gathering dusk," we are told. "The sun broke through the final shelf of clouds and bathed for a moment the dripping trees with blood. . . . He passed through the gap in the fence, past the torn iron palings and out to the western road, the rain still mizzling softly and the darkening headlands dawning off the day, heraldic, pennoned in flame, the fleeing minions scattering their shadows in the wake of the sun." Thus, in this first book we have the same images of bloody suns and fences and western roads as we find in *Blood Meridian* and *Pretty Horses*.

But this first book anticipates all the other books as well. We have a reference, for example, to "that being in the outer dark with whom only he held communion," anticipating the title and the theme of the second novel, and we have descriptions of McAnally Flats and the Knoxville market district, anticipating *Suttree*. Compare, for example, the description of John Wesley's journey through downtown Knoxville after he gets his hawk bounty to Suttree's after he sells his fish, or note old Arthur Ownby's comment to

John Wesley that "They's even a bounty on findin dead bodies, man over to Knoxville does pretty good grapplehookin em when they jump off of the bridge like they do there all the time," which forms the central action of the opening scene of *Suttree*. For that matter, think how John Wesley's bringing in dead hawks for bounty is like Gene Harrowgate's bringing in dead bats for reward in *Suttree* is like John Glanton's bringing in scalps as receipts in *Blood Meridian*. Like the fence pole that "grows" through the tree, there are numerous such images and actions embedded throughout all of McCarthy's novels.

I've noted that *Blood Meridian* is set primarily in 1849, and *All the Pretty Horses* in 1949, but the pattern continues in other books. The Green Fly Inn in *The Orchard Keeper* burns down in 1933 (the same year McCarthy himself was born), a hundred years after the kid is born and the same year Marion Sylder kills Kenneth Rattner in self-defense and Arthur Ownby sets up his vigil over Rattner's corpse in the insecticide pit. John Wesley Rattner is a baby when his father disappears, and when he heads west at the end of the book, he is fifteen or sixteen years old and it is 1948, the year before John Grady Cole goes to Mexico. *Suttree* begins in early 1950 and ends in 1955 when Cornelius Suttree leaves town, seeking his own new life.

The time schemes of *Outer Dark* and *Child of God* are less specific. *Outer Dark* takes place, one would guess, in the twentieth century, but the year is unclear and the world described comes more from folktale or myth than an identifiable locale, although east Tennessee seems likely. Lester Ballard in *Child of God* dies in the insane asylum in 1965, but we don't know how many years he has been incarcerated; we can again guess that his story takes place in the 1950s (one character, a Mr. Wade, described only as an "old man," says he was born in 1885, which can help us make a rough determination).

The point here is that not only does McCarthy tend to concentrate on mid-centuries (a chronological meridian, perhaps), but that his protagonists are most often young boys becoming men setting out onto their individual journeys, for good or ill, a pattern which is repeated in *The Crossing* (1994), his most recent novel. But I think this pattern also underscores another more significant point about McCarthy. Vereen M. Bell argued in his groundbreaking 1988 study, *The Achievement of Cormac McCarthy*, that McCarthy's characters are essentially unthinking, unreflective. "One strength of McCarthy's novels is that they resist the imposition of theses from the outside, especially conventional ones, and that they seem finally to call all theses into question," he wrote. This is still a prevailing reading of McCarthy's works. Denis Donoghue, for example, in his June 1993 *New York Review of Books* essay, repeats this contention. "The characters . . . are like recently arrived primates, each possessing a spinal column but little or no capacity of mind or consciousness," he maintains. "His episodes are produced not to be interrogated or understood within some large myth or other system of value. They are there to be sensed, to be seen. The appalling quality of each deed is its emptiness, as if it were done before anyone thought of any meaning it might have." I would suggest just the opposite.

Indeed, reading McCarthy's novels as intratexts rather than as separate, unrelated works makes it clear, I think, that his corpus does tell a definite story, and that story is as old as the hills of Tennessee and as profound as the deserts of the Southwest. Gail M. Morrison, in her recent essay on *All the Pretty Horses*, discusses the novel in terms of the quest myth. "Most of McCarthy's novels, despite their apparent episodic organization, involve both metaphoric and literal journeys which bring their voyagers inevitably into a series of conflicts and confrontations with themselves as well as with the various communities intersected by their wanderings," she writes. "And, in most of these novels, the central characters' journeys, however random in time and place they may be, are apparently rooted in dysfunctional families and troubled filial relationships."

To put it in somewhat more mythic terms, McCarthy writes about the passing down of heritage or the failure of that passage, the intergenerational communion which, like the fence holes in *Blood Meridian*, seems "less the pursuit of some continuance than the verification of a principal, a validation of sequence and causality." In *The Orchard Keeper*, we have three such generations, but none blood-related to the others (except by the act of violence). The true father, Kenneth Rattner, is killed by the man, Marion Sylder, who replaces him in paternal relationship to the son, John Wesley, while "grandfather" Arthur Ownby keeps watch, unknowingly, over the unidentified body of the failed and worthless father. But both Sylder and Ownby impart knowledge to the boy, who visits them both in their separate cells (prison and asylum), acknowledging their influence, before striking out on his own.

Culla Holme, like Laios, leaves his nameless infant son, begotten of his sister Rinthy, in the woods to escape his guilt but must face his own judgment before the dark strangers who judge him, again in the woods, with that same son as mute witness against the derelict father. Lester Ballard is that child betrayed—his mother run away, his father a suicide—left to find the father's dead body and to grow his own way into sorrow and perversity. (And lest we think Lester stands apart from McCarthy's other protagonists, compare him and his surroundings to John Wesley Rattner, who, I would maintain, is his healthier, saner counterpart in the same way John Grady Cole serves for the kid.)

Cornelius Suttree, alienated from his own parents, considers suicide but deserts his wife and only child to live alone and later finds the son dead and his wife mad with grieving. Suttree turns to look after another old man and another young boy as surrogates for his father and child and fails them both, each too late for saving and both bound for their own incarcerations.

"See the child" are the first words of *Blood Meridian*. The kid's father is a drunk. "The mother dead these fourteen years did incubate in her own bosom the creature who would carry her off. The father never speaks her name, the child does not know it." Thus divested of family or heritage, he heads west, there to meet Judge Holden, a variation of the same dark figure who rules over *Outer Dark*. "Dont you know that I'd have loved you like a son?" the judge tells the kid and subsequently "gather[s] him in his arms against his immense and terrible flesh," in a loving embrace of death.

Then compare the kid to John Grady Cole in *All the Pretty Horses*, whose mother has abandoned the family to pursue an acting career, and whose father and grandfather die in the same year. But here is a change. Both of these men have imparted to the boy a way of living, an attitude toward the world, which sustains him in the trials he undergoes.

A similar situation seems to be established in *The Crossing*, in which the boy, Billy, also learns and benefits from his upbringing before he, too, sets out on his own journey of discovery. Billy lies awake at night before leaving home, thinking about a wolf he is trying to trap: "He tried to see the world the wolf saw. . . He wondered at the world it smelled or what it tasted. He wondered had the living blood with which it slaked its throat a different taste to the thick iron tincture of his own. Or to the blood of God. In the morning he was out before daylight saddling the horse in the cold dark of the barn. He rode out the gate before his father was even up and he never saw him again."

The reference to the "blood of God" also reminds us that the search for the father can, in theological terms, become the quest for God, for grace. I don't want to turn McCarthy into an overtly Christian writer; although he makes compelling use of western Christian symbology, I suspect his own belief system embraces a larger and more pantheistic view. Vereen Bell has put it nicely in his *Southern Review* essay on *All the Pretty Horses*: "The word *being* still means something in McCarthy's writing. . .and his finest and simplest characters set their bearings by it in a way that determines their lives. It is greater than God Himself, and it is sacred." Bell later writes, "There can be no doubt that McCarthy is a genuine—if somehow secular—mystic;" but I think McCarthy is a mystic in the way his favorite writer Melville is a mystic, acknowledging and in fact honoring the majesty of the astounding and awful as well as of the simple and beautiful. As Garry Wallace recalled of a conversation with McCarthy, "He went on to say that he thinks the mystical experience is a direct apprehension of reality, unmediated by symbol, and he ended with the thought that our inability to see spiritual truth is the greater mystery."

And so I hold that Cormac McCarthy is no nihilist, that his works have meaning and theme, and his characters are made of much more than erect spinal cords. We often make of individual texts what we like, but each is a part of the larger mosaic, and the pattern of McCarthy's mosaic, to my eyes, is complex, profound, significant, and deeply moving.

WADE HALL

The Human Comedy of Cormac McCarthy

The postscript to Cormac McCarthy's *Child of God* tells about a man named Arthur Ogle, who is plowing his upland field one day when suddenly his plow and mules are snatched into a hole that opens in the ground. The poor farmer never finds his mules and plow, but the hole leads to a charnel house of horror where seven corpses lie rotting on stone ledges. It is the final revelation in a novel that, like McCarthy's six other books, relentlessly strips away the thin covering of decency and dignity in which we humans dress ourselves in a bold attempt to deny our caves of darkness. This concluding episode does for the novel what humor does for life and literature—it exposes snaked truth. A vital aid in McCarthy's fact-finding literary mission is humor, an ancient and present avenue to human truth.

The Greek masks of tragedy and comedy are cut from the same flesh. Only the facial lines are altered slightly to represent two basic ways of viewing the one human condition. Tragedy has traditionally dealt with human nobility and greatness under stress and at death. The tragic view, however, tends to be a highly contrived, nonrepresentational, and unrealistic view of human life. On the other hand, comedy insists on confronting human nature and behavior in all its dimensions. Indeed, any writer who attempts to portray life honestly and unvarnished will write comedy. The comic writer may reprove human weaknesses gently and compassionately in the manner

From *Sacred Violence: A Reader's Companion to Cormac McCarthy.* ©1995 by Texas Western Press.

of the Roman poet Horace or the old television series, "I Love Lucy." Most of our humor is such light comedy that scratches the surface so delicately that we may laugh comfortably at someone else and feel superior, failing to see that all humor is a mirror in which we can see ourselves.

Or the writer may attack human nature with bitter, devastating satire, in the manner of another Roman poet Juvenal or the Tennesse/Texas fictionist Cormac McCarthy. Indeed, even the superficial reader of McCarthy realizes that he is no purveyor of light comedy; therefore, we recoil at his ghastly exposés, especially when they are supposed to remind us that murderers, necrophiles, sadists, and all manner of misfits are children of God, pretty much like us. Whatever the approach, the humorist takes a close-up view of human littleness, human incongruity, human inconsistency, human inhumanity. The humorist knows that human life is filled with trivia, insignificance, and little and big acts of selfishness.

Reading McCarthy is sometimes like reading an Ionesco-like script of a grotesque theatre of the absurd, and we do not like to admit that we are characters in the play. We want to believe that most of life is decent, meaningful, and that it is ultimately important, regardless of how we may behave; and we fabricate fantasies about ourselves. According to George Santayana, humor is the perception of this illusion. Indeed, the horrors of existence, large and small, can only be confronted by humor. It is a constant reminder of our spotted, speckled, violent, and bloody natures; and so humor rips aside our civilized veneer and shows us how ridiculous and mean and ugly and selfish and violent we are much—if not most—of the time—not honest or heroic or kind, as we would like to think. Humor, therefore, takes us closer to *who* we are, especially if we don't wear too many layers of civilization, as is the case with McCarthy's characters.

But how can we live with such awful revelations, such truths about ourselves? What keeps us from going insane or going on a bloody rampage like Lester Ballard in *Child of God* or the deadly "liberators" in *Blood Meridian*? Our intelligence and understanding allow us to see our dark truths, and these same faculties give us the ability to survive our dark passions. We may, indeed, be the only species of animal that has or needs a sense of humor. It is the safety value in our arsenal of survival. Humor is thus at once a way of looking at the sordid side of life and a release from the tensions that build up when we consider the huge gap between what we hold to be ideal and what we must admit is reality.

This mine field between facade and substance is the fertile ground of humor. It is McCarthy's killing field which he tills with deadly accuracy. Like Conrad's Marlowe and Kurz, he dares to descend into our interior pits and confront the writhing horrors of our human condition. If, in fact, the final truth is horror, as Conrad suggests, how else can one react, except in a laughter that explodes out of the revelation? Perhaps such men are telling us that life's epitaph, the last sound of any self-aware person, is demonic laughter and not the optimistic note struck by Faulkner in his Nobel Prize address, as he extols man's "puny inexhaustible voice." Is the last human sound, therefore, like the "low laugh" of Poe's doomed and ironically named Fortunato from his wine cellar tomb in "The Cask of Amontillado"; "Ha! ha!—he! he!—a very good joke indeed—an excellent jest," followed by a chilling silence? Or maybe the human predicament is like the child's game of hide-and-seek, "a fond Ambush" that if proven to be meaningless, in the words of Emily Dickinson: "Would not the fun/Look too expensive!/Would not the jest—/Have crawled too far!" With such mentors who thus probe the dark reaches of the human consciousness, Cormac McCarthy is in choice company.

The ways of people and of their worlds, are as we have seen, the natural resources of the humorist, even in such odd corners as we find in Eastern Tennessee or in the border country of Texas and Mexico. When a novelist writes frankly about the way people look and talk and behave, he produces fiction that is true and humor that is natural and organic. This is the essence of Cormac McCarthy's vocation as a humorist. It is an element as basic to his novels as the air his characters breathe. It is as different from the wise-cracking, punch-line humor of the stand-up comedian as Las Vegas is from Knoxville or El Paso. McCarthy's humor emerges from his subject matter, his characters, and his plots and is sustained by these elements. You will find few quick laughs in his fiction because the humor is woven so intricately into the fabric of Tennessee or Texas life.

To the outsider, McCarthy's people and their world may seem culturally retarded and primitive. Perhaps they are—by national norms. But such people provide a more striking mirror in which we can see our own imperfections all the more clearly. In fact, it is the very uniqueness of life in the Southern Appalachians and in the Texas border country that makes it appealing to both writer and reader. We are intrigued by such exotic ways of speaking and living. When a close observer like McCarthy uses them for the surface stories of his fables of evil, we are all the more likely to believe them. After all, what can we expect from people like *that*? We don't talk like that. We don't behave like them. We don't practice incest or necrophilia or commit random murders. Do we? Surely he is not writing about us. We are not outlaws or headscalpers or hillbillies or rednecks. Are we? But that is precisely the point that McCarthy is making. It is the way of serious humor that first one laughs down at someone else, then gradually realizes that he is laughing at himself. The accidents of language, of looks, and of customs derive from a single human nature. And human nature is what McCarthy's novels are all about. From such regional raw materials, therefore, McCarthy has shaped fiction that transcends time and locale and speaks in a universal language to readers everywhere.

McCarthy's characters and locales may be outside the American mainstream, but his humor is related directly to two main movements, local color and the humor of the Old Southwest. Like the local colorists of the late nineteenth century, he reveals the folk and folkways of a particular region, though without the pathos and caressing sentimentality of the earlier writers. Tennessee local colorists Mary Noailles Murfree and Will Allen Dromgoole penned sketches that include forerunners of McCarthy's characters; whereas these women remained aloof and apart from the life they depicted and superior to it, McCarthy succeeds in portraying the low life from the inside out and with a great deal of sympathy and understanding.

McCarthy is closer kin, therefore, to the pre-Civil War humorists of the Old Southwest. These writers were usually professional men—lawyers, judges, physicians, educators, journalists—who recorded the rough-and-tumble masculine life around them during the "flush times" of the antebellum South. Such men as Joseph Baldwin, A.B. Longstreet, and Johnson J. Hooper wrote realistic sketches of the Old Southwest that stretched from Georgia across to Louisiana, East Texas, and Arkansas and up through Tennessee and Kentucky. It was a frontier territory where life was hard and violent, a Darwinian jungle where strength and ingenuity triumphed and the weak withered and died. These humorists published their documentary-like stories primarily in northern sporting journals intended for male readers like the New York *Spirit of the Times*, edited by William T. Porter.

Vestiges of this frontier survived well into the twentieth century in such isolated regions as East Tennessee. Here were a people and place that had, indeed, been recorded before, but were still waiting for the special talents of a Cormac McCarthy. Of all the earlier humorists, McCarthy is closest kin to a writer who, like himself, was born elsewhere but moved to Knoxville, Tennessee, when he was a boy. The Pennsylvania-born George Washington Harris (1814-1869) grew up and lived most of his life in Knoxville and in the 1850s and 1860s contributed a series of sketches of the *Spirit of the Times* that feature a coarse, vulgar, merciless prankster named Sut Lovingood, who calls himself a "nat'ral born durn'd fool" whose joy in life is to raise "pertickler hell." And that he does. Despite the restraints and taboos of nineteenth-century publishing, Harris was able to portray with a fair amount of realism the often crude and violent backwoods life of East Tennessee.

McCarthy's kinship with the Old Southwestern humorists ranges from his depiction of a mostly masculine society to his use of authentic regional dialect. Indeed, the title character of *Suttree* is not unlike McCarthy himself, an educated man who moves among, observes closely, and records the lowlife around him, like the Old Southwestern humorists. Perhaps McCarthy's most intriguing and successful novel, *Suttree* is a handbook in basic survival as the protagonist descends into an undergloom that is made, at least for the reader, bearable and enjoyable by humor. Suttree has left his marriage, his family, and his class and gone to live among a sordid subculture, which McCarthy describes extravagantly as a mix of "thieves, derelicts, miscreants, pariahs, poltroons, spalpeens, curmudgeons, clotpolls, murderers, gamblers, bawds, whores, trulls, brigands, topers, toss pots, sots and archsots, lobcocks, smellsmocks, runagates, rakes, and other assorted and felonious debauchees." Such an outrageous catalogue pays tribute to Dickensian lowlife as well as the American backwoodsman's love of outlandish words.

Indeed, spectacular use of language is a McCarthy hallmark which has sent many a reader to the *Oxford English Dictionary*. It is the raw, scatological language of his characters, moreover, with names like Trippin Through the Dew, Oceanfrog Frazer, J-Bone, Cabbage, Hoghead, Jabbo, and Bungalow, that helps to make their sad world endurable. These are people who love to play with language. This is the way that Kenneth Hazelwood (called Worm) refuses a homemade drink of whiskey: "The last time I drank some of that shit I like to died. I stunk from the inside out. I laid in a tub of hot water all day and climbed out and dried and you could still smell it. I had to burn my clothes. I had the dry heaves, the drizzlin shits, the cold shakes and the jakeleg. I can think about it now and feel bad." That's the way a latter-day Sut Lovingood would say it. Whether or not the well-read McCarthy has read Sut's frontier adventures, it is certain that he writes in the Lovingood tradition. Several characters even refer to Suttree as Sut. Coincidence? Maybe. Maybe not. What is certain is that Suttree is filled with raucous humor—just the kind that George Washington Harris would write today.

Similarities to the Old Southwestern humor are easy to find in all of McCarthy's novels. From Marion Sylder in *The Orchard Keeper* to the kid in *Blood Meridian* and John Grady Cole in *All the Pretty Horses*, the men survive by their wits. Like Johnson. J. Hooper's Simon Suggs, they know that "it pays to be shifty in a new country." They are independent men and boys who love their rough outdoor masculinity—trapping, hunting, making and drinking and selling whiskey, fighting, killing, and storytelling. Indeed, McCarthy has created a memorable gallery of characters who are the more humorous because they are behaving naturally. They are freedom-loving men who are suspicious of the law and outsiders, and they are men for whom excess is a way of life, from drinking to whoring to killing. Because literary humor often exaggerates even the usual distortions of nature, casual readers may dismiss McCarthy as a maker of grotesque parody. In fact, such depraved men as

Child of God's Lester Ballard and *Blood Meridian*'s Judge Holden seem to fit the pattern of grotesques worked by another twentieth century author, Sherwood Anderson, whose *Winesburg, Ohio* is filled with men who are controlled by a single passion.

More commonly, however, McCarthy's characters are going about what they consider the ordinary business of life, which seems grotesque only in the telling. Take, for instance, Ef Hobie in *The Orchard Keeper*. He is the scion of a clan which was a "whiskey-making family before whiskey-making was illegal" and spends time in prison for carrying on the family business. Less than a year after his release, he dies in a wreck in which he is thrown from the car and pinned under it. Well, actually, he dies some time after that accident. One day Ef is showing some people at the store his huge scar from the accident and is drinking an "orange dope":

> They performed a autopsy on me and I lived, he told them.
> Then he laughed and got down off the drink box, emptied his
> orange and reached to put it in the rack. The bottle clattered on
> the floor, he lurched once, wildly, collapsed into the bread rack
> and went to the floor in a cascade of cupcakes and moonpies.

Fortunately, he a wife and son to continue the family tradition—which they do until the authorities break into the smokehouse and find their unlicensed whiskey "and took Mrs Hobie, aged seventy-eight, off to jail, sending her back home only when it was discovered she has cancer of the duodenum." It is the ironic juxtaposition of all the facts in the case from distance that makes the incident seem comically distorted. Death is always slipping up on us, McCarthy suggests. So why not in "a cascade of cupcakes and moonpies"? We don't all die a dignified death of cancer at home in bed.

Another type of comic character finds a home in *The Orchard Keeper*. He is Earl Legwater, a man and a name surely worthy to join Faulkner's Flem Snopes in the annals of American literary scoundrels. Toadlike, spindle-legged, leering, and smirking, Legwater is the county humane officer. The character of this scalawag is established in one incident: "Most of the old men had been there the day he shot two dogs behind the store with a .22 rifle, one of them seven times, it screaming and dragging itself along the fence in the field below the forks while a cluster of children stood watching until they too began screaming." After a bogus war hero's body is discovered in a spray pit, Legwater spends three days sifting ashes to find the platinum plate alleged to have been in the murdered man's head. Unlike the more crafty Flem Snopes, however, he becomes the ludicrous butt of his own greed.

Two of McCarthy's most appealing comic characters are literary cousins, Gene Harrogate in Suttree and the ill-fated but winsome Jimmy Blevins in *All the Pretty Horses*. Harrogate, "a half daft adolescent" and a comic scarecrow, is part-time watermelon rapist, lizard racer, must bat killer, tunnel digger, earthquake creator, and telephone booth robber, and, like Blevins, a full-time loser. His string of failed attempts to get rich is travesty of the American dream of easy wealth. His tunnel under Knoxville leads not to a vault where he thinks "the city's wealth was kept," but to sewer main that he explodes with his homemade bomb into a volcano of human filth. All his comic attempts at success are a part of his struggle to survive in a world that denies safety and security to most—if not all—of its people. In *All the Pretty Horses*, when Jimmy Blevins joins John Grady Cole and Lacey Rawlins in Mexico, the balance is titled toward comic bravado and bloodshed. Their swaggering dialogue mocks the grownup boasting of renegades and desperados, and they play boyish games with the finality of adults.

Blood Meridian has a rogue's gallery of despicable men, most of whom are without any discernible redeeming features. There is obvious humor in their folkspeech, and there is one character with a vestige of decency, the kid from Tennesse who rejects the nihilism of the hairless giant called "the judge." Like Mark Twain's "sMysterious Stranger," the judge has sought to convert his band of mercenaries to a belief in life's nothingness. Life is merely a dance of death, he preaches, and the only "true dancer" is one "who has offered up himself entire to the blood of war, who has been to the floor of the pit and seen horror in the round and learned at last that it speaks to his inmost heart, only that man can dance." His bleak sermon fails to convert the kid.

Finally, there is in *Child of God* the foulmouthed and funny Lester Ballard, a necrophiliac who plays out grotesquely comic sex scenes with a corpse and outwits the authorities by taking them into a cave where he has hidden his stolen bodies and then leading them into a passageway too small for them to follow. He is completely amoral. Outside the common norms good and evil, right and wrong, he is free to behave as his nature wills, killing promiscuously, roaming the land in drag, and using his victims like manequins in some styleshow of the dead. His perversions are ultimately comic as he becomes a ridiculous Charlie Chaplinesque figure dressing in "outsized overalls."

Much of McCarthy's humor derives from the folkways and folkspeech of his unliterate characters. His countrified diction is especially effective when a company of boys get together—say, Warn Pulliam, John Wesley Rattner, and Johnny Romines in *The Orchard Keeper* or the boy expatriates, already noted, in *All the Pretty Horses*—as the boys try to outdo each other in their mastery of bragging and scatology. Moreover, for educated readers unfamiliar with folkspeech, there is color and comedy in such expressions as "Hot-toe-mitty" for God Almighty or "They Lord God" used as an exclamation or excrescent t's added to certain words to make "happent," "oncet," or "kilt." Sometimes even McCarthy as narrator can't resist a comic swipe. When Lester Ballard is accused of rape, he says of his accuser, "She ain't nothin but a goddamned old whore." The narration continues: "The old whore slapped Ballard's mouth."

Dialect is, of course, most effective when it is woven naturally into the narrative. In *Outer Dark*, when Rinthy is searching for her lost son, she meets an odd assortment of people on her journey, including an old widow with whom she stops to rest and talk. Rinthy asks, "Is it just you and the mister at home now?" This is how the conversation continues, somewhat erratically:

> Earl died, she said.
> Oh.
> I just despise a snake don't you?
> Yes mam.
> I'm like my granny that way. She always said what she despised worst in the world was snakes hounds and sorry women.
> Yes mam. . . .
> The old woman drew up the wings of her nose between her thumb and forefinger and sneezed forth a spray of mucous and wiped her fingers on the overalls she wore.
> Earl's daddy used to keep half a holler full of old beat-up hounds. He had to keep Earl's too. I won't have one on the place. Wantin to lay out half the night runnin in the woods with a bunch of dogs like somethin crazy. Ain't a bit of use in the world somebody puttin up with such as that. I run his daddy off too. Told him he'd run with hounds so hard and long he'd took on the look of one let alone the smell. And him a squire. They wasn't no common people but I declare if they didn't have some common habits among em. He's a squire ye know. Course that never kept his daughter from runnin off with a no-account that sent her back big in the belly and thin in the shanks and nary word from him ever from that day to this. Or doomsday if ye wanted to wait.
> How far are ye goin?

Enough said. This passage has the realism of a tape-recorded conversation.

Furthermore, folk humor is integrated into the narrative on every page. The beehiver whom Rinthy's brother Culla Holme meets on the road tries to find out where Culla comes from, and the following exchange takes place:

Never been thew Cheatham though?
Not to recollect it I ain't.
You would recollect it
Is that right?
That is right. He kicked with his toe the flat dried shell of a
wheelcrushed toad. They got the awfullest jail in the state.
I ain't never been in jail Holme said.
You ain't never been in Cheatham.

Among the many humorous techniques employed by McCarthy are
feigned seriousness and monstrous logic, as in *Child of God*, when Lester
Ballard goes to the store to buy some tobacco and groceries costing $5.10
and tries to charge it. This is the dialogue between him and the storekeeper:

Just put it on the stob for me.
Ballard, when are you goin to pay me?
Well. I can give ye some on it today.
How much on it.
Well. Say three dollars.
The storekeeper was figuring on his pad.
How much do I owe altogether? said Ballard.
Thirty-four dollars and nineteen cents.
Includin this here?
Includin this here.
Well let me just give ye the four dollars and nineteen cents and
that'll leave it thirty even.

The absurdity of the situation is, of course, immediately apparent; but
McCarthy carries it one step further, and like a latter-day Mark Twain,
pushes it over the cliff with a comic snapper:

The storekeeper looked at Ballard. Ballard, he said, how old
are you?
Twenty-seven if it's any of your business.
Twenty-seven. And in twenty-seven years you've managed to
accumulate four dollars and nineteen cents?
The storekeeper was figuring on his pad.
Ballard waited. What are you figurin? he asked suspiciously.
Just a minute, said the storekeeper. After a while he raised
the pad up and squinted at it. Well, he said. Accordin to my
figures, at this rate it's goin to take a hundred and ninety-four

years to pay out the thirty dollars. Ballard, I'm sixty-seven now.
  Why that's crazy.
  Of course this is figured if you don't buy nothin else.
  Why that's crazier'n hell.
  Well, I could of made a mistake in the figures. Did you want
to check em?

Lester Ballard is the occasion for most of the novel's humor in a story
that exploits the disparity between reader and character in examples ranging
from bathroom facilities to public executions. Once Lester answers a call of
nature behind a barn in a patch of jimson weeds and nightshade, where he
"squatted and shat;" then wiped himself in the country way with a stick. But
Lester is not the only source of comedy or horror. An old man routinely
describes a turn-of-the-century hanging of two condemned murderers:

> It was right about the first of the year. I remember there was
> still holly boughs up and christmas candles. Had a big scaffold set
> up had one door for the both of em to drop through. People had
> started in to town the evenin before. Slept in their wagons, a lot
> of em. Rolled out blankets on the courthouse lawn. Wherever.
> You couldn't get a meal in town, folks lined up three deep.
> Women sellin sandwiches in the street. Tom Davis was sheriff by
> then. He brung em from the jail, had two preachers with em and
> had their wives on their arms and all. Just like they was goin to
> church. All of em got up there on the scaffold and they sung and
> everybody fell in singin with em. Men all holdin their hats. I was
> thirteen year old but I remember it like it was yesterday. Whole
> town and half of Sevier County sing I Need Thee Every Hour.
> Then the preacher said a prayer and the wives kissed their
> husbands goodbye and stepped down off the scaffold and turned
> around to watch and the preacher come down and it got real
> quiet. And then that trap kicked open from under em and down
> they dropped and hung there a jerkin and a kickin for I don't
> know, ten, fifteen minutes. Don't ever think hangin is quick and
> merciful. It ain't.

McCarthy's people are, indeed, talkers. They love to tell stories and tall tales,
many of them based, rather loosely, on fact and experience. Like a Caucasian
Uncle Remus, Uncle Ather in *The Orchard Keeper* tells stories of earlier times
to a group of eager boys, including the tale of a panther that turned out to
be a hoot owl. Tall tales, in fact, add an heroic and mythic dimension to

McCarthy's fiction. Surely, without stretching the critical imagination too much, one could read *Outer Dark* as a tall tale about an Appalachian Adam and Eve and the birth of evil.

Maturation stories are also to be found in McCarthy's trunk full of archetypes. Stories by the humorists of the Old Southwest usually involved blood sports, such as a boy's initiation into the world of men when he learned to hunt and kill a fox, a deer, or a bear. Marion Sylder bonds as John Wesley Rattner's surrogate father in *The Orchard Keeper* partly as a result of their hunting experiences together. *All the Pretty Horses* is essentially a bildungsroman centered around John Grady Cole, who leaves his Texas home at sixteen and heads for Mexico, where he learns about love and death and many other things. Needless to say, the kid in *Blood Meridian* learns the depths of human depravity.

It is important to keep these comedies of human weakness and struggle through life in perspective. They are enacted against the backdrop of the ever-greening, enduring earth, which man foolishly tries to reshape and mold into something alien and poisonous. *The Orchard Keeper's* Uncle Ather represents the spirit of the clean, uncluttered wilderness, perhaps prelapsarian nature. Representing the human despoilment of nature, on the other side, are a spray-pit once used to mix insecticide and a government tank holding atomic waste atop a nearby mountain—like an ironic cathedral tower announcing itself to a fallen world. In a desperate and futile attempt to reclaim his natural inheritance, the old man shoots a giant X into the side of the tank. This keeper of a diminished orchard lost his wife years before to an itinerant Bible salesman and now lives alone with his dogs, until he is taken off to an insane asylum.

This natural background which the old man is trying to preserve—the woods, the mountains, the fields, the sky, the pastures, the rivers, and the animal life that inhabits them—this setting is not humorous. Only humans can be humorous, for only we have an intellectual capacity for choice that makes us accountable for our thoughts and deeds. Only we can knowingly and intentionally fail to live in right relationship with each other and with nature. The inanimate world has no will or choice. Neither do the animals. Through humor we are reminded that we may be the lords of creation, but we are here for a very short time; and our short span of years is further abbreviated and aggravated by our own foolishness.

Like serious comedians from Aristophanes to Dante to Faulkner, McCarthy records real life in a documentary fashion that only fiction can do so well. Reading one of McCarthy's novels—any one of McCarthy's novels— can lead to disgust and denial. But this master of the macabre asks, "You don't believe me? Then look at human history. Better yet: look inside yourself. Can't you do better? I believe you can." McCarthy may not be writing a contemporary divine comedy that eventually leads to paradise, but he's certainly doing a good job of taking us on the first leg—maybe leg and a half—of the trip filled with human follies. But, after all, it is always the trip that attract us, not the destination. There is no material for humor in paradise, for where there is no human folly, there is no humor.

We live two stages below paradise, but the desired way is toward the stars. Even the bloodbath McCarthy called *Blood Meridian* may properly be called a comedy of life, which means that death, its main subject, is life's ultimate absurdity and hence the ultimate comic character. In the words of e. e. cummings' epitaph for and tribute to that Wild Westerner and master sharpshooter Buffalo Bill, death is a formless, nameless, finally meaningless force he calls and ridicules as "Mister Death." Although humor points up life's absurdities, it is nonetheless finally about life, not death, as the Greeks knew so well more than two thousand years ago. One remembers that the women of Athens and Sparta go on strike so that life may conquer death in the sex farce that Aristophanes called *Lysistrata*. Just as *Suttree* continues to live in his suffering, absurd world even as he leaves Knoxville, so McCarthy commits himself through humor to life.

TIM PARRISH

The Killer Wears the Halo: Cormac McCarthy, Flannery O'Connor, and the American Religion

> If the red slayer think he slays,
> Or if the slain think he is slain,
> They know not well the subtle ways
> I keep, and pass, and turn again.
> —Ralph Waldo Emerson, "Brahma"

> I shot a man in Reno just to watch him die.
> —Johnny Cash, "Folsom Prison Blues"

D.H. Lawrence famously—and aptly—observed that "the essential American soul is hard, isolate, stoic and a killer," but his remark fails to explain the transcendental splendor that accrues to the killer American. Lawrence would almost certainly recognize the many killers afoot in the works of Flannery O'Connor and Cormac McCarthy as belonging to that "essential American soul," yet few critics have been willing to face the consequences of Lawrence's remark, just as the United States has always shielded itself from the violence of its history by recourse to a peculiar—and bloody—innocence. Likewise, critics of O'Connor and McCarthy have invariably had to wrestle with the peculiar combination of violence and redemption that suffuses each writer's fiction, seeking the former's extinction in the latter. If hardly anyone can deny the blood-thirst, even the perversity, that permeates each writer's work, then the obvious connection each writer

From *Sacred Violence: A Reader's Companion to Cormac McCarthy*. ©1995 by Texas Western Press.

forges between the violent and the sacred seems somehow to expiate us from acknowledging the identification we form with their bloody imaginings.

The French theorist Rene Girard has best clarified the relationship that pertains between violence and the sacred, and reminds us of the extent to which one term depends on the other instead of cancelling each other out. Not only does Girard teach us that violence and the sacred are inseparable; he shows that the urge to commit violence may well be at once the ground of our being and the cause of our being's ultimate dissolution. For Girard, the sacred becomes the means by which the community controls violence and therefore preserves the self. Thus, human history is a cycle which perpetually revolves around the key terms, or periods, or violence-sacrifice-redemption. Once a violent act occurs, there is virtually no stopping its contagion from spreading. "Men cannot confront the naked truth of their own violence without abandoning themselves," Girard writes as if fresh from reading *Blood Meridian*. He brilliantly interprets ancient texts, such as *Oedipus the King* and the Bible to make his case, his point throughout being that modern man has been so ingenious in finding ways to control his violent impulse that he mistakenly thinks he can separate himself from the elemental human desire to kill. Girard insists that we cannot escape our violent desires, we can only learn to contain them, ironically, through other self-consciously violent acts: "violence will only come to an end only after it has had the last word and that word has been accepted as divine." This is what Girard calls "the function of sacrifice," which requires not only a "surrogate victim," but, more importantly, "violent unanimity." Preventing murder with murder, in a symbolic slaying or sacrifice, keeps us from the abandonment to violence that results in mass destruction. In other words, our will towards destructiveness usually coalesces into a single symbolic murder instead of wholesale extermination.

As trenchant as Girard's reading can be on a broad humanist level, his axes shift when we examine the American self's capacity for committing the most unspeakable acts of violence as if he were partaking of sacrament or conferring grace upon a worthy supplicant. Works like *Blood Meridian* or O'Connor's "A Good Man is Hard to Find" depict communal violence wherein "violent unanimity" never coalesces into a sacrifice. Instead, the killer remains ready to kill again. Whereas Girard would insist that redemption can only be achieved through the "violent unanimity" of the community, *Blood Meridian's* "violent unanimity" expresses itself in a shared desire to commit more violence. McCarthy and O'Connor invert Girard's thesis. If the judge sacrifices the kid in the name of violence renewed, then O'Connor's Misfit sacrifices the grandmother in the knowledge that this murder will lead to others. Readers, however, prefer to see the kid and the grandmother as representatives of some sort of redemption, which somehow washes away the sins of the killers. Shielding our eyes from the killer, without whom the meaning of redemption could not occur, we walk with our martyred characters towards God's shining light. In this respect, most critics of O'Connor and McCarthy are Girardian readers—but misguided ones. Although Girard insists that redemption can only be achieved through the "violent unanimity" of the community, the "violent unanimity" in these authors' works unleashes further carnage. Redemption is an accident the grandmother stumbles into, or something that the kid receives only from the reader. Beyond these episodes, in the texts' extended universes, what comes next are assuredly more cycles of killing—with no redemption implicit in the process. Or let me put that another way: *murder is an American expression of the sacred.* American violence does not quite fit Girard's formula because our acts of violence—in our fiction and in our history—have constituted the expression, as opposed to the preservation, of self. Historian Richard Slotkin has argued that "regeneration through violence" is the dominant theme of American history; now, Harold Bloom's *The American Religion* dissects better than any other book on the American imagination the blessed landscape of the American's murdering soul. Before we examine the exemplary killers populating this landscape as depicted by McCarthy and O'Connor, killers who are likely to quote scripture as they kill, I will briefly sketch the contours of Bloom's argument.

Bloom does not directly address the issue of violence. However if, as Girard insists, violence and the sacred cannot be separated, then Bloom's explication of the "emptiness" of the American soul and its relation to God helps us to understand the sacred connotations of even a seemingly random act of violence. What might be dismissed as mere pathology endemic to the grotesque South, that quarantined section of the United States with its peculiar institutions, Bloom assumes to be characteristic of the nation as a whole: the overwhelming presence of religion in American life. Thus, Bloom unites the varied denominations of all Americans into a single religion which, loosely defined, inheres in each American's conviction that he is one with God. This is not as obvious as it sounds. Though we can speak of the American becoming one with God as a kind of ascension of the soul, we are truer to Bloom's gnostic reading if we think of this oneness as a sort of birthright. Neither God nor the American precedes or supersedes the other. Paraphrasing Emerson, the American soul is part and particle of God; God is part and particle of the American soul. Bloom writes:

> The American finds God to herself or himself, but only after finding the freedom to know God by experiencing a total inward

> solitude. [I]n perfect solitude, the American spirit leans again its
> absolute isolation as a spark of God floating in a sea of space.
> What is around has been created by God, but the spirit is as old
> as God is, and so is no part of God's creation. What was created
> fell away from the spirit, a fall that was creation.

American individualism pushed to its logical extreme, Bloom's formulation underscores the traditional argument that the American is a kind of innocent untainted by time or history, unrestrained by space, utterly free. The American does not merely find God within himself; he creates the God he finds within. "Build then your own world," the prophet Emerson famously admonishes, as if to exhort the American to wake up and recognize the power he shares with God, as if to say the world begins—is created—by you. This wisdom is at once terrible and exalting, empty the fulfilling.

The latter-day prophet David Koresh tapped into the same current that inspired Emerson, and the horror we express at what occurred outside of Waco in 1993 is actually the shadow we cast over our glint of recognition— and ecstasy. Were we to encounter Koresh in one of McCarthy's or O'Connor's fictions, doubtless his desires and actions would be represented as complicitous with our own. This is a hard truth to down, and as McCarthy's works collect critics like barnacles, they will no doubt, like O'Connor's, become encased within a reef of pious commendation. We would much prefer to discuss McCarthy's rapists, necrophiliacs, and murderers, in the same way that O'Connor and her critics discuss her moral and social outlaws: as redeeming agents, stairways to a heaven which may be pulled up after us when we have at last ascended to glory. We wish to be like Rayber, who is the only educated character in O'Connor's *The Violent Bear It Away* and perhaps the least likeable character in all of her fiction, to conquer the madness that courses within. We wish to be like *All the Pretty Horses'* John Grady Cole, wiping our blood-wisdom from our hands in a fit of expiation. We wish to say of our encounter with McCarthy's and O'Connor's characters, as Rayber does to his God-obsessed nephew Tarwater, I have fought the "freak"—Rayber's word to describe the older, prophetic uncle Tarwater—within and won. The American soul contains mystery and power to be sure, but the meanings to be found there are often too dark and perplexing to be brought to light.

Bloom shines light on this darkness in this remarkable reading of the "American soul" or "self," as embodied by the founder of the American religion, America's foremost prophet, Emerson, who knew that "[once you] place everything upon the nakedness of the American self, [y]ou open every imaginative possibility from self-deification to absolute nihilism." We might qualify Bloom's assertion to read that the naked American self is betrayed by any recognition that it cannot do otherwise than contemplate the alternatives of self-deification and absolute nihilism. For the American self, no middle ground exists between these paired terms; indeed, the terms become mutually inclusive. In *Wise Blood* O'Connor captures eloquently the strange emotional landscape the American self inhabits when Hazel Motes reacts to a policeman's mean spirited destruction of his church—embodied in the form of his car: "Haze stood for a moment looking over the scene. His face seemed to reflect the entire distance across the clearing and on beyond, the entire distance that extended from his eyes to the blank gray sky that went on, depth after depth, into space." O'Connor, typically, neglects to apprise us of the depths that may lie behind Haze's stare, preferring to have the blankness encompass him, but were we allowed more than a limited point of view we might read in his distant stare the thoughts of Cornelius Suttree: "there is one Suttree and one Suttree only" which means that "all souls are one and all souls lonely."

Suttree allows a different version of the American Religion, one that has little to do with violence, and may be closer to Bloom's original intention. When Suttree wanders in the mountains, shedding layers of civilization as he drifts, he perfectly evokes the Emersonian strain of "nature" in the American religion as illuminated by Bloom's argument:

> The water sang in his head like wine. He sat up. A green and reeling wall of laurel and the stark trees rising. . . . Suttree felt a deep and chilling lassitude go by nape and shoulderblades. . . . He looked at a world of incredible loveliness [where] everything had fallen from him. He scarce could tell where his being ended or the world began nor did he care.

The passage details Suttree's loneliness and his sense of equivalence with all creation with heartbreaking beauty. Here Suttree discovers what Bloom claims the American has always known, that "God loves her and him on a absolutely personal and indeed intimate basis." Bloom's insight is reinforced by the fact that the name "God" need not appear in the midst of Suttree's revery. Suttree's knowledge of the loneliness of each and every soul issues from his sense of being one with God. We might even say that he shares more in common with the itinerant preachers who wander through his world than he would care to admit. In his way Suttree, like Hazel Motes, houses himself within a church of one, but Suttree has gone that other avatar one better by fulfilling the logic of his fellow preachers' sermons: he is preacher/congregation/God dissolved into a single being.

As profound and as bloody as Flannery O'Connor's stories can be, her Catholicism, as many have pointed out, can make her stories and novels seem schematic, preordained, a way out of the terrifying American loneliness. As she wrote of John Hawkes, "the conflict between an attraction for the Holy and the disbelief in it that we breathe in with the air of the times" was behind every sentence she wrote. She goes on: "There are some of us who have to pay for our faith every step of the way and who have to work out dramatically what it would be like without [faith] and if being without would be ultimately possible or not." Yet, as Hawkes well knew, without the recognition of evil that was necessary to her characters' attainment of grace, her fiction would be little more than a religious tract, the teachings of St. Flannery. While O'Connor was dogmatic in her own interpretations so that she would not be interpreted as doing the devil's work, she too knew that the power of her fiction resided in the devil's working for her. "I suppose," she admitted, "the devil teaches most of the lessons that lead to self-knowledge."

For O'Connor, the devil clarifies the American soul's polar choices: self-deification or nihilism. Though we can find this choice tormenting so many of her characters, we shall examine one particular instance, the boy-prophet Tarwater of *The Violent Bear It Away*. Tarwater, a clinical schizophrenic as Harold Bloom notices, is accompanied by a dark double, named "Friend," who is most certainly the devil. Thus doubled, Tarwater can only choose between the cynical nihilism his Friend advocates and the apocalyptic religion of his great-uncle. His great-uncle's mission was to make Tarwater wise in the ways of prophecy:

> He made [Tarwater] understand that his true father was the Lord [a]nd that he would have to lead a secret life in Jesus until the day came when he would be able to bring the rest of his family to repentance. He had made him understand that on the last day it would be his destiny to rise in glory in the Lord Jesus.

One with God, the great-uncle again and again speaks words of fire to baptize Tarwater into the American religion and his one-to-one relationship with God. Thus, when his great-uncle dies, Tarwater's mission is to bury him and get on with the business of converting to Jesus Bishop, the idiot son of his other uncle, the agnostic Rayber, and if possible converting even Rayber himself. However, his Friend intercedes in the form of Doubt. He convinces Tarwater to commit the two acts which would betray his covenant with his great-uncle, and thereby violate his true heritage. But Tarwater burns his great-uncle's house in an effort to avoid burying the old man; later he seeks to abdicate both is heritage and his blood wisdom by trying to murder Bishop instead of baptizing the innocent child.

Yet, as happens so often in O'Connor's fiction. Tarwater's evil Friend unwittingly becomes an agent of grace, appearing in the guise of a traveler picking up the hitchhiking Tarwater, in flight from the scene of Bishop's murder, Tarwater notices "something familiar" about the "stranger," but cannot place him. After falling asleep upon drinking the stranger's whiskey, Tarwater wakes to find that he has been raped, "propped up against a log," his "hands tied with a lavender handkerchief," his clothes "piled neatly by his side."

There is, we see, a kind of symbiotic relationship between Tarwater's polar choices of self. This nihilistic act of the Friend awakens Tarwater to the possibility—nay, the reality—of his own self's deification. Arising from the scene of his defilement, Tarwater, to borrow a phrase the novel often employs, burns the scene of his rape clean, and it is clear that this violation has also burned him clean. Paradoxically, the devil's skewering of Tarwater has also purified him, making him fit to meet the terms of his covenant with his great-uncle. Penetrated by wisdom, Tarwater's "scorched eyes," O'Connor writes, "touched with a coal like the lips of the prophet, [w]ould never be used for ordinary sights again." This amalgam of violence, violation, and redemption provides the calculus to interpret the novel's other crucial moment, Tarwater's murder of the idiot boy, Bishop. Since the death of his great-uncle, Tarwater has been convinced by his Friend to believe that the only way he could escape the fate of becoming like his prophet uncle was by not baptizing Bishop. Tarwater feels the tug of his duty like the pull of the tide. After several missed opportunities, he can no longer sustain the tension of his obsession and he sets out to drown the boy to rid himself of his destiny; the drowning will be an act of freedom. In spite of himself—and here is an example of O'Connor's notion of "wise blood" surfacing with a vengeance— Tarwater discovers to his horror that the drowning becomes a baptism which realizes his covenant with his uncle. That this murder ostensibly "saves" Bishop is not the point; actually Tarwater is the one who is redeemed. Like a Pentecostal who becomes a channel for the Lord's unfathomable wisdom when "the Spirit" prompts him to speak in tongues, the "defeated" Tarwater is overcome by grace as he "cried out the words of baptism" over the dying boy.

Through a miracle that both disturbs and exalts, the innocence of the babe is transferred to the bloody hands to the murderer. By misreading representative acts of American violence such as this one, we have closed our eyes to what I will call the wisdom of the murder: the killer wears the halo— not the so-called saved. This strange compression of opposed meanings, wherein killer and saved are joined, of course recalls the climactic scene of O'Connor's masterful "A Good Man is Hard to Find," almost certainly the Ur-scene of her American universe. The Misfit at once murders and redeems the babbling grandmother. "She would have been a good woman," the Misfit remarks dispassionately of her slaying. "if it had been somebody there to shoot her every minute of her life." There is no truer expression of the will to violence in all of American literature—not even *Blood Meridian* quite matches it. As O'Connor would quickly remind us, this moment too is a perfect example of the devil's being an instrument of grace. What has not been noticed, and what O'Connor represses, is that the Misfit's words figure his own redemption as well as the grandmother's: if only *he* could be shooting someone every minute of her life, then he would be saved as well. Nothing, no creed, no church, no social institution, intercedes to prevent Tarwater from knowing the God that is within him, or the Misfit from recognizing the moment of redemption he shares with his victim. Where O'Connor, or Girard for that matter, would insist that these examples reveal the truth that there can be no return of the sacred without violence, I read her fiction to betray the uneasier truth that violence is an expression of the sacred.

Alone with his God, there before the creation, the American's most apposite expression of his wisdom occurs in a moment of simultaneous destruction and creation. When, in the last sentence of the novel, Tarwater sets out to the "dark city" to face the sleeping "Children of God" we know only that he goes to face them alone, sublimely so, on a mission to awaken them as he has been awakened. Indeed, there remains the possibility that the "dark city" is Tarwater's creation, a dark vision of Winthrop's emblematic "citee on the hill." When his mission is fulfilled Tarwater may indeed rise to kingdom come, but that kingdom, I think, will look a lot like the world of *Blood Meridian*. Though we can follow Tarwater only to the outskirts of the "dark city" with its "sleeping children of God." alongside the judge we see its population awakened and on the move, killing everything in sight.

This amazing novel, which resonates with the very greatest of American literature, a kind of unholy combination of *Huckleberry Finn* and *Moby Dick* (thereby making it truly holy—or holy as hell), recalls Melville's boast to Hawthorne that "I have written a wicked book, and feel spotless as the lamb." Hazel Motes' response to the destruction of his symbolic church, which was, of course, a church of one, is an apt evocation of Cormac McCarthy's fictional landscape: comic and terrifying at the same time. Haze voices what might serve as an introduction to the philosophy of many of McCarthy's characters: "Your conscience is a trick," he said," it don't exist though you may think it does, and if you think it does, you had best get it out in the open and hunt it down and kill it." This is the task that confronts the kid as well as the incestuous would-be killer Culla Holme of *Outer Dark*, and the necrophilic murderer Lester Ballard of *Child of God*. Each of these works is sustained by a succession of violent episodes, bloody broken rings which form a chain only in the sense that any number of rings may be bent to form any chain. And any chain may be bent to beat the bloody hell out of someone.

In this respect, McCarthy's ethic of violence is thrown into disturbing relief when compared with Mark Twain's characters, who also found their consciences to be a kind of menace which was nevertheless a repository for their best impulses. One of Twain's best and longest running jokes concerned how the conscience prevails in spite of itself. Huckleberry Finn, for instance, takes the most courageous moral stand in our literature without being able to explain adequately to himself why had must do it. His succinct, if inadequate, reasoning is compressed in his famous remark: you can't pray a lie. Moreover, Twain's unmatched understanding of the violence at the heart of the American character was overshadowed by his singular ability to deflate the threat this violence poses. This was the function of Twain's comedy, and *Huckleberry Finn's* Shepherdson-Grangerford feud is a case in point. An epitome of meaningless violence, these chapters evoke the horror of the American frontier while playing this horror for laughs:

> "Did you mean to kill him, Buck?"
> "Well, I bet I did."
> "What did he do to you?"
> "Him? He never done nothing to me."

A murder is made humorous; the moral is clear. This mixture of comedy and atrocity may be even more disturbing than McCarthy's in the long run, since it shows how easily Twain and his audience took such scenes for granted. Later Huck confesses that he can't even describe all the shooting he witnesses for fear it "would make me sick." His untainted innocence helps us to see that the murder is outrageous, but so is the comedy. Our laughter becomes at best a grim smirk, or better, a smirking grimness, which is close to McCarthy's ethos.

McCarthy's characters do not possess a conscience in the same sense that Huckleberry Finn does. Their actions seem to take place in a universe devoid of moral choice. Blood Meridian's opening scene, for instance, which introduces the fourteen-year-old kid whose mother died in childbirth and whose father is a drunk, clearly means to evoke the circumstances of Huckleberry Finn. Although the kid, like Huck, will witness a variety of horrible sights, a kind of perpetual Grangerford-Sheperdson fued, he is not revolted by what he sees, whereas Huck's revulsion is meant to elicit our moral sympathy; the kid's occasional moments of compassion are interpreted as signs of weakness.

Denis Donoghue preceptively writes of McCarthy's fiction: "His episodes are produced not to be interrogated or understood within some system of value. They are to be sensed, to be seen. The appalling quality of each deed is its emptiness, as if it were done before anyone thought of any meaning it might have." Donoghue's words are an effective antidote to Edwin T. Arnold's too hopeful claim that in McCarthy's work there is "a profound belief in trhe need for moral order." But Donoghue misses the mark by failing to discern a structure that explains the characters' actions. Blood Meridian would lose much of its power if it were not a history as well, and John Emil Sepich, in his Notes on "Blood Meridian," has identified some of its historical sources. Even a reader ignorant of the finer details of our war with Mexico should recognize this novel's mythographic evocation of Manifest Destiny, that dark historical twin of the American Religion. Donoghue, along with most readers, would probably agree that McCarthy had created characters who lived and breathed the lesson of Hazel Motes' statement that "your conscience is a trick." Certainly they have no conscience in the Sunday school sense of the term, but then again part of McCarthy's purpose is to depict what occurs when our Sunday sermons enter the fields of history, running amok. I would like to suggest that McCarthy's characters do not live in a moral void any more than Hazel Motes does; rather, their actions express the blood wisdom, so to speak, of individuals who have been baptized into the American Religion.

Except for Suttree, Judge Holden is the only character in McCarthy's fiction prior to All the Pretty Horses' John Grady Cole who provides a rationale for his actions. Just as the devil is Flannery O'Connor's guiding voice, so is the judge a guiding critical spirit. His attempt to propagate the philosophy of Nietzsche, a disciple of Emerson, represents the most coherent statement in McCarthy's novels of any moral order. Indeed, what the judge performs in the name of his philisphy is in a queer sense a testament to his desire to control everything within and beyond his ken. Americans are never far from the voice of God, and the judge in particular keeps his ear to the ground—literally:

> Books lie, [the judge]said.
> God dont lie.
> No, said the judge. He does not. And these are his words.
> He held up a chunk of rock.
> He speaks in stones and trees, the bones of things.

Throughout the novel the judge collects natural specimens, acting as a kind of proto-Darwin, as Donoghue points out. On one level, the judge is studying God, compiling evidence of His power and mystery. On a deeper level, the judge is communing with God and uncovering the diety within himself. Like God, the judge views the world as being made up of his own materials, remnants of his creation which he is free to make and remake as he pleases. To maimj, rape, kill, is, in effect, to feel God's dirt and blood beneath his fingernails. Moreover, the judge imparts this knowledge to his colleagues. In the scene quoted above, the judge's colleagues are trying to trip him up, but in the end they become "right proselytes of the new order." "I am God in nature' I am a weed by the wal," Emerson remarked in "Self-Reliance." Emerson might have been speaking for the judge when he declared that "the universe is fluid and volatile. Permanence is but a word of degrees. Our globe seen by God is a transparent law, not a mass of facts. The law dissolves the fact and holds it fluid." This transparent law is the judge's only moral guideline: "The truth about the world," the judge somewhere declares, "is that anything is possible."

Of course, neither the judge nor McCarthy's fiction can be understood soley in Nietzschean terms. As with Emerson, the judge has wagered his being on the uncertainties of transition. A student of power, he would agree with Emerson that "power ceases in the instant of repose." Emerson goes on: "It resides in the shooting of a gulf, the darting to an aim." At the end of the novel when the judge tells the kid, a la Yeats, that the dance is the thing, he reveals his thorough understanding that after what is tangible has disappeared, be that rocks or history or the dancers themselves, one thing reamins: transition, or the dance. Existing before time as Bloom tells us the American believes he does, the judge can realize the force of his divinity only in the moment of awakening, "a fall that was also a creation," as Bloom puts the matter. (Emerson remarks at one point "the first fall is into consciousness.") He offers his parable of the dance as a preamble to killing the kid and it is as if the kid and the judge are the only two characters left in the world. The judgment, in effect, justifies why he must sacrifice the kid:

> This is an orchestration for an event. For a dance in fact. The participants will be apprised of their roles at the proper time. . . . As the dance is the thing with which we are concerned and contains complete within itself its own arrangement and history and finale there is no necessity that the dancers contain these things within themselves as well. In any event the history of all is not the history of each nor indeed the sum of those histories and none here can finally comprehend the reason for his presence for he has no way of knowing even in what the event consists.

In effect, the judge admits that he needs the kid, even in opposition. For together they help to create the dance that enacts the cycle of violence which cannot end; whichcannot, ultimately, even be fully comprehended. Amid the swirl of the music and the dancing strangers, the kid and the judge have come to the end of their dance. "Do you believe it's all over," he asks the kid, before declaring that everyone is "gone under. . .saving me and thee." There in the dance hall the people who surround the judge have nothing to do with the book we have been reading, though of course the judge, adept dancer that he is, fits right in. In this scene we are nearing the end of a world. Killing the kid will not only end the novel we are reading, but the creation in which the judge has realized his divinity. This murder will complete the orchestration of the event the judge has been enacting, and the judge is apprising the kid of his role. If he tells the kid that none can finally comprehend the reason for his presence, then this is because the judge knows that in the next dance their roles might be reversed. Just as each act of violence enacts only a moment of transition to another such moment, so can the dance in which the judge and the kid participate never truly end.

The judge pushes Bloom's theory to its logical conclusiong as he is the only one of the band to survive. Donoghue remarks that the judge must kill the now mature boy because he cold have killed the judge and did not. Certainly the orgy of killing, which the better part of Blood Meridian depicts, ends with this choice: either the kid or the judge. The choice is between drawing back from violence and its consequences and following its logic to the bloody end. And this means "end" in its most terminal sense, for when everyone is killed the world which sustained and was sustained by violence ends as well. Whn the kid chooses to renounce killing, the judge sacrifices him not in the name of redemption, but in the name of unending violence. In perhaps the novel's most key passage, the judge tells the kid:

> You came forward, he said, to take part in a work. But you were a witness against yourself. You sat in judgement on your own deeds. You put your own allowances before the judgements of history and you broke with the body of which you were pledged a part and poisoned it an all its enterprise. Hear me, man. I spoke in the desert for you and you only and you turned a deaf ear to me. . . . It was required of no man to give more than he possessed nor was ny man's share compared to another's. Only each was called upon to *empty* out his heart into the common and one did not [emphasis added]."

Like Bloom or Emerson, the judge recognizes that the American's acts of self-expression are committed from within a terrible emptiness. Moreover, in emphasizing that they are alone in a desert, a veritable symbol of emptiness, the judge seems to be playing God, or Jesus, to the kid-as-supplicant. Certainly this scene refigures Bloom's map of the American soul, where the American comes to know his essential oneness with God before the creation of the world which is also a falling away from this original union. However, the kid refuses the judge's wisdom. He tries to tell the judge that it was he who held back, but of course it is the kid who continues to hold back for the rest of the novel, as he tries to renouce his identification with the judge and the emptiness he represents through gestures of kindness. Seeking out "pilgrims," victims of the sort of violence he once acted out, he tries to lead them "to a save place, some part of [their] country people who would welcome her." This murdering Huck Funn actually—and unaccountably—seeks the comfort of community.

A community that is not tied together by violence this novel will not allow—it would betray the meaning of the dance. That the judge and the kid act out the conclusion of their dance amid a community which seems unaware of their wxistence suggest the violence that underlies any American experience. The judge survives because he alone among the characters can appreciate the meaning of his survival, and the inexorable truth of his future. Telling the kid about the mystery of the dance prepares him the sacrificce the judge will offer by killing him. The kid does not know what the judge knows; his buried remorse for his actions—the many people he saved from danger in the years intervening since his last encounter with the judge—betrays his confusion over the sanctity of his deeds. On the other hand, the judge knows that when he kills the kid merely another transformation will have occured. He observes:

> For each man's destiny is as large as the world he inhabits and contains within it all opposites as well. This desert upon which so many have been broken is vast and calls for largeness of heart but it is also untimately empty. It is hard, it is barren. Its very nature is stone.

Recalling his earlier declaration that God speaks in stones, the judge here defines the American soul. His words describe its spiritual state in all its mixed-up richness and blankness. In killing the kid the judge has arrived at the last transformation within the cycle of violence the novel depicts.

SARA L. SPURGEON

"Pledged in Blood": Truth and Redemption in Cormac McCarthy's All the Pretty Horses

As many critics have noted, it is no coincidence that the action of *All the Pretty Horses* takes place exactly one hundred years after that of *Blood of Meridian*. In many ways, *Pretty Horses* is the offspring of that book, an elegy for a romanticized way of life, a code of honor, a mythical world birthed and brutally murdered in *Blood Meridian*—the world of the cowboy. In *Pretty Horses* we see the modern embodiment of the ancient myth of the sacred hunter—that of the sacred cowboy. The figure of the hunter engaged in holy communication with nature has, by the end of *Blood Meridian*, been replaced with that of the cowboy digging postholes, preparing to string barbed wire across the tamed body of the wilderness in order to populate with cattle what he so mercilessly emptied of buffalo. The figure of the cowboy personifies America's most cherished myths—combining ideas of American exceptionalism, Manifest Destiny, rugged individualism, frontier democracy, communion with and conquest of the natural world, and the righteous triumph of the white race. The mythic West and the frontiers of legend are familiar icons on the American cultural landscape.

The icon of the sacred cowboy is one of our potent national fantasies, viable in everything from blue jeans to car commercials to popular films. This mythic figure, however, like that of the hunter preceding it, is bound to crumble, for it is hollow at its core and stripped bare by McCarthy in *All the*

From *Western American Literature* 34, no. 1 (Spring 1999): pp. 25–43. ©1999 by the Western Literature Association.

Pretty Horses. As he slowly begins to recognize the fragility and falseness of his life, John Grady Cole seeks a return to the imagined innocence of the sacred cowboy of the mythic past.

The pervasiveness of images of the western frontier and its heroes is so extensive even one hundred years after the official close of the frontier, those archetypes have become important building blocks in what Lauren Berlant terms the national symbolic in *The Anatomy of National Fantasy*. A tangle of legal, territorial, linguistic, and experiential forces continually at work defining the nation and the citizen, the national symbolic is constructed through the production of national fantasy, those "images, narratives, monuments, and sites that circulate throughout personal/collective consciousness." Berlant argues that the space of the national symbolic serves to define nationality and identity not on the individual level, but on the level of national consciousness in the form of collective memory, popular stories, and official and unofficial histories. In United States, the national symbolic is filled with fantasy images from the frontier past. According to a Harris poll, John Wayne was the number one movie star in America as recently as 1995, well after his death. Garry Wills claims this is because Wayne personified the perfect fantasy frontiersman and was therefore "the most obvious recent embodiment of [the] American Adam. . . . the avatar of the hero in that genre that best combines . . . mythic ideas about American exceptionalism."

Like John Wayne, the iconography of the mythic West remains a potent form of national fantasy in part because, as noted in MacCannell, icons mark a gap or attempt to cover a problem the symbolic order does not solve. The issues and concerns associated with the western frontiers and borderlands of the past—colonialism, race relations, cultural and national identity, and human interactions with the natural world—are the same that currently vex modern America. They are, so to speak, dark spots on the geography of the national symbolic, disordered spaces still demanding to be rendered coherent through some structure of national fantasy, some new mythic formation that will impose control and order and reconcile the violent contradictions between rhetoric and reality these issues make apparent.

John Grady's quest signifies the gap in the national symbolic that the fantasy of the cowboy on the open range has never been able to cover. Unlike the random trajectory of the kid, however, John Grady's quest is made poignant for American readers by the fact that the imagined version of the cowboy code of conduct (honesty, loyalty, courage)—so wholeheartedly and unquestioningly accepted by John Grady at the start of the novel—is at once admirable and utterly untenable, full of contradiction and hypocrisy. As American readers, we cannot help but respond to the evocation of that myth through such a sympathetic and likeable character. This is, perhaps, one reason why *All the Pretty Horses* has been so often labeled McCarthy's most "accessible" work of fiction and why it is his first novel to appear on the *New York Times* best sellers list. Indeed, Vereen Bell notes, it is probable that "this novel has already sold more copies than all of McCarthy's previous novels combined."

The life John Grady has been living on his family's Texas ranch is a romantic fantasy, ubiquitously familiar to every American through innumerable novels, films, grade school history texts, beer and cigarette advertisements. It is nonetheless a mask, a rose-colored and stereotyped cliché of the national symbolic barely hiding the falseness at its core. That this particular myth strides about on feet of clay is made apparent not just through the imminent sale of the ranch, but through the persistent return of all that this version of national fantasy attempts to deny and repress, the truth of its conception so brutally revealed in *Blood Meridian*. McCarthy lovingly evokes that myth and at the same time strips away the layers of fantasy that make belief in it possible.

The violent past thrusts itself into the present in *Pretty Horses* almost immediately, as the novel opens with John Grady leaving the funeral of his cowboy/rancher grandfather to ride

> the western fork of the old Comanche road coming down out of the Kiowa country. . . . the ancient road was shaped before him in the rose and canted light like a dream of the past where the painted ponies and the riders of that lost nation came down out of the north . . . all of them pledged in blood and redeemable in blood only. . . . nation and ghost of nation passing in a soft chorale across the mineral waste to darkness bearing lost to all history and all remembrance like a grail the sum of their secular and transitory and violent lives.

The very people scalped for profit in *Blood Meridian* to allow for white settlement—the nation made ghost so that generations of Gradys and Coles could run cattle—limn with darkness and blood the wholesome myth of that most privileged of western icons, the independent rancher. The vanished Comanches traverse the gap in the national symbolic left bare by this version of national fantasy that resolutely ignores the reality, the noninnocence, of its own history. They are "pledged in blood and redeemable in blood only," but so is the nation replacing them and riding the same trail, side by side with their ghosts. John Grady, in his innocent acceptance of the noninnocent myth of the sacred cowboy realizes only faintly this debt of blood, and not at all that it will fall on him to pay if he wishes to redeem himself from the hollowness, falsity, and self-deception (sweetly romantic though it may be) of that myth.

This metaphorical joining of one ghostly dream with another is established again through the image of the vanished, and now thoroughly (and safely) romanticized, Comanches. John Grady's father, another dying cowboy/rancher, tells him, "We're like the Comanches was two hundred years ago" in an attempt to soften the loss of the ranch, to evoke the presence of one "dream of the past" to join in mourning the passing of another, one equally "secular and transitory and violent." But it is yet another memory of the past, which comes to John Grady as he sits at his dead grandfather's desk, that best signifies not only the persistent return of history through the liminal spaces of myth, but also the lesson John Grady must finally learn about the deceptive nature of the world seen through the blinders of national fantasy. As he sits in the darkened office, he can see through the window "[t]he black crosses of the old telegraph poles yoked across the constellations passing east to west. His grandfather said the Comanche would cut the wires and splice them back with horsehair." In the illusion created by the splicing of what has been severed, McCarthy demonstrates the difficulty of seeing the world not as one would wish it to be, but as it actually is. While the wire may appear whole, it is nonetheless not functional. To paraphrase the Dueña Alfonsa, this is the difference between what is true and what is merely useful to believe, between the dream and the reality, myth and history. This is the world that lies waiting between the wish and the thing.

It is John Grady's naive and romantic inability to distinguish the truth—defined by the Dueña Alfonsa to be not "what is righteous but merely what is so"—which moves her to pay his and Rawlins's way out of prison but also, ultimately, causes her to reject his suit for Alejandra's hand. As she tells John Grady before she begins her tale, "You will see that those things which disposed me in your favor were the very things which led me to decide against you in the end." Her entire monologue, the history of her life, is told for John Grady's benefit, and indeed, John Grady is a sort of male version of her young and idealistic self. Her journey may be seen as a tightly compressed parable of his.

As their stories start, both are seventeen years old, romantic, idealistic, enamored of a moral code of justice and honor in a world built upon justice and corruption; both are believers in a nostalgic myth, a form of national fantasy that shows them, as Alfonsa puts it, "how the world must become if I were to live in it." Therefore, it does not allow them to see the world as it really is. The danger of such deliberate, albeit romantic, blindness is illustrated by the fates of Gustavo and Francisco. These two fellow idealists are tortured and shot by mobs directed by the corrupt General Huerta. At the same time, the ambassador at the American embassy fails to forward to President Taft a frantic telegram written by Francisco's mother to ask the United States to intercede on her son's behalf.

Despite the way in which many have read the novel, this is not a matter of juxtaposing innocent American romanticism with the brutal, violent realities of an inherently corrupt Mexico. American culpability in Mexican history and politics is clearly established in *Blood Meridian* and openly alluded to in *Pretty Horses*. I do not believe that McCarthy is attempting to posit America as the site of modernity and Mexico as simply a dream of the romanticized past, as Vereen Bell suggests, although John Grady may initially see it in just that way. Bell writes in "Between the Wish and the Thing the World Lies Waiting" that "John Grady and Rawlins escape for a time the dissociating effects of the technology and capital of the new American order, but what they get from their adopted ancient culture is an attractive but totalitarian hierarchy—the autocratic rule of families, at best, and at worst, of brute power instead of law. In Enlightenment terms, a dignified ancient culture is also, inescapably, a primitive one." McCarthy has gone to great lengths, however, to point out that Mexican culture is no more "ancient" or "primitive" than American culture. Do the roots of Mexican culture stretch back to pre-Columbian indigenous peoples? John Grady rides through the ghosts of just such peoples on his own ranch and is watched by their living descendants upon his return to Texas. Is John Grady a nomad without a home in Mexico? He's still a homeless wanderer when he recrosses the border, and the brute power of law, explained to him by his father's attorney, has still robbed him of his patrimony. He is as helpless before its implacable and pitiless advance as he is before the corrupt captain in the Mexican jail. Neither can be cajoled, neither can be reasoned with, neither shows mercy or the slightest acknowledgement of John Grady's wishes, his code of honor, his view of how the world should be rather than how the world is.

In other words, the myth of the sacred cowboy, which demands that a worthy young man should end up with a ranch of his own, a lovely young wife, and "all the pretty horses" simply by virtue of being Anglo, male, a cowboy, and the descendant of colonizers, functions in neither world, and this is McCarthy's point. If we fall into the trap of believing that the code of the sacred cowboy was valid at some romanticized time in America's past, we will naturally assume that in an equally romanticized "old Mexico," where John Grady has symbolically traveled back in time, it will once again function properly. The world will be as the myth says it is. Reality, of course, proves the world to be far different. As Bell acknowledges, there is no escape possible, because "there is no human place outside of time, and where human places are there are also the constructs and institutional artifacts of history."

This is as true, however, for the United States as it is for Mexico. It is not some ancient or primitive quality in Mexico that defeats John Grady; it is the hollowness and blindness of his faith—or, more properly, the hollowness of that myth upon which he has chosen to place his faith. Like the peasants in Alfonsa's tale who desperately attempt to sell objects no one wants, John Grady clings to the values of a myth that hides the true nature of the world. He refuses or is unable to recognize that the falseness of the sacred cowboy is equivalent to the broken bits of machinery the peasants gather from the roads. The peasant's faith in a myth, in this case their belief in the value of all things associated with the industrialized world coupled with a profound ignorance of the true nature of that world, strengthens but also dooms them. The courage to see the world without ignorance and without faith, essentially without sentiments however attractive they may be, is what the Dueña Alfonsa wants John Grady to find through the story of her own life and the history of Mexico.

The United States and Mexico are not opposite ends of some nostalgic timeline here. They are, more properly, mirror images of each other. What John Grady and Rawlins find restored to them in Mexico is simply a magnification of what they left behind in Texas—cowboys and charros, ponies and grullos, ranch house and hacienda. Yes, there is a social hierarchy in Mexico, but the Mexicans dealing with John Grady and Rawlins are simply more honest than the Americans in acknowledging the class differences that molded the lives of the two boys from the start in Texas. John Grady's family owns an 18,000-acre ranch, and it is John Grady who takes his meals privately in the kitchen of the hacienda while Rawlins stays in the bunk house. In fact, those breakfast scenes at La Purísima are nearly identical to the ones in John Grady's ranch house in Texas, right down to the paired Mexican women cooking and serving him his food. When the padrón of the prison asks if he learned to speak Spanish from servants, John Grady maintains, "We didnt have no servants. We had people worked on the place." There is, of course, no practical difference between the two, but John Grady is vainly attempting to uphold another facet of the sacred cowboy myth as it has been used to construct the national symbolic—that class hierarchies do not exist in America in general, but most especially not in the American West, where a somehow truer and purer form of American democracy is supposed to have eliminated such corrupt, old-world cultural manifestations.

The sacred cowboy as a modern expression of the sacred hunter is connected to Annette Kolodny's definition of an American pastoral. Although she traces the figure of the yeoman farmer, I would argue that the hunter/cowboy figure holds far more sway in the American imagination and the national symbolic simply by virtue of its romantic and mythic air. Nonetheless, both figures have much in common; along with the idea that both possess a special connection to the natural landscape comes the fantasy that they created a classless and egalitarian society in "New World." Kolodny agrees with Harold Toliver that the diction of much American literature has had "a tendency to level 'all social elements to an Arcadian democracy'." To her mind, that creates an appeal to "that quality of fraternal and communal democracy that has always been an element of [the] pastoral." But far from contrasting American egalitarianism with a Mexican caste system, for McCarthy Mexico merely illuminates the hypocrisy of the American myth.

John Grady lacks money when he reaches la Purísima, and that is doubtless Alejandra's father's main objection to him, because the padrón recognizes immediately that while John Grady and Rawlins may have equally empty pockets, they are not social equals or members of the same class. The padrón becomes a sort of foster father to John Grady, while he is never more than an employer to Rawlins. In this way, Alejandra and John Grady are also more like mirror images than opposites. Like the young Alfonsa, they both still see the world as they wish it to be, from the privileged position of their social classes, cocooned in the fragile paradise of their respective ranches, where the descendants of the peoples their ancestors conquered are now servants and outcasts. (Interestingly, even their mothers appear to be twinned, with both women preferring to live in cities and seemingly incapable of understanding their offsprings' desire to stay in the country.) Alejandra and John Grady are shielded, at least initially, from having to face the world without their sentiments, clinging like the peasant from the countryside to bolts and "wornout part[s] of a machine that no one could even know the use of." Like the young Alfonsa, neither of them can see that what may appear innocent, right, whole, is, like the telegraph wire, unsound and nonfunctional, merely an illusion of the real. Alejandra in the end sees the futility of refusing to select "between the dream and the reality," and this eventual acknowledgment marks her with the sadness John Grady sees at their final meeting, just as Alfonsa tells him she is marked through the loss of her fingers, and as John Grady will mark himself with the redhot barrel of his own pistol.

There is some disagreement among scholars as to what, if any, lesson John Grady (and presumably McCarthy's reader) learns after his adventures in Mexico and his discourses with the Dueña Alfonsa. Tom Pilkington claims the realization that "the individual is alone in a cold, indifferent universe . . . appears to be the sum of John Grady's experiences in the novel." Vereen Bell asserts that the point of the novel is "whether John Grady can endure such gratuitous tribulation with his hardheaded boy's idealism intact," while Dianne Luce in "When you Wake" disagrees with Bell and argues that on the contrary, John Grady's "idealism misleads him sometimes so seriously as to compromise his integrity. I think the point of the novel is more whether John Grady can understand and accept the consequences of his own choices . . . without abandoning himself and thus breaking faith with others." What John Grady must abandon, however, is not his idealism per se, but rather his blind faith in a mythic construct hiding from him the true nature of the world—and therefore also the knowledge of his proper place within it.

The second half of this equation, however, which Luce identifies as not "breaking faith with others," is even more difficult to attain than the simple recognition that we are alone in a world that is not always what it appears to be. The Dueña Alfonsa has come to terms with the nature of the world as she sees it. Gustavo told her that "those who have endured some misfortune will always be set apart but that it is just that misfortune which is their gift and which is their strength and that they must make their way back into the common enterprise of man for without they do so it cannot go forward and they themselves will wither in bitterness" Alfonsa continues her discourse with John Grady, saying, "Long before morning I knew that what I was seeking to discover was a thing I'd always known. That all courage was a form of constancy. That it was always himself that the coward abandoned first." And yet we know that the price Gustavo paid for rejoining "the common enterprise of man" is violent death at the hands of a mob he had sacrificed his fortune to aid. Gustavo, in effect, reached out for the world again with both hands. Alfonsa, however, seems to have achieved an almost Zen-like equilibrium. She grasps the world with one hand and disengages from it with the other, never allowing herself to be pulled either into paralyzing bitterness or blind idealism. This is the constancy she identifies as courage. She tells John Grady,

> You spoke of my disappointments. If such they are they have only made me reckless. My grandniece is the only future I contemplate and where she is concerned I can only put all my chips forward. . . . I know what she does not. That there is nothing to lose. . . . I dont know what sort of world she will live in and I have no fixed opinions concerning how she should live in it. I only know that if she does not come to value what is true above what is useful it will make little difference whether she lives at all.

Alfonsa sees through the facade of the various myths constructing her world, that of Mexicans "mad for society," of the Spanish who believe in nothing unless it be made to bleed, of the romantic and idealistic notions of social justice she embraced in Europe. But unlike John Grady's father, who, having seen the world "right at last. . . .as it had always been," is destroyed by the sight, Alfonsa is moved to action, strengthened rather than weakened by the knowledge that "there is nothing to lose," or, perhaps more properly, that all one loses is the sentimental blinders of myth. She releases her hold on any belief about what the future should look like but holds on, firmly, to the reality of its existence through her love for Alejandra.

John Grady struggles down the hard road to reach such a place himself through the final section of the novel. He begins to realize the hollowness of the myths into which he has poured his faith even before his long dialogue with Alfonsa, as he lies in the prison after the knife fight and feels a child's sorrow welling up inside him that "brought with it such pain that he stopped it cold and began at once his new life and the living of it breath to breath." But while his new life, seen without the rosy filter of the mythic fantasy through which he has always viewed the world, might be said to begin here, his own place within that world is still unclear. No new mythic structure has emerged to replace the old one, and this is perhaps the most important part of the Dueña Alfonsa's lesson for John Grady—that to distinguish what is true from what is useful to believe means to discard all the myths one's culture holds dear and make one's way in the world alone, with nothing but one's own courage to call upon, and all without ever falling into hopeless bitterness. This sort of existentialist epiphany, however, will never leave one unmarked, or even entirely whole. Such knowledge exacts a price, leaving one arguably reduced—like Gustavo with his glass eye and the Dueña with her missing fingers.

John Grady's task then is to come to terms with this loss, signified for him by the loss of Alejandra, and to the rest of the world (represented by the Texas judge to whom he confesses) by the pistol-burned scars on his leg. He must somehow achieve the balance that will allow him to rejoin the common enterprise of man in order to determine his place within a world now completely altered and yet totally unchanged. John Grady's first step in this process occurs when he tells his and Rawlins's story to the children outside of Torreón. Just as the Dueña Alfonsa's story was a sort of compressed parable of John Grady's, here John Grady is reifying, reducing, and compressing his own story for the children. "He told them how they had come from another country, two young horsemen riding their horses, and that they had met with a third who had no money nor food to eat nor scarcely clothes to cover himself and that he had come to ride with them and share with them in all they had." The story is presented as a parable, distilled down to its mythic parts, and its inherent recognition of the role of myth in shaping the world reflects John Grady's internalization of at least part of the Dueña Alfonsa's lesson.

It is also apparent that he cannot entirely let go of the magical vision of the world as it is constructed through the myth of the sacred cowboy. There is romance and adventure in the image of "two young horsemen," and within that mythic structure and under that sanitized code, what is right is more important than what is so. What is so is that John Grady is riding the horse given to him by the Dueña Alfonsa. What is right is that he recover his own horse, no matter how foolish or blindly romantic his attempt to do so may be. The fact that he does recover his and Rawlins's horses, and Blevins's as well, feels right to generations of American readers raised on Zane Grey and *Gunsmoke* and immersed in the parameters of a national symbolic constructed by such fantasies, even while we recognize the stupidity behind it.

Upon his return to Texas, John Grady is caught between two visions of the world, unable to return to the safe confines of the mythic past and as yet equally incapable of seeing how he must live his life in the future. He exists in a liminal space beyond myth, but not yet within history, a space within which "he felt wholly alien to the world although he loved it still." His unfixed liminal status, betwixt and between myth and reality, truth and history, Mexico and the United States is figured by his physical appearance, like "some apparition out of the vanished past"—with his horses, guns, Mexican serape, and his inability to properly assess his relationship to the world to the point where he must ask what day it is, surprised to discover it is Thanksgiving. His quest to return Blevins's horse to its rightful owner is more properly a quest to release himself from the last hold of the myth of the sacred cowboy, signified in the national symbolic by the image of the horse. His confession to the judge does nothing to alleviate his pain, since what he receives from the judge is essentially the same lesson given to him by the Dueña Alfonsa: the task of fixing a way for himself in the world is one he must accomplish alone.

As if to reify for him the empty and dead status of the sacred cowboy myth and the impossibility of the innocent return to a non-innocent past, the last image within the narrative is John Grady riding among the living descendants of the ghost nation of the Comanches, camped in their wickiups among the pumps of the Yates oil field, as he watches a solitary bull in the empty and lifeless desert "rolling in the dust against the bloodred sunset like an animal in sacrificial torment."

There is no neat and happy ending here. John Grady "[p]assed and paled into the darkening land, the world to come," but whether he has found the epistemology that will enable him to live within that world or if he will simply vanish into it is not clear. One may well ask at his point, given the rather simple trajectory of the plot, what lifts this story above the level of a dime novel Western or a simple coming-of-age tale. Oddly, or perhaps appropriately, the answer seems to revolve in part around horses. Vereen Bell notes that "[t]he deepest continuity with life in this novel is through horses," but horses resound here with a symbolic significance that functions on a number of metaphysical, even mystical, levels. Horses are inextricably linked to the mythic cowboy within the national symbolic. More so even than the cow or the gun, the horse defines the cowboy's status as sacred, special, uniquely American. (And, of course, Mexican as well, as McCarthy is certainly aware. The common Spanish term for *gentleman* is *caballero*— literally *horseman*.)

Advertisers have long realized the appeal inherent in this popular metaphorical connection, as a quick glance at any ad for Marlboro cigarettes, the best-selling brand both in the United States and abroad, makes clear. Even Ford Motor Company's major sellers carry the names Pinto, Mustang, and Bronco—distinctly western terms for horses. Americans have long been trained to respond to the image of cowboys and their horses, and if the mounted cowboy signifies the will of the American people in action, taming the wild West and conquering the wilderness, the horse symbolizes the cowboy's connection to that wilderness. Within the national symbolic, the cowboy's horse signifies both the mythic West and all the national fantasies that have become attached to it. And in an uneasy juxtaposition, the image of a herd of wild horses thundering across some dramatic western landscape has become one of the primary mythic signifiers by which we refer to wild and untamed nature. The tension uniting these images is lurking off-screen, so to speak, behind the wild herd and just out of our sight: the cowboy with his lasso, the empty corral, the waiting saddle, bridle, bit, and spur. The process of breaking the wild horse, branding it, claiming and utilizing it in the further subduing of nature through fences, cattle, roads, for instance, follows unseen, behind the image of the wild herd. It is a complex and powerful metaphor of desire and domination, of colonialist nostalgia and Manifest Destiny. Again, Kolodny has identified this paradox as inherent in the American pastoral. She writes that "[i]n the course of civilizing the landscape . . . man makes of it his helpless victim and inevitably betrays an earlier or hoped-for intimacy." This destruction of the dream in the act of achieving it, which Kolodny says becomes one of the major themes of American fiction, sounds a "note of nostalgia for an irrevocably lost pastoral landscape." And yet that loss, she argues, impells us "both to continue pursuing the fantasy in daily life, and, when that failed, to codify it as part of the culture's shared dream life."

For McCarthy, the image of the wild, free herd and the mounted cowboy in pursuit of it, is a metaphor through which to explore the deceptive matrix mapping the relationship of modern Americans to the land and the difficult metaphysical problem of being in the world—the very question, on riding out of Mexico, John Grady still struggles to answer. If the Dueña Alfonsa is there to teach John Grady about the dangerous blindness of myth and the necessity of recognizing the truth, horses serve to teach him the nature of that truth and how one should finally live with it.

The horse breaking episode at the hacienda is an ironic foreshadowing of the experiences John Grady will go through later in the novel. The stablehand, Luis, tells him that "the souls of horses mirror the souls of men more closely than men suppose" but that while all horses share a common soul, sadly "among men there was no such communion." John Grady's first act at La Purísima is to break the communion among the wild herd, to force them to "reckon slowly with the remorselessness of this rendering of their fluid and collective selves into that condition of separate and helpless paralysis." Soon they are all roped and motionless "with the voice of the breaker still running in their brains like the voice of some god come to inhabit them." The illusory communion John Grady feels with his life and his history through the comforting myth of the sacred cowboy is broken in Mexico, and he is left by Alfonsa like the hobbled horses in the corral, still alive but divided and paralyzed. To regain a sense of being, of connection to the world, a sense of the proper order of things and his own place within that order, John Grady must learn to recognize the mirror of his own soul within that of horses, representing for McCarthy what Bell terms an "invisible bond with the powers of the earth." Horses represent the sacred, and for McCarthy that most often means the world of nature, or as Tom Pilkington says, "McCarthy's horses . . . represent the vital life force of the universe. They stand for what *is*, pristine and unfallen nature in its most elemental form."

The world of men and the world of nature are not really separated for McCarthy, and the task of reconnecting those worlds drives many of his characters. The complex forces that bind them together—that illustrate the nature of truth and life and being in the world—are revealed to John Grady through two important dreams. In the first, he is shown both the collective nature of the soul of horses, who never question their relationship with the natural world, and his own connection to it through them.

That night he dreamt of horses in a field on a high plain where the spring rains had brought up the grass and the wildflowers out of the ground and the flowers ran all blue and yellow far as the

eye could see and in the dream he was among the horses running
and in the dream he himself could run with the horses and they
coursed the young mares and fillies over the plain where their
rich bay and their rich chestnut colors shone in the sun and the
young colts ran with their dams and trampled down the flowers
in a haze of pollen that hung in the sun like powdered gold and
they ran he and the horses out along the high mesas where the
ground resounded under their running hooves and they flowed
and changed and ran and their manes and tails blew off of them
like spume and there was nothing else at all in that high world
and they moved all of them in a resonance that was like a music
among them and they were none of them afraid horse nor colt
nor mare and they ran in that resonance which is the world itself
and which cannot be spoken but only praised.

The language in this single remarkable sentence is patently spiritual,
mystical, even biblical. John Grady touches the sacred in the world through
the body of horses, which by the end of the dream he has become. Words and
language, the providence of the divided souls of men, are inadequate here.
The world cannot be spoken, and it is the attempt to do so—to construct a
world through the deceptive structures of myth rather than to experience it
directly—that veils the true nature of the world, drowns out the music and
resonance of it, brings chaos and disorder. Pilkington implies that for
McCarthy, nature itself is violent and chaotic. He compares *All the Pretty
Horses* to R. G. Vliet's novel *Soledad, or Solitudes*, which takes its epigraph
from a Wallace Stevens poem: "We live in an old chaos of the sun." "This is
existentialism in a nutshell," Pilkington says, "since nature is chaotic,
meaning and order must be forged from within the individual." I would
argue, however, that it is not nature that is chaotic for McCarthy; rather
chaos is introduced into natural order by disordered humanity, signified in
John Grady's "breaking" of the wild horses at the La Purísima corrals in
accordance with the blinding and destructive myth of the sacred cowboy, a
myth disguising not only its own violent and disordered nature, but the true
nature of the world and its effect on it as well.

The dream of the Eden of horses is paired with a second dream later in
the novel, after John Grady has spoken with the Dueña Alfonsa about the
importance of truth. He has already returned to Encantada to seal back his
and Rawlins's horses and has not entirely come to terms with the loss of the
mythic world that had sustained him.

In his sleep he could hear the horses stepping among the
rocks and he could hear them drink from the shallow pools in the

dark where the rocks lay smooth and rectilinear as the stones of
ancient ruins and the water from their muzzles dripped and rang
like water dripping in a well and in his sleep he dreamt of horses
and the horses in his dream moved gravely among the tilted
stones like horses come upon an antique site where some
ordering of the world had failed and if anything had been written
on the stones the weathers had taken it away again and the horses
were wary and moved with great circumspection carrying in their
blood as they did the recollection of this and other places where
horses once had been and would be again. Finally what he saw in
his dream was that the order in the horse's heart was more
durable for it was written in a place where no rain could erase it.

The symbolism here, with the artificial order of the human soul
revealed as false and transitory, is fairly obvious, but the irony, of course, is
how this knowledge can help John Grady, who is, after all, a man and not a
horse. He may run with horses in his dreams, but when he awakens, he still
must find a way to live within the world of men, chaotic and disordered as
that world may be. Simply loving horses and the natural world they
represent, as John Grady does from the outset, is obviously not enough, and
this quest, carried on in the liminal spaces of the plot of *Pretty Horses*, and
within the guise of a genre commonly famed for its lack of metaphysical
concerns, is what finally drives the action—not lost loves, roundups, cattle
drives, or prison-yard knife fights—and it is the complexity of this search that
makes the novel, despite its "accessibility," so typically McCarthy-esque and
so important in understanding how and why the icons and figures of the
mythic West continue to wield such power in popular American culture
today.

In *Pretty Horses* McCarthy has manipulated the most familiar forms of
national fantasy, icons constructing the most basic images commonly held in
America of identity, nationality, and culture to make the coming-of-age of
John Grady a story that speaks to the coming-of-age of a nation and causes
the sorrowful and necessary death of a national fantasy. The ending here is
ambiguous, not necessarily hopeful. As promised in the opening chapter,
John Grady has redeemed himself in blood from the nostalgic blindness at
the heart of the sacred cowboy myth, but whether this redemption is enough
to carry him forward into the world to come remains obscured and unspoken
at the close of this novel.

It becomes tragically clear, however, in his final fate in *Cities of the Plain*.
In fact, it is evident from the opening scene of this third book in McCarthy's
borderlands trilogy that the mythical world of the sacred cowboy is dead and

gone, scarcely viable even in the imaginations of those who wish to live in it. In the first scene, John Grady, Billy, and several other cowboys employed on a small ranch in southeastern New Mexico sit in a whorehouse in Juarez, across the border from El Paso, calling each other "cowboy" over and over, in a sort of desperate incantation, as though they are trying to banish the impending seizure of the ranch by the U.S. military as part of its base at Alamagordo and their own inevitable unemployment and obsolescence. However, their constant naming of themselves and their profession is futile, the invocation of a world and an identity already vanished. The opening scene is lively and humorous, full of comic verve, but the feeling is that of a B-grade Western, as if John Grady, Billy, and the others are acting out a scene at once familiar, nostalgic, but already a cliché, more fantasy than reality. The heart of the ranch where they live and work, Mr. Johnson's daughter, Margaret, is dead before the narrative begins, and Mr. Johnson himself is like a walking ghost, slowly falling into senility, wandering off into the desert in the middle of the night dressed only in his nightshirt and having to be led back to the house. It is John Grady who looks after Mr. Johnson in his increasingly common attacks of confusion. John Grady sits up with him at the kitchen table until morning for it to appear that the old man simply got up early, though all the hands on the ranch are aware of their employer's condition.

Although this is a kind-hearted act—attempting to mask the disintegration of the old cowboy (and his way of life, along with his doomed ranch)—it is an early hint that John Grady has chosen to ignore the lesson the Dueña Alfonsa attempted to teach him. He chooses to see the world of the ranch in the way he wishes it to be, not in the way it is. Again, the plot of *Cities of the Plain* is simple and straightforward. John Grady convinces himself he is in love with the pretty, young whore, Magdalena, whose long black hair makes her resemble Alejandra. She is killed by the pimp who manages the whorehouse as she tries to run away to marry John Grady, who in turn challenges the man to a knife fight in order to revenge Magdalena's murder. John Grady, the last real cowboy, who has adhered to the cowboy code throughout the novel, dies along with the ranch and the imagined way of life they both represent.

In effect, however, John Grady has committed suicide, both literally and figuratively. In order to get close enough to stab the pimp, John Grady deliberately allows the man to give him a fatal wound, and in order to deny the truth he sees before him every day on the ranch, that the myth upon which he has structured his life is hollow at its core and shattering to pieces around him, he chooses time and time again to ignore what the world shows him and to cling blindly to a vision of things as he would like them to be. He is unable to move into the future without the comforting blinders of myth, as the Dueña Alfonsa has done, and, unlike her, chooses death rather than truth. As the Dueña Alfonsa told him three years earlier, it is always himself the coward abandons first.

To call John Grady a coward may seem far fetched. After all, he has exhibited great physical courage and is presented in both novels as an entirely good-intentioned and likeable character, one of the few in McCarthy's works. But the fate he chooses for himself in *Cities of the Plain* succinctly answers the question left hanging at the close of *All the Pretty Horses* where John Grady disappears ambiguously into "the world to come."

The myth of the sacred cowboy and the structures of the national symbolic it supports are, in the end, an epistemology of death, dashing and romantic without doubt, but hollow, false, blood-stained, and too frightened of the truth to see the world as it is, or to live in the one to come. Through the tragic figure of John Grady and the choices he makes, which lead inevitably to death, McCarthy challenges his readers to look clearly upon the consequences to the natural world and to American culture of the acceptance of the figure of the sacred cowboy as one of our defining myths. *Cities of the Plain*, with John Grady's life and death in its narrative, continues McCarthy's radical revisioning of American history and identity as it has traditionally been defined in the Western.

BARCLEY OWENS

Thematic Motifs in Cities of the Plain

> "Our plans are predicated upon a future
> unknown to us."
> —from *Cities of the Plain*

Who's afraid of the dark? We all are, or should be. Compared to other animals with more developed senses of hearing and smell, as well as enhanced night vision, we are limited by our inability to see clearly in the dark. Being afraid of the dark is as primal as fear gets. We have been cowering around campfires since the first evening of mankind—and not just to stay warm. There might be dangers lurking out there beyond the perimeter of our light: big cats, bears, wolves, crocodiles, snakes. Ancient common sense, a sixth sense, warns us to be wary of the night. Seeing has always been our best way of discerning what is actual. To see is to believe; blindness is fear. But to the most daring and romantic of us—poets, cowboys, and lunatics—night is more like a different shade of day, a place to muse and ride and dream. Some of us are blind to the dangers of night because we cannot see the darkness.

For McCarthy's cowboys, the night bodes ill. In the dark, Billy flicks the switch on the barn lights and is jolted by the current running through faulty wiring. Shaking his arm in pain, he recalls past misadventures: "Ever time I reach for that son of a bitch I get shocked." The larger "son of a bitch" in

From *Cormac McCarthy's Western Novels*. ©2000 by the Arizona Board of Regents.

this novel is Mexico, and the faulty switch presages a return to the theme of romantic tragedy across the border. Mexico at night is wholly alien to a cowboy's daytime existence. In the stark light of day, ranching is simple, straightforward, and rewarding. As Billy aptly puts it, a cowboy's work ethic is to "put in a day's work for a day's wages. . . . Daybreak to backbreak for a godgiven dollar." And Billy, like any Adamic hero living in a cowboy's Eden, understands the life-sustaining, redemptive rewards of an honest day's work. In a burst of exuberance he gushes, "I love this life. You love this life, son? I love this life. You do love this life don't you? Cause by god I love it. Just love it." Billy affirms the value of Mac's ranch and of having a stable position. The wanderlust of the first two novels is absent here; after all their journeys, John Grady and Billy have finally found a home. For readers familiar with the other novels in the Border Trilogy, Billy's top-of-the-morning exuberance for ranch life recalls the lost paradises of the pair's childhood family ranches and of Don Héctor's hacienda. In *Cities of the Plain*, McCarthy raises the stakes to tragic proportions. He locates his two cowboy heroes several years after the close of *All the Pretty Horses* in a ranch paradise outside El Paso, replete with all the familiar trimmings: cows, horses, dogs, and all the biscuits and gravy and scrambled eggs and grits and sausage and preserves and *pico de gallo* and butter and honey his men can eat. There is much to lose here.

From the beginning, McCarthy laces the text with motifs from one of his favorite themes: man's inability to predict far-reaching consequences of his actions. Upon a first reading of the novel, most of the oblique motifs are fleeting, such as the moment that follows Billy's expression of love for a cowboy's life: "The sun was blinding white on the dusty windshield glass." Only later does one realize that this detail is part of a repeating pattern of blindness from reflections. Shortly thereafter, a coyote trots along the crest of a nearby ridge, paying no attention to the men. Billy notices the coyote first: "I want you to look at that son of a bitch." The phrasing connects this scene with the faulty light switch, which is also a "son of bitch." John Grady underestimates the coyote's abilities when he suggests going for his rifle and taking a shot. Billy informs him that the coyote would "be gone before you get done standin up." Unsettled by such an unnatural sight in "the middle of the day," John Grady wonders, "You think he seen us?" and Billy answers with typical western aplomb, "I don't expect he was completely blind." John Grady's surprise and desire to reach for a gun underscore his misunderstanding of night creatures as well as his preference for direct action. In contrast, Billy establishes himself as the older voice of experience and restraint.

Small, unsettling moments resonate in the episode leading up to the incident when an owl crashes into the ranch truck. Late at night, on the road back to the ranch, Billy drives past a stranded truckload of Mexicans in need of help. After continuing on without stopping, he abruptly changes his mind and turns back, remembering a time eleven years before, after Boyd had been shot, when he and his brother were helped by such people. The brothers were rescued from the "worst day of my life," as he explains to Troy: "We was on the run and he was hurt and there was a truckload of Mexicans just about like them back yonder appeared out of nowhere and pulled our bacon out of the fire." In playing the good "Samaritan," as Troy puts it, Billy pays some interest on a past debt. However, Troy, who does not trust Mexicans as a general rule, suspects that nothing Mexican should be taken at face value. Although this blatant comment surprises Billy—who replies "Why would anybody lie about goin to Sanderson Texas?"—its truth is later borne out by the novel's denouement, which, as in *All the Pretty Horses* and *The Crossing*, involves an existential hero who defies authority. Against all odds and sensible advice, John Grady persists in acting according to his own will. He will sacrifice all for love. Unforeseen troubles presage John Grady's eventual martyrdom. When Billy turns back to help the Mexicans fix a flat tire, he inadvertently sets in motion events leading to the accident with the owl.

Billy and John Grady share an affinity for Mexican folk *campesinos* and a faith in their country hospitality. Like cowboys, campesinos live close to the land and are poor, hardworking, and honest. They also live according to a machismo code of honor and suffer at the hands of authority. Likewise, campesino culture endows young rebels with legendary status. The songs of the Border, known as *corridos*, celebrate the exploits of cowboys who willingly pit themselves against corrupt landowners or Anglos. Fighting oppression, these antiheroes sacrifice themselves in a hail of bullets as martyrs to the people's causes. Travis speaks for cowboys in general as he fondly recalls frequent trips into Old Mexico:

> Mostly I just visited. I liked it. I liked the country and I liked the people in it. I rode all over Chihuahua and a good part of Coahuila and some of Sonora. I'd be gone weeks at a time and not have hardly so much as a peso in my pocket but it didnt make no difference. Those people would take you and put you up and feed you and feed your horse and cry when you left. You could of stayed forever. They didn't have nothin. Never had and never would. But you could stop at some little estancia in the absolute dead center of nowhere and they'd take you in like you was kin.

While John Grady looks out over the beautiful landscape, "the green line of the river breaks and range on range [of] distant mountains," he muses nostalgically about his own adventures in Mexico, telling Billy, "Those

people would take you in. Hide you out. Lie for you. No one ever asked me
what it was I'd done." Although both men retain a love for campesino
culture, in *Cities of the Plain* Billy has outgrown his youthful, naïve attraction
to Mexico's romantic possibilities. At twenty-eight, he is nine years older
than John Grady, more travel-worn and world-weary. In contrast with John
Grady's youthful optimism, the tone of Billy's reply reveals bitterness over
the loss of the wolf and his brother Boyd: "I went down there three separate
trips. I never once come back with what I started after." Billy is more wary of
life's vicissitudes and no longer yearns for adventure or love. He has become
practical over the years, settling into the comforts of electric light and stable
ranch life. His character in this novel is a dramatic change from the young
existential hero who rescued a wolf in *The Crossing*, as he now joins the ranks
of reason and caution, much like Rawlins in *All the Pretty Horses*. Billy is old
for his twenty-eight years, and has learned "hard lessons in this world," like
Mr. Johnson, who tells John Grady the hardest lesson in life is "that when
things are gone they're gone. They aint comin' back," citing the extinction
of wolves in the Southwest as an example. Of course, in *The Crossing*, a much
younger Billy has learned firsthand the impossibility of saving even one wolf.
In his new role as pragmatic older brother, Billy advises John Grady to give
up his impossible, romantic dreams, to stop playing the fool, to see things as
they really are, not as he wishes them to be. Billy himself has ignored such
advice several times as a young man, as has John Grady in *All the Pretty
Horses*. Throughout the Border Trilogy, the existential, Adamic hero never
takes the path of least resistance. Instead, he behaves according to the
unyielding ethics required in the cowboy's code of honor, in which a man is
expected to act spontaneously from the heart while stubbornly ignoring all-
too-certain ramifications of the deed.

   Billy will not leave a truckload of campesinos stranded. Instead, he turns
around and helps the Mexicans repair the flat. On this night, at least, he will
act heroically, like John Grady, and not worry about the unforeseeable
consequences of kindness. He owes a debt to the Mexicans for helping his
brother Boyd. McCarthy gives us a visual clue to this incident's connection
with the Mexican prostitute Magdalena in the description of the Mexicans'
truck, which has a faulty taillight with a short in it, and thus winks "on and
off like a signal." The faulty wiring of the taillight is doubled in the wiring of
the barn light, which shocks Billy when the flips the switch. It also finds a
resonance later in a Juárez café scene, where a "man with a strange device"
asks John Grady if he wishes "to electrocute himself." The motif of winking
reappears in the winking eye of Magdalena's ominous servant and the sudden
appearance of Eduardo's knife in the climactic fight. By connecting "the old
one-eyed criada," whose blinking eye makes her appear "to be winking in

some suggestive complicity" to "a wink of light off the blade," McCarthy's overlapping images make the symbolism clear: the night of Mexico is full of winking hazards, and stopping to act the part of Good Samaritan entails fatal consequences.

Soon after Billy stops to help the Mexicans, an owl slams into the truck, breaking the windshield, "a sudden white flare" recalling the earlier sun "blinding white on the dusty windshield glass." The "laminate of the glass" is "belled in softly." In death, the owl sprawls "cruciform" across the "wrecked glass" like an "enormous moth in a web." With symbolism suggesting a Christlike crucifixion, the "soft and downy" bird, "its head slumped and rolled," is hung by the men on the wires of a nearby fence. The owl incident also foreshadows John Grady's nighttime plunge into the fatal knife fight with Eduardo. The fractured windshield of Billy's truck prefigures John Grady kicking in the doorglass of Eduardo's car, which is described in similar terms: "The glass was laminated and it spidered whitely in the light and sagged inward." John Grady replays the role of the crucified owl, which is normally at home in the night until it is unexpectedly blindsided by a car. Finally, shortly before their last night together, John Grady and Magdalena may be seen in the description of two owls: "Two owls crouching in the dust of the road turned their pale and heartshaped faces in the trucklights and blinked and rose on their white wings as silent as two souls ascending and vanished in the darkness overhead."

The small pathos of the owl accident is one of many such unnatural occurrences involving blindness followed by the sudden tragic clarity of death. Blindness can be interpreted as both the literal condition of inability to see and the figurative condition of being unable to foretell the future. Both omens are bad. The identity of the owl, whose death disturbs Billy and Troy, is richly connotative, suggesting Billy's dead brother, Boyd; Troy's dead brother, John; and the future death of John Grady. Blindness in foreseeing the consequences of doomed love raises the mythic stakes to tragic proportions. A pastoral hero loves unwisely, which inevitably leads to an existential moment, a choice between paternal advice and youthful passion. Pastoral poets—from Sidney and Shakespeare to Yeats and Graves—have demonstrated the pattern. True love is an unquenchable, eternal force of human nature. It is sexual and ideological, like an Adamic hero who sacrifices the safety of his father's Eden for Eve's love. And he never sees the consequences. A pastoral hero is blinded by his own willful idealism—unable to see the folly of his actions and unwilling to accept the advice of more level-headed friends.

Various characters in *Cities of the Plain* demonstrate the power of true love. Mac's love for his dead wife continues unabated, as does Mr. Johnson's love for his dead daughter. The unfulfilled promise of love can be seen in the old rancher who picks up John Grady even as he goes to fight Eduardo. When, speaking of his wife, he tells the boy, "There aint been a day passed in sixty years I aint thanked God for that woman," it underscores the extent of John Grady's tragic loss: a lifetime with Magdalena that is never to be. Love's power over John Grady is such that he will not—cannot—give it up. As Troy says about Grady, "I reckon he just don't like to quit a horse." As we have seen in *All the Pretty Horses*, in John Grady's passion for Alejandra, in the cowboy's pastoral scheme of things a horse is a lot like a woman. When Billy tells Troy that he once lost a horse he "was awful partial to," Troy's double-entendre rejoinder, "It's easy to do," applies to women as well. Horses and women inspire cowboys to existential acts of true love.

Blindness from reflections at night proves fatal. As Billy and Troy drive back to the ranch, a jackrabbit freezes in the road and is hit. This leads to Troy's tall tale about killing a hundred jackrabbits on a wild road trip. Figuratively, the jackrabbits represent John Grady's blindness to reality. Recalling his night rides with Don Héctor's stallion, John Grady says, "I used to love to ride of a night . . . You'll see things on the desert that you can't understand." When he is asked what sort of things are in the night, he explains that horses can see a lot more than their riders and intimates that a horse's vision is more reliable, a vision into the deeper meaning of life itself: "I aint talkin about spooks. It's more like just the way things are. If you only knew it." Like a jackrabbit, John Grady is attracted to the night and its dangerous reflections. At one point, Billy directly warns the younger man about riding at night: "Ride him blind through the brush tryin to beat me back. Get him snakebit and I don't know what all." But John Grady replies with characteristic cowboy machismo, "It takes a special hand to ride him in the dark. . . .A rider that can instill confidence in a animal," This kind of blind faith in his nocturnal abilities indicates John Grady's tragic flaw, hubris, which leads him to search for Magdalena in the dark, dangerous lights of Mexico. During his meeting with her, he opens his heart completely, confiding to her his past, the events described in *All the Pretty Horses*. He tells her about the old Comanche trail and "how he would ride that trail in the moonlight in the fall of the year when he was a boy." Later, he tells her about his plans to rescue her from Eduardo and blithely reassures her there is nothing to fear. Despite previous lessons about the dangers of Mexico, he has not yet learned to be afraid of its dark.

One plausible explanation for the long gaps between McCarthy's novels—years in length—may be the richness of intricately associated motifs that they require. He works and reworks a novel to achieve figurative saturation, adding visual and verbal cues until every scene resonates with symbolic overlays. In *Cities of the Plain*, such thematic motifs all point in one direction: toward the final knife fight.

In the ribald humor of the novel's first pages, it is easy to overlook the small details of the setting: "Out in the street the rain slashed through the standing water driving the gaudy red and green colors of the neon signs to wander and seethe." The rain violently cuts like knives through the gaudy, wet silk-shirt-like neon lights, green and bleeding with red. And just so we don't forget later on, in the "bloodred barlight" the cowboys salute "some fourth companion now lost to them." Thus an intimation of John Grady's death is already present in their toast. Images of rain, red lights, and red carpet proliferate in McCarthy's descriptions of the streets and whorehouses of Juárez. As they walk up Juárez Avenue, "the lights of the bars and cafes and curioshops bled slowly in the wet black street." The trolley tracks "shining in the wet lamplight" run "like great surgical clamps" toward the ominous "dark shapes of the mountains." The pouring rain that floods the streets and soaks their boots at several points in the narrative parallels the loss of blood in the climactic knifefight. When John Grady returns to La Venada to look for Magdalena, a "small drip of water falling from the ceiling into puddles in the bloodred carpeting" suggests the dripping of blood from wounds. Later, in John Grady's dream, the velour curtains are "as red as blood." And on the last night of his life, he stands and watches "the sky to the west blood red where the sun had gone." Many such small details reward a close reading.

The color blue takes on ominous meaning when it is associated with the "blue walls and a single blue bulb" in the corridor leading to Eduardo's office and his "sleek oiled head blue in the light" during the knifefight. The truckload of Mexicans helped by Billy are silhouetted against the "deep burnt cobalt of the sky." The cabdriver who hails John Grady while he is searching for Magdalena has "a blue suit of polished serge" and an umbrella with a sheet of "blue cellophane," under which "the driver's face was blue." As John Grady and Mr. Johnson discuss the topic of marriage, the sky turns "dark and blue." When Billy helps John Grady paint the old mountain shack with an ugly bright blue, he unwittingly symbolizes Eduardo's ownership of his dream. When Magdalena flees the hospital by running out into the dangerous streets of Juárez, she seeks "some favored inclination in the blue light of the desert stars by which she would stand revealed for who she truly was." But the stars hold no such promise, as their blueness symbolizes Eduardo's possession. On the morning of her death, Magdalena hopefully puts on a blue dress and regards "herself in the dimly lit mirror," like a doomed Virgin of Guadalupe: the cab that arrives at the café—the one in which Magdalena unknowingly rides to meet Tiburcio instead of John Grady—is also painted blue. Blue portends the disaster in Mexico, a blue corridor leading to Eduardo. In the end, as Billy carries John Grady's body in his arms through the streets in the "gray Monday dawn," a group of schoolchildren "dressed in blue uniforms" witness the lonely funeral procession and bless themselves in "gray light."

The colors green and gray represent, respectively, the dreams of John Grady juxtaposed with grim reality. Like F. Scott Fitzgerald's use of a green beacon in *The Great Gatsby*, green symbolizes John Grady's hopes for a better life. This color's first association with John Grady's dreams is implied in the description of the "live belt of green" that runs down the Rio Grande valley, contrasted with the "fenced gray fields" and "gray dust" of the "gray furrows." Gray is the absence of life in a dead landscape seen close up. McCarthy doubles images of the old grayness of dawn throughout the novel. In Juárez, the gutters run with "a grayish water," and in the White Lake, in the "gray light" of a new day, the tattered reality of the whorehouse becomes apparent: "stains on the carpet, worn places on the arms of the furniture, cigarette burns." In contrast, at night the cities on the plain appear so pretty, deceptively scintillating "like a tiara laid out upon a jeweler's blackcloth." The word *tiara* is also used to describe the chandelier in the White Lake, connecting the glittering lights of the city with the glass lights of the brothel. The beckoning "aura of the lights" is beautiful, but in the grayness of day, one can see more clearly: "The desert plain lay cold and blue below them in the graying light and the shape of the river running down from the north through the break of gray winter trees lay in the pale serpentine of mist. To the south the cold gray grid of the distant city and the shape of the older city across the river like stampings in the desert soil." Notice that in the cold light of day, the desert also reveals the ominous blueness associated with Eduardo. From high in the upper range, Billy and John Grady see the "thin standing spire of smoke . . . rising vertically in the still blue morning air" and Billy remarks how it looks "different from up here. Always looked different. It was different." The American cowboys' idealistic dreams of the "green line of the river breaks" is lost in the "pale serpentine of mist" and "range on range the distant mountains of Mexico" signifying a "future unknown." All the pretty lights of the city at night contrast with the squalid "cold gray grid" of the streets by day. McCarthy extends the symbolism by showing John Grady with his arm around a bloody dog with "four bloody furrows along her flank" that has returned to camp "bearing witness to things they could only imagine or suppose out there in the night." The dog's bloody furrows hearken back to the description of the landscape's gray furrows, which also foreshadow Eduardo's four bloody cuts spelling out the letter E in John Grady's thigh during the knifefight. Likewise, as Magdalena leaves the White Lake for the last time, the city lights are described as a breathtaking reflection of the heavens, "burning on the plain like stars pooled in a lake." The illusion of beauty here is undercut by the word *pooled*, which has echoes in the autumn pools of dead leaves and the "pools of rainwater" during the knifefight.

When John Grady and Billy look out over the surrounding countryside from high in the upper range of the Jarillas, they see the "green of the benchland below" and the "thin straight line of the highway and a toysized truck" and the "green line of the river breaks." The first night he makes love to Magdalena, John Grady notices the light running like "a river over her naked shoulders," connecting the green of the river to his dream of true love. Yet on the first page of the novel, McCarthy has already intimated the end of the green dream in the bleeding of green neon. When Magdalena awakens from her epileptic fit on the steel table, she runs out through a "gray metal door" and escapes through a "long green corridor dimly lit and stretching away to a closed door at the end." Her fate is thus sealed symbolically by the grayness of the door as a harsh reality closing off the green corridor of love. The day of Magdalena's death, John Grady rides into the high country one more time and contemplates the lonely landscape: "To the south the thin green line of the river lay like a child's crayon mark across the mauve and bistre waste. Beyond that the mountains of Mexico in paling blues and grays washing out in the distance." The "crayon mark" and "mauve" echo the description of Magdalena's "painted child's mouth" and the naïve childishness of John Grady's romantic dream. The thin green line of love is reflected in the landscape as youthful desire, another kind of idealistic " picturebook" (*All the Pretty Horses*), an impossible dream when faced with the "paling blues and grays washing out in the distance."

Yellow and red, white and blue, gray and green, circles and webs, night and day, reflections and blindness—all these thematic motifs are carefully woven into the novel's overlapping images, forming a densely figurative tapestry. The color yellow connects the mirror in La Venada, the "yellowing glass of the old Brunswick backbar," to the "yellow leaves" that "turn and drift in a pool," to Magdalena's yellow lamplight, to "the yellow bulb screwed into the fixture over the back door," to the "yellowed finger" of the blind man. The yellow associations all point to the false hopes engendered by John Grady's ardent green love for Magdalena. The green leaves turn yellow in the fall, where they end up dying in the pool, which is doubled in the black pools of rainwater outside the White Lake on the night of the knifefight. On his way to get some answers from Eduardo, Billy stands under a "green and yellowed tiled arch," which in McCarthy's arcane encoding gestures toward the disastrous mixture of green dreams and yellow deceptions. The morning after the knifefight, as John Grady lies dying of his wounds, Billy sets out to find help: "As he trotted out across the vacant lot he looked back. The square of yellow light that shone through the sacking looked like some haven of promise out there on the shore of the breaking world but his heart misgave him." It is too late. In the "gray dawn" the "stars had dimmed out and the dark shapes of the mountains stood along the sky." The false hopes of yellow and the glittering promise of stars fade into the gray morning of a grim Mexican reality. When Billy returns a few minutes later, John Grady is dead.

The blind pianist, like so many of McCarthy's anchorites, offers vague, misleading advice: "You must persevere. To persevere is everything." While this kind of simple idealism appeals to John Grady's stubborn machismo, which drives him to follow his heart and never give up—on a horse or a woman—it is bad advice, especially given the ominous context of the next lines:

> My belief is that she is at best a visitor. At best. She does
> not belong here.
> Among us.
> Yessir. I know she don't belong here.
> No, said the blind man. I do not mean in this house. I
> mean here.
> Among us.

John Grady gives no clue that he understands what the blind man has just intimated: that he and Magdalena will soon die. John Grady walks back "carrying the blind man's words concerning his prospects as if they were a contract with the world to come," yet he is unable to act on the truth he has been told. Later, when John Grady asks the blind man to stand in as Magdalena's godfather, the blind man refuses because he believes that Eduardo will kill her. At this revelation, John Grady demands that the blind man tell him what to do. Instead he is given a strangely direct yet evasive riddle: "You must understand. I have no certainty. And it is a grave matter." The word *grave* works as a double entendre to signify that in the course of the world's events the matter is already settled. Magdalena will die. At the end of this conversation, McCarthy uses a dialogue between John Grady and the blind man as a direct expression of his theme:

> You think I'm a fool.
> No. I do not.
> You would not say so if you did.
> No, but I would not lie. I don't think it. I never did. A
> man is always right to pursue the thing he loves.
> No matter even it if kills him?
> I think so. Yes. No matter even that.

But this is an impossible outcome for the youth to accept. All of his success in life has been improbable and hard-earned—training horses, chasing wild dogs, fighting in Mexico. He gives no quarter to the possibility of failure. On the ranch, his honesty and determination have paid rich dividends, garnering him the respect of other men in the region. His refusal to give up on the "owlheaded" colt leads Billy to predict, "I got a suspicion that whatever it is he aims to do he'll most likely get it done." When John Grady alertly spots that a horse is lame in the right foreleg and won't allow delivery, he has to stand firm against another man's insistent prodding that he take the horse anyway. Six times John Grady firmly denies the man's request, and the incident almost escalates into a fight. But the owner of the injured horse is so impressed by John Grady's keen judgment that he tries to hire the young man, full-time or part-time, whatever he can get. Billy, the voice of reason, tells him to do it, that it's a good deal, but John Grady's loyalty to Mac is like his loyalty to horses and women. He will work for only one man at a time. Once he's made up his mind, he never quits a horse. In a clash of wills, John Grady always stands firm, true to his word according to his best judgment. This quality can be admirable and, at times, can make the difference between failure and success. In the dog hunt, John Grady leads the way on a precarious route to the top of the mesa by tying his jacket over the horse's head to calm it. Here again, blinding the horse takes on thematic overtones, connecting with John Grady's willingness to go to any lengths to succeed, even if it means self-imposed blindness. Going into Juárez to make love to Magdalena and planning a future with her is another kind of blind deception, one he is unwilling to admit when confronted by older voices of reason. After the rousing dog hunt, when John Grady and Billy go back after the pups only to discover an unmovable boulder on top of the den, John Grady is the one who won't give up. With great effort and at his own peril, he rigs an impromptu lever and winch to tip the boulder over. And it works. Through sheer determination and quick wits, John Grady wins the day.

But the night is a different story. When he insists on pursuing unorthodox, extreme measures at night, he becomes as foolish as those frozen jackrabbits. One night after spraining an ankle, John Grady wakes everyone on the ranch with a crazy attempt to train the colt in the middle of the night. Billy upbraids him, asking, "What the hell's got into you? . . . You can't even see to rope the son of a bitch," and Oren labels it all a "bunch of damned ignorance." John Grady, however, is not chastened and only replies, "It wasn't any of your business." The phrase "son of a bitch" and the inability to see constitute additional links with blindness, the faulty light switch, and the peculiar coyote as other unnatural events. Another incident demonstrating John Grady's fallibility at night is his loss of a chess game to

Mac, a player whom he usually beats during the daytime. When Billy asks John Grady if he slacked up "on him just the littlest bit," he answers "No. I don't believe in it." John Grady never quits, never changes his mind, never slacks up, not even a little bit.

John Grady's penchant for always standing his ground adheres to the manly code of the Old West. Thus it is not surprising that he finds common ground with Mr. Johnson, the old cowboy. Mr. Johnson also wakes up others with crazy antics in the night, and it is John Grady who goes out to get the old man, who is dressed only in his hat and boots and a "long white unionsuit . . . like the ghost of some ancient waddy wandering there." John Grady defends the old man's behavior, ignoring Billy's comment "That's pitiful" and telling Mac, "He aint loony. He's just old." Noticing that John Grady and the old man "have a lot in common," Billy warns the boy to not "be hangin around him so much." But John Grady enjoys listening to Mr. Johnson's stories of the Old West, tales about going on cattle drives to Abilene and, suitably enough, of once being shot at while bringing some "stolen horses we'd recovered" out of Mexico, mirroring John Grady's experiences in *All the Pretty Horses*.

One of McCarthy's persistent themes in the western novels is the certainty of dark fate. Although his characters are unaware of what the future holds, McCarthy's last sentence in the main text of *Cities of the Plain* returns to determinism: ". . . the woman stepped once more into the street and the children followed and all continued on to their appointed places which as some believe were chosen long ago even to the beginning of the world." The circle motif represents chosen paths as closed orbits. McCarthy's symbolism here departs from traditional understanding of the circle as a representation of eternity—as in the wedding ring, the stone circles of England, and the Aztecs' calendar, *la Piedra del Sol*. The clocklike circles of the sun and moon arching across the dome of sky have long suggested celestial eternity. However, McCarthy uses circle images to indicate the inscribed birth and death of each individual. In *Blood Meridian*, the "tethered coin" of one's life is destined by an invisible string to fly out into the night and, at a designated time, to return again into the hand of an appointed death. In *Cities of the Plain*, circle images especially predominate in the description of a young man's funeral, as witnessed by Magdalena after she has seen John Grady for the last time. The scene strikes her as a terrifying epiphany of coming tragedy, causing her to collapse into an epileptic fit:

> The cart rattled past and the spoked wheels diced slowly the
> farther streetside and the solemn watchers there, a cardfan of
> sorted faces under the shopfronts and the long skeins of light in

the street broken in the turning spokes and the shadows of the
horses tramping upright and oblique before the oblong shadows
of the wheels shaping over the stones and turning and turning.

The young man, pale and newly dead, of course prefigures John Grady's fate,
something made more clear by the ominous presence of the "blind maestro."
Later in the night Magdalena tells a woman, "in three days' time the boy she
loved would come to marry her," suggesting the promise of a risen savior, a
Christ. But the turning wheels of the funeral cart are full of the closed lines
inscribing only circles within circles. Within the circles there is no promise
of an afterlife, no Christ, no salvation, no other possibility except certain
death. Even the straight shafts of light are caught and broken in the 'brutal
fate of the wheels' circling, "turning and turning." The circle image is also
seen in the face of the clock in Mac's house, which McCarthy carefully
describes at several points in the narrative. After a conversation about
marriage, John Grady sits pondering the horizon: "Through the window far
to the south he could see the thin white adderstongues of lightning licking
silently along the rim of the sky in the darkness over Mexico. The only sound
was the clock ticking in the hallway." The clock's loud ticking at night is the
sound of time passing, regulated and parceled into small, discrete units. The
ticking, like the hands of the clock sweeping around in circles, is immutable
fate, a future already decided. John Grady hears the ticking sound again in
his dream of the young girl dead on a "palletboard like a sacrificial virgin,"
describing it as a "periodic click like a misset metronome, a clock, a portent.
A measure of something periodic and otherwise silent and vastly patient
which only darkness could accommodate." The deadliness of circles is finally
made evident in Eduardo's circular motions during the knifefight, as
McCarthy uses the terms *circled* or *circling* no less than seventeen times.
McCarthy's interconnecting symbols are woven so tightly into his
descriptions that one begins to notice a complex web of thematic motifs
embedded in almost every line.

McCarthy's use of thematic motif is perhaps most noticeable in the
novel's frequent references to mirrors. John Grady first sees Magdalena
framed in a yellow "backbar glass," a beautiful girl with downcast eyes and
long black hair that she sweeps back as he watches; later, at the White Lake,
he repeatedly looks for her in the "glass of the backbar." At first he sees only
the reflection of "a tall woman in a diaphanous gown," who looks like "a
ghost of a whore." This small detail is doubled later in Magdalena's half-
crazed night journey through the dangerous streets of Juárez, when she is
wearing only a sheer white shift. At one point the car lights cast "her slight
figure up onto the walls in enormous dark transparency with the shift burned

away and the bones all but showing" and further on "in the glare of the headlights" she appears "like some tattered phantom routed out of the ordinal dark and hounded briefly through the visible world to vanish again into the history of men's dreams." The danger of the onrushing headlights in Juárez also hearkens back to the unfortunate jackrabbits and the owl accident, with its image of "an enormous moth in a web," an image that is reinforced here by the mention of "a millermoth that patrolled [a lightbulb] in random clockwise orbits." With only enough money to buy a drink at the White Lake, John Grady keeps an eye on Magdalena by watching her in the bar mirror and thinks perhaps "she had been watching him." In another mirror, the one-eyed criada and Josefina look at Magdalena critically. Here McCarthy takes great care to denote the difference between the real girl and the mirror's image:

> She [Josefina] studied the girl and she studied the girl in the mirror. The criada had stepped back and stood holding the brush in both hands. She and Josefina studied the girl in the mirror, the three of them in the yellow light of the tablelamp standing there within the gilded plaster scrollwork of the mirror's frame like figures in an antique flemish painting.

In thematic terms, this passage's reiteration of the words *mirror* and *girl* juxtaposes reality with the false reflections of hope. Because the two images, one real and the other unreal, tend to look alike, the two attending women check back and forth to make sure of their handiwork. What they see in the mirror is a pretty picture framed in gold. And it is this pretty, false mirror image that dominates the scene, lending the picture a gilt-edged unreality. As Magdalena continues to stare at herself in the mirror, the woman's eye winks "in suggestive complicity," an unnatural sign which, like the faulty taillight, foretells a tragic end.

Unlike John Grady, however, Magdalena is not so easily fooled by the false hopes of the pretty mirror image. When the criada suggests the fantasy of marrying a rich man and living in a fine house with beautiful children, the girl does not answer.

> She looked across the old woman's shoulder into the eyes in the glass as if it were some sister there who weathered stoically this beleaguerment of her hopes. Standing in the gaudy boudoir that was itself a tawdry emulation of other rooms, other worlds. Regarding her own false arrogance in the pierglass as if it were proof against the old woman's entreaties, the old woman's

promises. Standing like some maid in a fable spurning the offerings of the hag which do conceal within them unspoken covenants of corruption. Claims that can never be quit, estates forever entailed. She spoke to that girl standing in the glass and she said that one could not know where it was that one had taken the path one was upon but only that one was upon it.

At times, this storybook Cinderella clearly sees the harsh reality of her world. Her epileptic convulsions, which the other women consider sacred, the divine touch of God, are moments of deathly clarity, in which she is literally seized by the violent, bloody truth of her coming demise. In the conversation with the criada, the old woman is puzzled by the talk of life's paths, and Magdalena explains simply, "Cualquier senda. Esta senda. La senda que escoja," which translates, "Any path. This path. The path that is chosen." Unlike John Grady, who lives in the bright green world of the American ranch, a cowboy paradise, Magdalena is a woman of the night, a prescient owl who understands her blue destiny, her tragically closed circle of fate. She wants to believe in John Grady because she loves him, yet she remains a figure of pathos, one who knows about the unreality of gilded reflections.

Reflections appear throughout the novel. Eduardo's office has a desk of "polished glass" and "a low coffeetable of glass and chrome," which resemble the reflections from Tiburcio's "greased hair" and the "glossy sheen" of his black shirt. Yet the shiny blackness of Tiburcio contrasts with the clean white leather couch and cream-colored carpet of Eduardo's furnishings. The implications is that Eduardo and Tiburcio are twinned images of each other, alike in their deceptive reflections yet different in social status. As the boss, Eduardo fancies himself a businessman who has risen cleanly above the greasy dealings of his henchman, who has the base duty of working directly with the whores and collecting money from customers. But this illusion ends on the night of the knifefight, when Eduardo's head glistens blue with oil, like Tiburcio's, even as he complains that he should be past "fighting in alleys with knives."

Small moments in the novel work as thematic motifs. When Billy goes to the White Lake to gauge Eduardo's reaction to John Grady's proposal to buy Magdalena, he likewise watches the women in the backbar mirror and is suddenly startled by Tiburcio, who materializes "standing at his left elbow like Lucifer." When Billy takes a cab ride while investigating John Grady's disappearance, the cabdriver looks at him in the mirror, which would be innocent enough except for the connecting detail of the cabdriver's watching Magdalena in the mirror on her death ride. At the White Lake, as John Grady looks for Magdalena in the "glass of the backbar," a cockroach creeps up the counter of the bar, in between the bottles, and ascends "to the glass where it encountered itself and froze." The cockroach is fooled by its own false image and, like the jackrabbits, freezes in an intractable position. John Grady likewise fails to question the false reflections in the mirror. In the directness of the daylight, out in the raw elements of nature, he is a true cowboy hero, a strong-willed man, the best hand on the ranch. He never second-guesses his judgment concerning horses or wild dogs. He stubbornly stays with his plan to get the boulder off the pups' den. Once he has made a decision—and all of his decisions are spontaneous and from the heart—he stands by it until the end. But at night, across the border in Juárez, in the glittering world of mirrors, blue cabs, and one alluring girl, he is out of his element. John Grady's unshakeable sense of his own infallibility is more than a stubborn streak—it is the fatal flaw that undoes all of the green dreams of his ranch paradise.

Readers of *Cities of the Plain* will soon notice a structural anomaly setting this novel apart from McCarthy's previous westerns: the permanence of its locale. The characters are no longer nomadic, and the action remains centered around Mac's ranch and the whorehouses of Juárez. In particular, John Grady has set down roots and has plans for staying on at Mac's ranch for the duration. The looming possibility of an army takeover of the property hints at the impermanence of this position; in fact, Mr. Johnson guesses that eventually the army will take "the whole Tularosa basin." But the main characters, like John Grady in Mexico, remain oblivious to this fate. Until the army takeover, they will persist. This novel's uncharacteristic permanence of locale strengthens the narrative in a couple of ways: first, by demonstrating how much John Grady has to lose, and second, by juxtaposing the peaceful dream of pastoralism against the violence of Mexico. John Grady's green pastoral dream of happiness has already been half-fulfilled. In a way, he has recouped many of the losses incurred in *All the Pretty Horses*. He is no longer haunted by memories of Alejandra or the deaths of Blevins, the inmate, and the Mexican captain. His position on the ranch as a favored son of Mr. Johnson and Mac has given him another chance to have paternal authority figures. His respect for Mr. Johnson equals the respect he had as a boy for his pioneering grandfather, who, like Mr. Johnson, survived the dangers of the frontier. And Mac is even more suitable as a surrogate father than his real father had ever been. Mac willingly offers advice, plays chess, loans money, and admires John Grady's horsemanship. All John Grady needs to complete this version of the American Eden is an Eve. But this is where, once again, he rejects all advice and falls into hubris—precisely the original sin he had been guilty of at Don Héctor's hacienda in *All the Pretty Horses*. There also, John Grady established himself as a top hand, a man who knew and loved horses; there also he risked everything for the love of Eve. With both Alejandra and Magdalena, however, he fails to devise a workable plan of action and pays the price in a knifefight. In *All the Pretty Horses*, he wins by killing the inmate and thus lives to dream again. In this novel the hubris proves tragic in a classical sense and is therefore fatal.

The cowboy hero, in all his pastoral glory, decidedly qualifies as an American version of the noble figure worthy of tragedy. Although John Grady is not royal in an Aristotelian sense, he meets the larger-than-life requirements of the tragic hero with his status as the best hand on the ranch. As the primary icon in the American pantheon of heroes, the cowboy represents the quintessential man. John Grady's simple dream of fixing up the shack for his Mexican bride replays the pioneer's dream of forging a garden-paradise in the wilderness; as in *All the Pretty Horses*, McCarthy offers a version of the western myth of progress. With Magdalena by his side and a steady position on Mac's ranch, John Grady would have everything he needs. But this everything, this potential happiness, is doomed from the moment he chooses Magdalena as his Eve by a fatal paradox: Magdalena is controlled not by God but by Eduardo, and to oppose Eduardo inevitably means to lose Magdalena.

By restricting the narrative to Mac's ranch and Juárez, McCarthy has come full circle: the end of the trail is its beginning. The protagonists of *Blood Meridian* and the Border Trilogy represent the American wanderlust for adventure, the whole westering manifesto that promises so much and serves as the centerpiece of American mythos. We all have felt the mythic impulse for heroics: to love, to rebel, to get back to nature, to stake out turf, to build a little place we can call our own. But if such dreams fed the pioneering of the West, they are certainly not the whole of reality, not the entire history. In reality, the Old West was often a violent and lawless place of massacres and Darwinian "right by might," the Old West of *Blood Meridian*. In the Border Trilogy, McCarthy's vision of Mexico embodies the violence of the Old West. Mexico is the glittering night dream of adventure and a gray land of death. The hard lessons of McCarthy's westerns teach us that the green hopes of youthful dreams—all the pretty horses, Alejandra, the she-wolf, Blevins, Boyd, the scintillating lights of the cities, Magdalena in the mirror—are fanciful chimeras, mere reflections in the night, the artifice of lamps and neon, which bleed and die in a gray dawn.

DIANNE C. LUCE

'They Aint the Thing': Artifact and Hallucinated Recollection in Cormac McCarthy's Early Frame-Works

From the outset of McCarthy's career, his work has embodied his meditation on the value and difficulty of recapturing the past. He repeatedly suggests the ambiguous function of the historical artifact in its capacity to evoke or to displace the thing of which it is a record, the primacy of memory and imagination over mere record, the paradoxical frailty of memory. His work also implies that the will to rewrite history may drive the imagining of the past.

This pattern is central to McCarthy's earliest known work, the short story 'Wake for Susan,' in which an old gravestone prompts Wes' act of creative imagination. It recurs in the graveyard scenes that frame *The Orchard Keeper*, and the similarities in the relationship of narrative framework to bracketed story suggest that the sketch is an early working out of some of the formal and thematic characteristics of the novel. With similar thematic weight, the frame appears again in the William Chaffee scenes opening and closing McCarthy's screenplay, *The Gardener's Son*. In all three, artifacts of the past—gravestones, ruins, photographs—both evoke the past and obscure memory, but the search to re-imagine the past is valorized.

'Wake for Susan' was published in October 1959 in *The Phoenix*, the literary supplement to the University of Tennessee student newspaper, *Orange and White*. 'Wake' is the story of a young man's coming to terms with

From *Myth, Legend, Dust: Critical Responses to Cormac McCarthy*. ©2000 by the Manchester University Press.

human mortality and natural transitoriness through his act of creative imagination, an act triggered by his contract with the autumn woods and certain found or sought-after historical objects. 'Wake' is also a portrait of the artist's creative awakening. Wes has been hunting squirrels on a crisp October morning, and the story begins with his rising from the base of a 'towering shagbark hickory,' a muted Rip Van Winkle echo faintly hinting that in Wes' prior life he has been less fully awake than he is about to be. The allusion may also imply that what follows is as much dream as experience— a distinction that is of little significance to the unfolding of the story except that the suggestion of Wes' dreaming reinforces the emphasis on imagined experience.

As Wes makes his way slowly homeward, where his Saturday chores await, he notes the woods' autumnal decay together with artifacts of human culture from an earlier era: the 'dead leaves'; the 'damp leaf-carpeted woodland floor'; 'the remnants of an abandoned quarry' (an adumbration of the quarry visited by Lester Ballard in *Child of God* and, with its algae covering, of the old insecticide pit where Ather Ownby watches over the corpse of Kenneth Rattner in *The Orchard Keeper*); the old railbed with its 'rotting ties' and its 'sagging rails . . . rusty with disuse.'

Increasingly these artifacts impinge on Wes' attention, and when he finds 'a flattened hog-rifle ball,' his progress home halts. 'He scraped the mud from the oxidized lead and examined it. Well. Wes wondered when it had been fired, who had fired it, and at what, or whom? Perhaps some early settler or explorer had aimed it at a menacing Indian. More likely it had been intended for game for a table of some later date, when the Indians were all gone.' Close observation, knowledge and wonder come together. In a Keatsian moment, the ball's reticence, the very incompleteness of its evocation of the past, elicits the act of imagination in the susceptible boy: 'As Wes examined the rifle-ball, the woods became populated with ghosts of lean, rangy frontiersmen with powder-horns and bullet pouches slung from their shoulders and carrying long-barreled, brass-trimmed rifles with brown and gold maple stocks.' Though it leads to no epiphany, Wes' imagining the ghosts of frontiersmen prefigures and causes his second, more extended and affecting act of recovery: 'It was probably the discovery of the rifle-ball that prompted him to look for the burial plot.' No longer heading home, Wes 'pocket[s] the relic and walk[s] quietly through time-haunted woods', now seeking out the old cemetery with its attendant 'rich and lonely haunted feeling' and inviting it to awaken his powers of imagination.

However, not only is the historical artifact provokingly 'mute', but memory itself is elusive and incomplete: Wes finds that 'The cemetery was not exactly where he remembered it. But while he recognizes that the burial plot is forgotten by most—'especially forgotten,' he thinks—he perceives the life of Susan Ledbetter, buried there, as accessible to his memory because her gravestone is inscribed with the year 1834, and '1834 was a year one could remember, not like 1215, or 1066, but a real year.' Obviously, the memory Wes wishes to access is not personal recollection but historical construct: a 'memory' that imaginatively assimilates personal experience and knowledge with the evidence offered by tangible remnants of the past such as the rifle-ball or Susan's gravestone. The years of the Magna Carta and of the Norman Conquest, etched into schoolboys' memories, cannot truly be remembered because Wes knows directly too little of those eras: they are inaccessible to his historical imagination, and he thinks he can make no construction of these years. Less remote in time and space, the year 1834 has left behind more perceptible artifacts in the landscape, in his culture; so when Wes finds the burial plot, he perceives that 'The bearded stones themselves seemed arrested in that transitory state of decay which still recalls the familiar, which pauses in the descent into antiquities unrecognizable and barely guessable as to origin.'

The story of Susan that follows is precisely a constructed thing, a story constructed by Wes out of the familiar and inspired by the gravestone's laconic and therefore mysterious inscription: 'In this year . . . the Source of Life has reclaimed His own.' What prompts Wes' imagination to wake for Susan rather than any other buried in the plot is her age at death. Pondering the engraved dates, Wes realizes, 'Susan had lived on the earth a full seventeen years.' The closeness of their ages awakens his subjective identification, and thus the grave marker elicits Wes' imagining of history: 'From a simple carved stone, the marble turned to a monument; from a gravestone, to the surviving integral tie to a once warm-blooded, live person. Wes pictured Susan.' He creates her story not as a record or document with claims to authority, but as an act of historical imagination that honors both the testimony of the artifact and the concerns of the artist (much as McCarthy himself would later create *The Gardener's Son* and *Blood Meridian*).

These concerns are hinted first in Wes' imagining Susan as an attractive and marriageable young woman 'blue-eyed and yellow-haired, soft and bright in her homespun dress,' capable and comfortable with her household chores, a nurturing girl who watches 'with womanly pride' as her brothers eat a plentiful and well-prepared country meal. Wes' subjective involvement is self-mockingly telegraphed when he thinks, 'Susan should have a lover, and the lover looked strangely like Wes.' (As in many of McCarthy's more mature works, the narrative voice of 'Wake for Susan' is ambiguous, the line between a removed authorial voice and an involved narrator often deliberately blurred. In this story, I would argue, Wes is to be read as a projection of the author's persona as Susan's lover is a projection of Wes.' The story of their doomed courtship is the story of Susan's lover/Wes more than of Susan. She experiences death; Wes, participating as her imagined lover, confronts the transitory nature of life and is transformed by the experience.

Susan's story begins in the warmth of summer, but it soon partakes of the autumnal images Wes perceives in the woods around him on this October Saturday. As the youth and Susan fall in love and he experiences sexual urgency, Wes imagines the youth tutored by nature in the voice of 'wind-tortured trees that spoke in behalf of the silent stars':

> You walk here, as so many others have walked. The ancient oaks have seen them. The lifesap courses through these twisted limbs as it flows hot through your veins—for awhile. . . .You walk here. Moonwarmed and wind-kissed, you walk here . . . for awhile.

The trees warn the youth to recognize mortality and seize the day: a lesson that Wes' historical perspective on Susan's fate allows him to absorb from nature perhaps for the first time, although his experience as a hunter has prepared him for it. As artist Wes communicates his new insight to his alter ego, Susan's lover, putting the warning back into the mouth of nature.

But as Wes shapes his story for dramatic irony, both Susan and her young man heedlessly enjoy the vigor of their lives, high-spirited with the 'seductive promises' of the 'tingling air' and the sense of well-being evoked by a bountiful harvest. Although she too is urged on by her sexual feelings, Susan feels no larger urgency about their marriage: 'she was willing to permit him to take his time. The question of her future was settled quite agreeably and her youth told her all was well. Give him time; all will be well.' The young couple are like the cottonwood spoken of by the wind-tortured trees that '*cares not for the trees that sucked at this damp earth before its birth, but only for the earth, and the sunwarmth, and the seed.*' For both, as Wes repeatedly affirms, 'it was a very good time of year.'

However, Wes is less naive than the young pair, if only because the historical/authorial perspective carries the advantage of hindsight/foresight. Wes interrupts his story of Susan with a parable of fox and chipmunk, probably invented but perhaps a vignette he witnesses as he sits in the deserted cemetery. The paragraphs preceding this tale-within-a-tale oscillate between the present and 1834, suggesting that Wes is actively mediating the insights derived from the two sets of circumstances. He abruptly breaks away from his description of the young man's satisfaction with his daily life, recapping the lecture of the trees and foreshadowing the thematic resolution of his story of Susan:

Diurnal forces carpeted the forest floor with thick layers of
chunchy [*sic*] brown leaves, torn from the half-naked trees. Long
enough these leaves had shaded the wooded ridges and slopes.
Now they returned to the earth to decay and so provide life and
sustenance for their unformed successors. Long enough, leaves.

'Long enough, leaves' becomes a refrain as Wes assimilates his invented story
of Susan with his recognition of the flow of time and natural cycles in his own
life. This refrain is immediately followed and counterbalanced by the refrain
Wes associates with Susan and her young man: 'The year was 1834, and a
very fine year it was. It was fall, and that is a good time of year.'

The two refrains are succeeded by the story of the fox and the
chipmunk, which, like the trees' warning, embodies naturalistic truth. The
fox pursues the chipmunk because he needs a meal; the chipmunk tries to
elude the fox. Trapped in a crevice where the fox cannot grasp him, the
chipmunk dies from the clawing of the fox and is left 'for the smaller
carnivores.' Wes begins this subplot of his story with the assessment that it is
a 'minor tragedy', suggesting that next to the tragedy of Susan's unfulfilled
life with her suitor and her premature death, the tragedy of the chipmunk or
the fox is insignificant. But the ending of the parable, with its emphasis on
the continuity of life up and down the food chain, calls into question its very
status as tragedy. Although the squeamish may flinch at the idea that the fox
'scraped and clawed at the chipmunk until it was bloody and lifeless', neither
animal is granted tragic stature. Wes narrates the story more from the fox's
perspective, stressing his missed opportunities and his whine of frustration,
but against this he balances the chipmunk's victim status and the pathos of its
death. The emotional impact of these creatures' wasted efforts and death
finally is neutralized as the fox trots off to try for a meal elsewhere and the
chipmunk feeds other life forms. Wes apparently comes to a new, naturalistic
perspective on mortality even as he imagines this tale.

It is a perspective that prepares the reader for the end of 'Wake' and
prepares Wes psychologically to resume his story of Susan, though it does
not reduce his empathy for her and the young man. Indeed, he narrates this
story too for pathos: his last image of Susan is of her undressing for sleep
thinking, 'She would see him again tomorrow night.' Then, because the
'mute stone' gives Wes nothing more on which to hang the conclusion of his
tale, he momentarily retreats into a romantic perspective, identifying fully
with Susan's suitor and his loss: 'The stars came back; if their luster paled, it
was because a part of beauty was no longer there to receive them. In his eyes
they swam blurred and distorted in a salt sea. The year was 1834 and it was
October.'

The gravestone, which has been a bridge to the past, brings Wes back to the present, and he breaks his identification with Susan's lover to wonder how she died, noticing that the marker 'left no testimony.' Now that his story of Susan is completed, though, he experiences catharsis: 'He threw his arms around the unyielding stone and wept for lost Susan, for all the lost Susans, for all the people; so beautiful, so pathetic, so lost and wasted and ungrieved.' As he heads home, 'drained and empty', he sees the dead leaves animated by the wind, dancing 'in a travesty of life.' But his story has done its work. He smiles, picking up the naturalistic refrain, 'Long enough, leaves', and walks home, 'towering even among the lean trees.'

Though it carries few hints of the master of style and tone that McCarthy was to become, 'Wake for Susan' is a rather intricate experiment in narrative strategy, and with hindsight we can say it is a remarkable introduction from the author of *The Gardener's Son, Blood Meridian*, and the Border Trilogy of McCarthy's concerns with history as both material and muse for works of the imagination. As character, Wes is a prototype for John Wesley Rattner in *The Orchard Keeper* and William Chaffee in the narrative frame of *The Gardener's Son* as these young men seek beyond the artifacts and records of history to come to imaginative apprehensions of the past. As an artist figure, Wes is McCarthy's prophetic self-portrait—a man whose intellect and wonder are engaged by the ambiguity of relics of the past and who seeks to bring the past to life through the narrative act while entertaining no illusion that his invention represents what actually happened. Recently Bernard Schopen has written of *Blood Meridian's* 'shaping voice' as a subjective one that 'literally constructs as it speaks to us', a 'consciousness in search of meaning', a narrator who 'is not just recounting past events but also brooding over them, uncertainly searching for meaning within them.' The narrative voice of *Blood Meridian* is far more complex and sophisticated than that of 'Wake for Susan', and it remains cloaked in anonymity rather than presented as a character-narrator in any frame but for the one whispered in the opening invitation to 'See the child'; but surprisingly some of its defining characteristics are adumbrated in the persona of Wes in this early story.

The framing of a story of earlier days by scenes in a cemetery, where a young man contemplates the gravestone of a dead woman and attempts to remember/imagine the past, recurs in McCarthy's first published novel, *The Orchard Keeper* (1965). The young man is John Wesley Rattner (almost a namesake of the protagonist of 'Wake for Susan'), returned to Red Branch in the fall of the year, to visit his abandoned childhood house. Like Billy Parham returned home to find his parents gone, murdered, in *The Crossing*, and Robert McEvoy returned to Graniteville to discover his mother has died in *The Gardener's Son*, John Wesley confronts evidence that in his absence the life and people he had known have slipped into the irretrievable past. At the ancient, abandoned house, itself a relic, he observes that 'Old dry leaves rattled frail and withered as old voices, trailed stiffly down . . . like . . . curling ancient parchments on which no message at all appeared.' After sitting for a while under one of the trees in the yard, an echo of the beginning of 'Wake', he rouses himself and sets off to the graveyard to confirm what the deserted house has suggested, rather like Wes' seeking out the burial plot after finding the rifle-ball. John Wesley reaches the cemetery in late afternoon. There he finds his mother's gravestone, but only after some search, as the men who have been cutting a tree into lengths and who show him the fence '*[g]rowed all up in that tree*' in the prologue have finished their work and departed in the evening hours of the closing chapter. Reading the inscription on the stone, John Wesley thinks, 'It was like having your name in the paper'—this terse and public record of a human life and death.

Like Wes, John Wesley reads the stone for information that is of subjective importance, in this case that his mother has been dead for three years. Then 'He reached out and patted the stone softly, a gesture, as if perhaps to conjure up some image, evoke again some allegiance with a name, a place, hallucinated recollections in which faces merged inextricable, and yet true and fixed.' In 'Wake' Wes embraces Susan's gravestone after it has evoked his 'memory' or 'hallucinated recollection' of the year 1834 when she was courted by a young man like himself and died; but John Wesley's touch is more tentative 'as if perhaps' the stone could evoke image, allegiance, recollection. And when he touches it he finds it 'a carved stone less real than the smell of woodsmoke or the taste of an old man's wine'—images he associates with his mentors Sylder and Ownby. As a defining influence on his character, his mother is less real to him than either of these men who have shaped his life and values, and thus her marker provokes no imaginative recovery of her story. The scene would seem to back away from the idea established in 'Wake for Susan', that an object from the past can speak to the memory and imagination. Yet John Wesley's thought affirms the possibility of hallucinated recollection that mingles and even mangles images, yet somehow remains 'true and fixed', suggesting at its very end that all of the narrative between the framing scenes in the cemetery has been John Wesley's partly remembered, partly imagined reconstruction of his past—and his father's, Sylder's, and Ownby's. As he walks in the cemetery looking for his mother's marker after speaking to the workers, John Wesley recollects and invents the story that is this novel. By the time he finds his mother's gravestone, the story has done its work and 'he no longer cared to tell which were *things done and which dreamt*'; he does not need the marker to evoke again the hallucinated recollection.

In some of the same ways in which Wes' presence is felt in the story of
Susan, but much less obviously signalled, John Wesley's narrating presence
can be detected in the story that disjointedly unfolds between the opening
and closing frames of *The Orchard Keeper*. Especially in the early scenes—
where John Wesley imagines the character of his father Kenneth, the youth
of Marion Sylder, and the confrontation between them that explains his
father's disappearance—details from his own frame-time experience inform
the narrative, just as Wes' experience in the autumn woods becomes an
integral part of his story of Susan. Like both Rattner and Sylder, John Wesley
has just traveled back to Red Branch, quite likely by the Atlanta-to-Knoxville
roads on which he imagines the two older men. Parallel images occur in the
first moments of the story proper and in the end-frame's description of John
Wesley's walk from his old house to the graveyard. In both the sun is setting,
'reddening the western sky.' John Wesley steps off the 'buckled asphalt' to
watch wobble past 'slowly, laboriously' an old negro on a mule-drawn wagon
that 'shimmered in waves of heat rising from the road.' Kenneth Rattner
turns on 'the blazing strip of concrete' to watch a pickup truck 'struggling
toward him.' Once past, the pickup appears to have been a 'fleeting mirage';
John Wesley's wagon dissolves 'in a pale and broken image.' The blown
leaves that seem to John Wesley messageless parchments are transmuted in
his revery into the 'dusty newsprint and candypapers pressed furtively into
the brown wall of weeds' edging the highway where Kenneth hitchhikes.
Both John Wesley and Kenneth head toward forks in the road.

As John Wesley imagines a past for his friend Marion Sylder, a time
prior to their meeting, it is in one respect strangely like his own yet
transformed with wishful thinking: for Marion, John Wesley invents a
prodigal return, the men in the Green Fly Inn not recognizing him until he
calls the bartender by name and Cabe studies him while 'the face of the lost
boy grew in the features of the man standing at the bar.' John Wesley's own
return to Red Branch is to a community incapable of recognizing its prodigal
sons, and his salute to the man and woman in the car is not returned, an event
that leads directly into the elegiac assertion of the last paragraph that the old
people 'are gone now.'

If John Wesley is in this sense the narrator/inventor of the novel, then
the relationship of the narrative strands focused on Rattner, Sylder, and
Ownby, which readers often find only tenuously linked through the boy's
association with each, is clearer. John Wesley as author of his 'hallucinated
recollection' mediates the stories of his biological and chosen fathers,
bringing them together in ways the three men themselves do not recognize
and which may have only partial basis in historical reality. In doing so, John
Wesley accommodates his past, especially the void that has been his father,

known to him through his memory of being treated to a soda pop on the eve of his father's disappearance, the lionizing stories told by his mother, the old photo of Captain Rattner in his military uniform, 'soldier, father, ghost,' but mostly through his absence. With the construction of his story, John Wesley affirms the values he has learned from Sylder and Ownby and confirms their influence on his adult character. The hallucinated recollection fulfills his pledge to his mother that he will 'never forget' while it imaginatively frees him from her charge that he avenge his father. He reinterprets his meeting of Sylder and Ownby, the men whom he imagines respectively killed and hid his father, as fulfillment of her specific demand that he 'find the man that took away your daddy' and of her prophecy that he will find a way. He does find a way.

Imaginatively reconstructing the past he has experienced and remembers, John Wesley exorcises the ghost of his father. He makes young Sylder his father's executioner, a psychologically true representation of Sylder's having replaced Rattner in the life of the boy as he neared adolescence, mentoring him as he mastered the masculine world of hunting and as he entered an adult world requiring ethical choices. By making Rattner an opportunist on a par with Gifford and Legwater, and worse, a highwayman and potential murderer, John Wesley refutes not only his mother's suspect history of his father, but also the historical testimony of the photo of Kenneth as an officer. He does so to absolve Sylder of the projected guilt of killing his father, and to absolve himself for his disloyalty to a father who has existed for him as little more than icon or artifact. In finding a way to question now the suspect versions of the past that he had not known how to reject as a child, John Wesley makes a necessary step toward self-reliant adulthood.

The role John Wesley imagines for Uncle Ather as guardian of Rattner's corpse is also psychologically healing. Watching over the corpse, the bones, the physical artifact of his dead father, Ownby performs for John Wesley the obligation placed on him by his unhealthy mother; and through this rite in some mysterious way Ownby anneals the Rattner family's loss. Ather's watch absolves John Wesley from meeting the gaze of the father who watches relentlessly from the photo on the mantel; by remembering the corpse, Ather frees John Wesley from having to remember a father who is mere ghost, from being haunted all his life by a task he can never complete. In John Wesley's imagination, his father's remains are respectfully guarded until they are dissolved, burned away, effaced. He even imagines his own innocent participation in the effacement, as the boys' tipsy experimentation with fire results in the burning of the cedar and the bones it hides. The detail of the corpse's entombment in the insecticide pit, concealed by vegetation, derives from young John Wesley's witnessing of the rabbit that fell down the well and died though he tried to feed it, remaining a vivid and moving image etched in his memory: 'He went away and he could see for a long time the rabbit down in the bottom of the well among the rocks with the lettuce over it.' That he 'remembers' Ather's performing the requisite death-watch rather than reporting the corpse to the authorities accords with Ather's other characteristics as challenger of impersonal civil law and institutions, champion of human values, and patient repository of the past in John Wesley's actual knowledge of him.

As suspect as Judge Holden's pronouncements always are, his claim in *Blood Meridian* that the death of the father is the son's birthright resonates nevertheless with this aspect of *The Orchard Keeper*. Whatever the judge's purpose and whatever the kid may derive from his statement, McCarthy's first novel suggests that before a boy can become a man, his father must be cut down to size. If the father's mortality masks his fallibility rather than revealing it, the child is doomed to remain a child in the shadow of an icon, never to inherit the mantle of manhood. In reconstructing the history of his father, imaginatively filling the gaps so as to reject the suspect construction foisted on him by his mother, John Wesley transcends his own past.

The narrative voice of the frame itself reinforces and affirms the value of imagination as a supplement to the irretrievable past. The framing image of the fence grown into the tree that provokes such wonder and admiration from the workers is, from this perspective, an image of John Wesley's story: a blending of dead fact with living imagination so that the fence/material fact is seen to 'grow' and live with the tree/created story it informs. As the novel ends, the tree and fence are both down, and the tone is unabashedly elegiac as John Wesley heads 'out to the western road.' With his leaving, like those of his three fathers ('Fled, banished in death or exile, lost, undone'), no 'avatar, no scion, no vestige of that people remains.' *The Orchard Keeper* ends as 'Wake for Susan' does: both protagonists walk away from cemeteries into their futures, leaving behind the artifacts of the past that have attended their healing hallucinated recollections—the laconic monuments with their terse reminders of a past that was or might have been and out of which successive generations of the strange race to come will make what their imaginations can: 'myth, legend, dust.'

McCarthy was not done with this motif; he revisits it fully in his screenplay *The Gardener's Son*, his first historical work in the usual sense of the term. Written in 1975–76 while McCarthy was also working on *Suttree*, and aired on television in January 1977, the screenplay was not published until 1996—and then in a version that differs both from the shooting script held by the South Caroliniana Library of the University of South Carolina and from the filmed version. (The widely available published version represents an earlier draft than the shooting script; in the discussion that follows, I will cite the published version except where the shooting script differs in ways relevant to the hallucinated recollection themes and image clusters.) Although cuts were made in the filmed version, many elements of the hallucinated recollection pattern appear in McCarthy's script as written: the frame structure, the monuments, cemeteries and ruins, the protagonist's return to a changed world, the autumnal imagery, the provoking silence of historical records, the musing on the act of recovery. Perhaps inevitably, the motif also shows up in the 'research newsletters' or progress reports director Richard Pearce submitted to the Alicia Patterson Foundation in New York in 1975, during the period of McCarthy's collaboration on the film. As a historical work, *The Gardener's Son* as McCarthy wrote it brings front and center the themes of the difficulty of recovering the past and the reticence of surviving artifacts; it develops in new ways the notions that histories and even contemporaneous records are suspect and that artifacts can efface the reality of which they are the traces; and it reaffirms in the face of this the validity of the search to recover the past through the human faculties of memory and imagination.

McCarthy's unfilmed opening frame of *The Gardener's Son* introduces the search for the past in a brief conversation between the Timekeeper, an old employee of the Graniteville mill, now a keeper of the documents encrypting the mill's past, and a young man who like John Wesley in *The Orchard Keeper* remains unidentified until the end-frame. There it becomes clear that he is William Chaffee, grandson of Mrs. Gregg and nephew of the man Robert McEvoy has killed, and thus the subjectivity of his motive to recover history is revealed. But the opening frame just hints that the young man seeks information about a past event that may concern his family, and that he is somehow connected to the Greggs. Still, this prologue establishes far more directly than the opening of *The Orchard Keeper* that the enacted tale to follow is the story the young man has sought to re-collect. (Without it, the film itself relies on a frame of script informing the viewer that the dramatized events are historical, a clumsy device but crucial to the audience's understanding of the film.) Further, McCarthy's opening frame announces the idea that the documents kept by the mill will be of themselves insufficient tools in the recovery process: as spokesman of the Past and for the millworker class, the Timekeeper warns the young man that he will not find what he seeks in the mill archives: 'They're just boxes of records. There's some old pitcher albums here somewheres . . . They aint the thing. Old papers or pitchers. Once you copy something down you dont have it any more. You just have the record. Times past are fugitive. They caint be kept in no box.'

This notion, embodied in the script primarily in the frame which was not to be filmed, is a dominant theme in Pearce's newsletters chronicling his and McCarthy's research process. The first one, received by the foundation on April 7, 1975, describes the ceremony marking the return to Graniteville of the monument that had originally been the gravestone of William Gregg, founder of the Graniteville mill. (His wife, Marina, had moved the monument and the bodies of William and James to Charleston with her in 1876; see *The Gardener's Son.*) Pearce quotes from the speech of Dr. J. W. Speake, the black secretary of the South Carolina Methodist Conference, whom he ironically labels 'the Methodist Secretary of Industry' because of this occasion Speake appeared as apologist for Gregg and for the mill's treatment of its workers even while he articulated the principle of the subjectivity of historical accounts:

> The truth is, the history we know and read was made and written largely by those who do not share out point of view. We in all likelihood would have held with them but for the light of events that have for some of us flashed a spotlight of new understanding upon many of the pages of our history. Those of us making the history of our present order are in the presence, no doubt, of mistakes as tragic as those behind us, if indeed our mistakes are ever behind us.

Speake continues: 'the ultimate end of all social relations must be that man may come to himself enriched, perfected, complete—thinking the true, willing the right, loving the good. This is and must be the key to judgement upon all social and economic institutions and the measurement of politicians and statesmen.' Undermining Speake's ceremonial account of William Gregg's industrial experiment, Pearce declares his intent to explore

> both sides of Graniteville's industrial revolution, that is, both her public mythology of monuments and ceremonial heroes, and at the same time her private underworld of ghost villains and legendary characters, family histories and photographs, each preserved and passed down through the generations family by family in solemn testimony to this extraordinary period on our economic history.

We do not know the precise date on which McCarthy joined in the exploration, and he may have had no influence on this first newsletter in April—Pearce says that he contacted McCarthy in spring 1975 and received a responses 'few weeks' later—but the statement makes it clear what their shared venture was to be, and the later newsletters and the screenplay as written are fully consistent with it.

The sixth newsletter, dated October 8, 1975, when McCarthy was surely working on the project, demonstrates even more explicitly that the film was to break with the received interpretation of the Gregg murder recorded in contemporary documents and the celebratory 1928 biography of William Gregg by Broadus Mitchell. Pearce juxtaposes passages from the biography describing Robert McEvoy, 'the bad boy of the village', with the admonition of historian Jesse Lemisch that 'No contention about the people on the bottom of society . . . even approaches being proved until we have in fact attempted a history of the inarticulate' and with a fragment of the trial transcript that is used in the screenplay:

> . . . AND IT BEING THUS SOLEMNLY DEMANDED OF THE PRISONER ROBERT MCEVOY IF HE HATH ANYTHING TO SAY WHY THE COURT SHOULD NOT PROCEED TO AWARD EXECUTION OF THE JUDGMENT PRONOUNCED AGAINST HIM . . . HE SAITH NOTHING.

Like the dead Susan Ledbetter in 'Wake', like the absent Kenneth Rattner in *The Orchard Keeper*, Robert McEvoy in his life as well as his death is one of the inarticulate. Both screenplay and film establish in the trial sequence that McEvoy cannot speak for himself and that no one in a position to control either his destiny or the public records that become his remains will speak for him. Thus the figure of William Chaffee, the young man of the frame, becomes another author-surrogate like Wes and John Wesley. The story told in the screenplay is Chaffee's attempt at a history of the inarticulate, as the screenplay itself is McCarthy's: a history that requires sympathetic identification and creative imagination to fill the gaps and compensate for distortion in the artifacts and monuments. That Pearce, and perhaps McCarthy too, felt the Chaffee frame could be eliminated from the film attests that, despite what was lost in the deletion, the story as imagined by the author and the story as imagined in Chaffee's framing perspective are essentially identical. As in *The Orchard Keeper*, the framing perspective as 'voice' is nearly imperceptible in the dramatic action, and no line is established between authorial stance and meditations of McCarthy's 'narrators'. To borrow a phrase from McCarthy's play *The Stonemason*, the hallucinated recollection has its *'right autonomy'* that transcends the subjectivity of its character-narrator. The 'voice' that communicates it in novel or screenplay is authorial, even omniscient, so that the construct carries an author-ity far beyond the historical evidence of document or artifact.

McCarthy's strategy in the screenplay and even Pearce's in his newsletters are similar to that of Herman Melville in such works as *Billy Budd* and 'Benito Cereno', where Melville's imagination is brought to bear on historical incidents and in which the conclusions juxtapose official legal depositions or newspaper accounts with the tales' 'inside narratives', more psychologically complex and sympathetic interpretations of the crimes of the characters and the natures of their victims: narratives that carry more authority than the appended documents they unmask. That McCarthy had *Billy Budd* specifically in mind as he wrote of McEvoy is suggested by the direct echo of Vere's response after Billy strikes and kills Claggart: "'Fated boy," breathed Captain Vere in tone so low as to be almost a whisper, "what have you done!' " In the screenplay, Mr. Giles, far less sympathetically than Vere, asks Robert McEvoy after he has shot James Gregg: 'You wretched boy, what have you done?'

The difficulty of capturing a true story of the inarticulate is embedded in the shooting script and film's graveyard scenes in which Mrs. Gregg and her son James puzzle over the monument the Greggs have erected to an anonymous 'little boy' who came to Graniteville alone and soon after died unknown. As in 'Wake for Susan', here is a monument without memory, provoking wonder but offering no answers other than those the strangers who witness it are able or willing to imagine. For Mrs. Gregg it is a monument to her family's bond to the community of millworkers: 'He must have had relatives somewhere . . . We tried to find out. Sent up to Columbia. It's hard to know what God would mean by such a thing. It seems a hard way to tell us to love one another.' James projects a different interpretation: 'He was probably run off from somewhere;' and to him the gravestone is a monument to his family's burden of responsibility for an unworthy class of millhands. The Greggs' interpretations are subjective, as are those of Wes and John Wesley, but they are more fleeting, less meditative than those of McCarthy's narrator-heroes. Rather like the tomb of the unknown soldier, the little boy's gravestone commemorates an abstraction to those who have erected it and maintain it, not a personal memory. It remains a mute icon, and for the Greggs it prompts no hallucinated recollection of the inarticulate. But the scene functions as so many of McCarthy's parables: the unknown child is an emblem of the anonymous and ungrieved millworkers in general and of Robert McEvoy in particular (whose grave is, if anything, more anonymous than the little boy's since it has no marker at all to prompt speculation (*The Gardener's Son*); and the screenplay's frame, with its depiction of William Chaffee's search for an understanding of the past and a history of the inarticulate McEvoy, stands in direct opposition to this little vignette.

Along with the screenplay's many images of cemeteries, gravestones and corpses, photographs take on a special weight in the leitmotif of artifacts. In their research, Pearce and McCarthy found period photographs of the mill, the Greggs, and Graniteville residents, many of which are reproduced in the newsletters. However, these photos are not used in the film, which opens with a long cinematic shot of the mill through morning mist. Although the screenplay calls for a *'Series of old still shots of the town of Graniteville and of the people'* after the frame scene and the credits, the plan clearly was not to use the period photos but still shots from the film itself: *'These are to have to look of old sepia photographs and may look stiff or posed. They comprise an overture to the story to follow, being shots of the characters in the film in situations from the film itself, so that they sketch the story out in miniature to the last shot of an old wooden coffin being loaded into a mule-drawn wagon and a shot of the town.'* This overture extends the introductory frame, and the stills of the film's characters represent the visual artifacts from which William Chaffee partially constructs his new understanding of Robert McEvoy's murder of James Gregg. Using historical photos would have undermined the film's 'right autonomy' by suggesting to the viewer that the film itself is mere construct with less authority than the historical documents. Instead the contrived stiffness of the film's photos, presented as authentic, suggests the suspect authority of photographs as documents of the lives they are meant to capture and validates Chaffee's imaginative construction that transcends the photos' limitations.

Like gravestones, photographs can be mementos, but as the old Timekeeper says, 'they aint the thing.' Like the court records and histories, they are—for all their illusion of objectivity—man-made and second-hand representations. The photographer who makes Robert's formal portrait and offers to share the proceeds with the McEvoy family if Robert will permit him to sell copies is an embodiment of the biased documentarian of the inarticulate; the cast of characters tellingly describes him as 'good-natured, perhaps clumsy with his equipment' and directs that 'He should not appear obsequious' in his relations with his subject. As the photographer thoughtlessly turns to personal profit the fate of his community's ghost villain, he contributes to the creation of a false myth, a false picture of Robert McEvoy—one that conceals his crippling but that fixes him for all time in his notoriety. This is a reversal of the effect of the formal photograph of Kenneth Rattner is his captain's uniform, a heroic picture of his father that John Wesley decides is a lie, noticing the fleshy face that the captain's bars and rakishly slanted cap cannot quite obscure.

The still photo, then, holds the status of mere artifact, and as a snapshot frozen in time it violates the truth of the living being it seems to capture. This failing of the frozen artifact is hinted again with the mysterious whittler silently and furtively at work in the hallway of the jail as Robert McEvoy is hanged and placed in his coffin. He works in wood, and if he whittles a likeness of McEvoy, it can be but a poor substitute for the living—as the wooden leg Robert is shown whittling and carving for himself early in the shooting script and film is a poor substitute for and reminder of the lost flesh and bone. In her conversation with William Chaffee in the closing frame, Martha McEvoy tells him that her father refused to have a photograph made of his dead wife: 'he didnt want to remember her dead,' and he erected no marker over Robert's grave for fear that it would be disturbed. Martha shows Chaffee a photo of her brother, probably the one taken at the end of his life by the photographer. It is clear she has wanted mementos of her family. But by the time Chaffee comes to see her in the state hospital, when Robert and her mother have been dead for many years, she has changed her mind about the artifact: 'Sometimes I wish I'd not even kept it. That lawyer said that the image of God was blotted out of his face. That's what he said about Bobby. I ort not even to of kept it. I think a person's memory serves better. Sometimes I can almost talk to him. I caint see him no more. In my mind. I just see this old pitcher.' Martha's affirmation of memory over artifact and William Chaffee's affirmation of sympathetic imagination together restate the value of hallucinated recollection that had informed McCarthy's framed works from the beginning. Chaffee tells her that before he had gone in search of the truth, 'It was just a family story. It was like something in a book. It didnt seem like real people.' And this is why he has come to see Martha. His gesture echoes Martha's earlier visit to his grandmother Mrs. Gregg to commiserate her loss, and it reflects his compassionate understanding of the McEvoy family achieved through contemplation of the records and artifacts thoughtfully and imaginatively enough to transcend their falsehoods.

The screenplay suggests that while records and artifacts may embody the distorted views of their creators, they are nonetheless the fragments out of which we may apprehend the past if we read them closely, sympathetically, and in context. The furtive and inarticulate whittler working in his poor medium may nonetheless create an icon to stand in opposition to the icon made by the clumsy and indifferent official photographer. Perhaps the whittler is to be compared with Melville's rude balladeer whose 'Billy in the Darbies' counterbalances the more literate received account of Billy Budd published in a naval chronicle and 'for the most part written in good faith.' Certainly the film, with its moving pictures, counters the still photos and suspect accounts of the nineteenth-century custodians of history. The screenplay's frame calls attention to its story of Robert McEvoy as a construct like the stories 'hallucinated' by Wes and John Wesley—perhaps no more historically valid than theirs but, like theirs, given weight and authority by the 'narrating' persona. McCarthy once spoke of the film itself as an imaginative construct: 'The kid was a natural rebel, probably just a troublemaker in real life. But in our film he has a certain nobility. He stands up and says, "No, this is intolerable and I want to do something about it."' It did not concern McCarthy that the film might not be a 'true' representation of the historic Robert McEvoy. He and Pearce sought the nobility and humanity in the inarticulate boy who was hanged for murder, and sought it in precisely the artifacts and records that would deny McEvoy worth.

The concerns of these early works about imaginative acts of historical recovery do not receive as much focused attention in McCarthy's writings which abandon the frame structure, but they resurface in minor ways in *Suttree's* imaginative reconstruction of his family's past through the prompting of artifacts such as photographs or old houses, and in *Blood Meridian*, where the judge, who draws artifacts in his book and then destroys the originals, and who kills birds in order to draw them, demonstrates that the 'creative' act has the potential to efface history or life itself while inscribing it. However, in *The Crossing*, where the larger narrative frames several subordinate storytellers and their tales, McCarthy reshapes his earlier artifact material in the gypsy's brooding tales of the airplane he says he has been commissioned to recover. Billy meets the gypsy while he is journeying back to New Mexico with Boyd's bones. The gypsy implies a parallel between the bones and the wreckage of the airplane and admonishes Billy, 'La cascara no es la cosa' (The husk is not the thing), an echo of the old Timekeeper's assertion to William Chaffee about old pictures and records. Uncomprehending, Billy asks him to go on with the third history of the plane as he has promised. And the gypsy replies:

> The past . . . is always this argument between counterclaimants. Memories dim with age. There is no repository for our images. The loved ones who visit us in dreams are strangers. To even see aright is effort. We seek some witness but the world will not provide one. This is the third history. It is the history that each man makes alone out of what is left to him.

What is perhaps most crucial to recognize in the narrator-heroes of the earlier frame-works is McCarthy's articulation of the kind of historical imagination to which he aspired from the beginning of his career. In all his work, his major characters are delineated as seekers after insight or non-seekers. Repeatedly, his works affirm the value of the search that demands man's inner resources—his compassion, his courage, his honesty, his spirit— even while many of them depict the lost or the non-seeking. McCarthy's narrator-heroes work through or circumvent the artifacts and records of the past to transcend obscurity, reject falsehood, and find insight. This insight is of another nature altogether from dead fact or the dry bones of history; though it gives these data their due, it insists that 'they aint the thing.'

CHARLES BAILEY

The Last Stage of the Hero's Evolution: Cormac McCarthy's Cities of the Plain

> I want a hero: an uncommon want,
>   When every year and month sends forth a new one,
> Till, after cloying the gazettes with cant,
>   The age discovers he is not the true one.
>   (Byron, Don Juan, *Canto the First* lines 1–4)
>
> In my youth's summer I did sing of One,
> The wandering outlaw of his own dark mind.
>   (Byron, *Childe Harold's Pilgrimage. A Romaunt*, Canto the
>   *Third* lines 19–20)
>
> Where's the all-american cowboy at?
>   (McCarthy, *Cities of the Plain* 3)

Lord Byron and Cormac McCarthy: a curious yoking. Certainly critics have remarked the echoes of Homer, Shakespeare, Melville, and Faulkner in the novels of Cormac McCarthy, but none, insofar as I know, cites Byron. *Cities of the Plain*, however, makes the connection to Byron unavoidable and, considering its position as the last of the Border Trilogy, also inevitable. The heroic character of the knight from the courtly love romances of the Middle Ages inspires *All the Pretty Horses*. The tragic hero of ancient Greek and Renaissance drama inspires *The Crossing*. Proceeding naturally from the

---

From *Myth, Legend, Dust: Critical Responses to Cormac McCarthy*. ©2000 by the Manchester University Press.

131

courtly hero through the tragic hero, the anti-hero, developed by Byron in such works as *Lara, Childe Harold's Pilgrimage*, and even the comic *Don Juan*, provides the inspiration for *Cities of the Plain*. And as the first two novels deconstruct the models on which their heroes are based, so the third deconstructs the most recent heroic model, the anti-hero, to prepare the way for the emergence of a new hero.

Harold Bloom and Lionel Trilling, editors of Romantic poetry and prose for *The Oxford Anthology of English Literature*, claim that Byron provided in his hero's persona 'a thoroughgoing transvaluation of values,' the hopelessness of which was 'precisely prophetic of . . . recent literature.' In fact, the self-satirical *Don Juan*, though it was on the surface a comic take-off on Byron's other darker works, only masked Byron's loss of belief in a conventional heroic attack upon life. Responding to the social, economic, and scientific developments of his age, Byron sensed the irrelevance of the romantic and optimistic heroes of previous times, and produced instead the High Romantic hero. Reserving some discomfort for the seeming selfishness and cruelty of the character, he nevertheless followed his own instincts to what critics have come to call the anti-hero. Thus, when I use the term 'anti-hero,' I do not mean the clumsy, often inept character of the picaresque novel that started the tradition, nor do I mean the tortured, raging, mysterious, Satanic Byronic hero of Byron's own serious work, so popular later in nineteenth-century fiction. You will find no Tom Jones or Heathcliff in the Border Trilogy. Instead, I mean the character of highly developed sensitivities, the 'wandering outlaw' intent on self-realization and personal salvation, capable of great courageous moral action in the cause of human freedom, whose unconventional impulses rise from some inherent spiritual core, one (in Byron's words) whose 'madness [is] not of the head, but heart' (*Lara*). This description might easily apply to John Grady Cole and to Billy Parham in *Cities of the Plain*. And just as Byron became disillusioned and, in lament, debunked the previous heroes as incompatible with a world that is too much with us, so does McCarthy lament even the anti-hero, made finally irrelevant in a world corrupted and degraded by advancing science and nuclear technology. Moreover, McCarthy's work clearly views this anti-hero sifted through the tradition of the American novels of the late nineteenth and twentieth centuries. Hence, it is only natural—evolutionary—that Byron's desire for a 'hero: an uncommon want/When every year and month sends forth a new one' should transvalue to the question of McCarthy's last novel: 'Where's the all-american cowboy at?'

Let me begin with the first layer of this argument, which, because of time and space, must at best comprise only some brief comments, *All the Pretty Horses* is a courtly romance. John Grady Cole, the knight-errant, wanders into the wilderness and falls in love with an unattainable lady of a distinctly higher aristocratic class. He performs for her as a knight should, displaying a God-given talent for martial skills—in this case, taming horses. When he comes to dinner at the hacienda after the first day of braking horses, the vaqueros treat him with the reverence due a saint. In the Saltillo prison, he even engages in direct tournament combat, in which homemade knives become swords and metal cafeteria trays become shields. In his futile attempt to win Alejandra's hand, John Grady plays chess, in all its medieval imagery of knights and bishops and kings and queens, with her great aunt Doña Alfonsa, who at one point addresses him directly: 'Beware gentle knight.'

The lady Alejandra is the epitome of the courtly lady who inspires John Grady's heroism. Not only do her looks and social position establish her as the idealized embodiment of perfect beauty, but the religious imagery with which McCarthy presents her associates her clearly with the Virgin, just as the lady of the courtly romance is a version of the Madonna. Her home is the Hacienda de Nuestra Señora de la Purísma Concepción (the Estate of Our Lady of the Immaculate Conception). In a contest to prove his worth, one that echoes the chess game with Doña Alfonsa, John Grady plays pool with her father, Don Héctor, the hacendado (a sort of landed baron). The poolroom, once the hacienda's chapel, has never been desanctuarized. As Don Héctor says, 'What is sacred is sacred.' They play on holy ground. The ritual of the lovers' secret affair is to ride into the mountains by moonlight and stop on the shores of a lake. On one occasion, she literally becomes Our Lady of the Lake (evoking both the Arthurian legend and the Virgin Mary), emitting the celestial light of the Madonna:

> The water was black and warm and he turned in the lake and spread his arms in the water and the water was so dark and so silky and he watched across the still black surface to where she stood on the shore with the horse and he watched where she stepped from her pooled clothing so pale, so pale, like a chrysalis emerging, and walked into the water . . .She was so pale in the lake she seemed to be burning. Like foxfire in a darkened wood. That burned cold. Like the moon that burned cold.

Finally, when John Grady parts with his friend Rawlins to return to make one final bid for Alejandra, Rawlins asks him why: 'On account of the girl?' John Grady's reply unites the spiritual and physical aims of the cowboy as romantic knight: 'The girl and the horses.'

Likewise, *The Crossing* takes classical tragedy as its model. The works of literature it self-consciously echoes are *Hamlet* and *Oedipus the King*. In terms of the novel's plot structure, the opening initiation tale concerning Billy Parham and the wolf (though it seems complete in itself) actually sets up the Oedipal and Hamletesque nature of the story of the next two crossings. After the burial of the wolf, Billy returns to New Mexico to find his family's ranch abandoned. During his absence, an itinerant Mexican Indian, whom he had unfortunately directed to his home for a secret meal, has murdered his parents and looted the ranch. Without reflection, Billy collects his fourteen-year-old brother Boyd, and the two of them cross the border to retrieve the horses, their only inheritance and their dead father's property. From this point on, even through the third crossing, the *Hamlet* parallels become undeniable. For one thing, like Hamlet, Billy is a dispossessed son whose father's murder took place while he was away. Second, out of moral responsibility and guilt, he must reclaim what the dead father, in the son's absence, has been robbed of. Other details support this same view. Namely, along the way, he encounters a troupe of traveling actors. And the core event of the third crossing is a gravedigger's scene when, discovering that Boyd has died in a gunfight, Billy personally digs up his brother's bones.

As McCarthy knows, if *Hamlet* is present, then *Oedipus* is present. McCarthy has set this connection up in Billy's first crossing, accompanied by the pregnant she-wolf. In this section Billy not only discovers himself (the initiation), he also asserts himself Oedipally against his father. Billy follows his father's orders as he sets traps for the wolf, knowing that, to protect the cattle, his father will kill her. But no sooner does Billy set the traps than he contrives to check them alone, Acting from an Oedipal impulse, he replaces his father, and when he captures the wolf, instead of bringing her back to the ranch as his father has instructed, Billy steals his father's wolf (a female and a mother) and pursues his own course. Moreover, the Oedipal significance of his father's death, Billy's fault because he led the Indian to the ranch, seems again unmistakable. In the second crossing, having 'killed' his father and stolen his 'mother,' Billy goes after the horses—like Oedipus and Hamlet, to claim what remains of his father's kingdom, the primogeniture he has been denied. Although he loses the other horses, he does hold onto his father's personal horse, Niño, which he rides until the book's end. Can one imagine a more Freudian, Oedipal image? Further details corroborate this reading. The book is a veritable mine of blind soothsayers, all of whom warn Billy that truth is 'seen' only in blindness and that the greatest temptation is *orgullo*: pride, hubris.

So *All the Pretty Horses* presents the courtly knight as hero. *The Crossing* presents the tragic man as hero. In sequence, *Cities of the Plain* presents the anti-hero, introduced by Byron and developed in the American novel. The first clear indication of the heroic nature of the action lies in the enterprise that is the focus of the plot. As in *All the Pretty Horses*, the enterprise is to save a lady and enshrine her in a kind of chapel. This time, the lady is Magdalena, held in the cruel and degraded like of a prostitute by the dark pimp Eduardo. John Grady falls in love with her, but her Mexican nationality and the life that traps her make her as unattainable to him, really, as Alejandra in *All the Pretty Horses*. He means, however, to marry her and bring her to a little house on Mac McGovern's land, a cottage that he paints blue, the color of the Virgin, and that he decorates with nothing but a crude *santo*. This time everyone in the novel knows the enterprise is doomed, even Billy, who becomes his cohort, but John Grady continues despite the obstacles because he is driven by his sense of heroic mission. This dedication to his mission is that kind of madness that Byron identifies in his assessment of Lara—the 'madness . . . not of the head, but heart.' The idea that this mission amounts to madness, though presented comically, suffuses Billy's reactions to John Grady's request that Billy help and act as courier to buy Magdalena from Eduardo. Variously he says: 'Shit . . . Smile or something, will you? Goddamn. Tell me you aint gone completely crazy . . . Do you know what they're goin to do with you? They're goin to hook up your head to one of them machines and throw a big switch and fry your brains to where you wont be a menace to yourself no more . . . You're in a dangerous frame of mind, son. Did you know that? But, as I said, it is a madness of heart, the driven quality of the hero. In his own defense, John Grady says, 'I feel some way like I didnt have nothin to do with it. Like it's just the way it is. Like it always as this way . . . There's some things you dont decide. Decidin had nothin to do with it.' Even Eduardo, the enemy pimp, says of John Grady that he is 'in the grip of an irrational passion.' Both of the figures of aged wisdom in the book. . .Mr. Johnson and the blind maestro—advise John Grady to follow his heart, no matter the consequences. According to Mr. Johnson, 'I think you ought to follow your heart, the old man said. That's all I ever thought about anything.' In the next scene, juxtaposed as if for emphasis, when John Grady asks the maestro if he is a fool to try to marry Magdalena, the old man replies:

> A man is always right to pursue the thing he loves.
> No matter even if it kills him?
> I think so. Yes. No matter even that.

This driven quality makes John Grady a hero from another sphere, a spiritual world where the values of good prevail. Like the references to his madness, the assessment of his 'other worldliness' fully informs the book. One of his fellow cowboys, Troy, defines that quality prophetically early in the story when he talks about his brother, another cowboy of John Grady's ilk, who fell in love with a whore: 'There's a kind of man that when he cant have what he wants he wont take the next best thing . . . I think he [Troy's brother] loved that girl. I think he knew what she was and he didnt care . . . I think he was just lost. This world was never made for him. He outlived it before he could walk.'

Moreover, as in *All the Pretty Horses*, the action of the story is knightly. If anything, John Grady is the more fully developed knight. His martial powers with horses become unsurpassed and unsurpassable, a mystical association with the horses' souls. He has also become the undefeatable chess player, moving the knights and bishops of the board about with the strategy of the schooled and experienced master. And, of course, the knifefight, the duel, of *All the Pretty Horses* is repeated in the climactic, bloody confrontation with Eduardo, in which John Grady rises to become a filler, a cuchillero—for which I can find no exact English equivalent. But he becomes the 'expert wielder of the knife blade.' Metaphorically, he becomes the swordsman, the fencer, the knight.

Furthermore, he exercises this martial, if irrationally driven expertise, again as in *All the Pretty Horses*, in the cause of the lady, the Madonna. Magdalena is another version of the courtly lady, her cause made more desperate by the horrors of the world that entraps her. Her physical description, her pale skin and lush black hair, suggest Alejandra from the previous novel. She is also Our Lady of the Lake, only this time from the whorehouse named the White Lake. She has the beauty of the courtly lady, but the world has made her a whore. In a neat exchange, while her criada dresses her, the old woman whispers, 'Como una princess [Like a princess] . . . Como una puta [Like a whore], said the girl.' McCarthy provides an interesting touch in the one-eyed criada who attends Magdalena. She corresponds to Doña Alfonsa, the imperious dueña of *All the Pretty Horses*. But what a degradation! She also suggests the nurse/servant figure of traditional courtly romances, like Angela the Old of Keats' 'Eve of St. Agnes' or Juliet's nurse. The Madonna/Magdalene dichotomy that McCarthy chooses to characterize Magdalena should not be confused with the archetypal attitudes toward women expressed in Jung's universal symbols or the dialectic poles of Levi-Strauss's structuralism. Magdalena is clearly the innocent Virgin stained and degraded by the modern world. She tells her own story: at thirteen sold into prostitution to pay a gambling debt, resold by the church where she sought protection, resold another time by the police after they abused her. She is Magdalena, the holy whore, victimized by the church and state. Even her epilepsy, which seems at first a blot on her perfection, McCarthy offers up in the biblical sense as part of her spiritual mysticism, what he calls 'the dormant sorcerer,' finally prophetic and visionary. Just prior to her murder, barely warding off an attack, Magdalena cups her palms before her eyes and, in the darkness, sees 'herself on a cold white table in a cold white room.' When she dies, she dies clutching a *santo*, the only relic she has brought from her earthly life. Her name also associates her with the other female, saint-like figure of the novel. Mr. Johnson's dead daughter, Mac McGovern's dead wife, whose spiritual presence hangs over the ranch like a guardian angel, was named Margaret, a derivative of the name Mary, and shortened, of course, to Maggie. Margaret, Maggie, Magdalena, Mary Magdalene, Saint Mary—they all become one in the spiritual fusion of the novel.

For all its nobility, what dooms the enterprise and, finally, what dooms John Grady himself is a completely degraded world. Both the physical and spiritual worlds in which the hero must act make true, successful heroism impossible. The urban world encroaches on the wilderness, and the urban world is rotten—El Paso and Juárez, the cities of the plain, Sodom and Gomorrah. The arena for the cowboy/knight's heroism quickly and irreversibly diminishes. Some of these degradations I have already mentioned. The Madonna is forced into prostitution. The aristocratic dueña has descended to the cowardly one-eyed criada. The lake has become a whorehouse. But not only that, the cowboy's way of life is reduced and disappearing in the face of advancing, destructive technology. The American government has commandeered the wilderness for nuclear testing. The romantic wilderness has changed, losing both its romance and its spirituality. McCarthy briefly comments on what the West was and what it has become in recalling the history of old man Johnson: 'He'd been born in east Texas in eighteen sixty-seven and come out to this country as a young man. In his time the country had gone from the oil lamp and the horse and buggy to jet planes and the atomic bomb but that wasnt what confused him. It was the fact that his daughter was dead that he couldnt get the hang of.' Mr. Johnson's daughter was, of course, Margaret, the spiritual ideal (perhaps the actual spirit) of the ranch country, and she is dead. The warrior spirit of the wilderness has also passed. At another point in the novel, Mr. Johnson discusses the poisoning of wolves, the animals presented somehow as fit opponents for the cowboy in his struggle against nature. The wolves, spoken of with respect and dignity, of course, hark back to the associations of the wolf's nobility as a natural creature in Part I of *The Crossing*. Mr. Johnson mourns because the passing of the wolves has stolen the noble character of both the country and the cowboy's work. He says, 'when things are gone they're gone. They aint coming back . . . it had always seemed to me that somethin can live and die but the kind of thing that [the wolves] were was always there. I didn't know you could poison that. I aint heard a wolf howl in thirty odd years. I dont know where you'd go to hear one. There may not be any such a place.' The story plays this judgment out. When the cowboys face predators that threaten their cattle, they face not wolves, but scavenging wild dogs that, like the puppy John Grady retrieves from their den, can be easily domesticated, unlike a wolf, to a pet.

What is the upshot of this degradation of civilization, and the spirit and character of nature? It makes the heroic attack upon life impossible. As anticipated in Byron's presentation of the anti-hero, the enterprise of the modern hero—chivalric or tragic—makes him a 'wandering outlaw' (*Childe Harold's Pilgrimage. A Romaunt, Canto the Third*). This is, in fact, the very language McCarthy uses. Billy says to John Grady:

> I just wonder if you even know what a outlaw you are.
> Why?
> Why do I wonder it?
> Why am I a outlaw.
> I dont know. You just got a outlaw heart.

On top of that, the hero's wandering shrinks to retreat, not a search for new heroic adventures, but an escape from the horrors of a corrupt and repulsive world. After Magdalena's murder, John Grady says to another cowboy he encounters on the range: 'I wish I could ride . . . I wish I could . . . I'd ride and I'd never look back. I'd ride to where I couldn't find a single day I ever knew. Even if I was to turn back and ride ever foot of that ground. Then I'd ride some more.' It is the state of mind of the modern hero: 'I've been thataway, said the rider.' The point is that all heroes—courtly or tragic or 'anti'—now wander in alienation from the modern world. But where?

Let me insert a qualification at this point. I do not mean to imply that the Border Trilogy, *Cities of Plain* included, is simplistically a Byronic dirge for the passing of the hero. For one thing, *Cities of the Plain* is distinctly an American novel, not Byron's High Romanticism. It belongs to that literary genre called the Western, after all. But the truest homage to its American ancestors it pays in the fact that it is a buddy novel in the truest sense of its American ancestors. The symbiotic relationship between its two protagonists makes it such. The previous novels anticipate that characteristic—the fusion of the two buddies into one hero—in the relationships between John Grady and Lacey Rawlins, between Billy and Boyd. And surely the closeness of the friends and the brothers lends psychological credence to the bond between Billy and John Grady. But the first two books function merely as feelers toward the fully realized union of the heroes of *Cities of the Plain*. In both of the earlier books, the pals, Rawlins and Boyd, disappear well before the novels end, leaving the heroes alone in their adventures. Not so in *Cities of the Plain*. The heroes are together, at least in spirit, until John Grady dies. Their familiar address to each other is the single word 'bud.' Less than halfway through the novel, Billy, who in his older wisdom has advised the younger man, ceases to play the skeptic about John Grady's mission and agrees to approach Eduardo about buying Magdalena. He enters the enterprise. Here McCarthy begins a stylistic convention of the novel that prevails up to John Grady's death. He begins each new scene solely with the pronoun 'he.' The reader must read well into the scene to discover whether 'he' refers to John Grady or Billy; in each section, initially it could refer to either. The ambiguity begins to merge the two characters. Then, they begin to share duties both to Magdalena and to the tasks of the cowboy. For instance, they paint the little house together. They ride the range together. When they go after the wild dogs that have ravaged the herd, they almost become the same person. First, pursuing the last of the dogs, they trade horses as they execute the difficult climb to the mesa, thus blurring their separate identities. And when they rope the leader of the pack, the repugnant yellow dog, they do it in simultaneous, unspoken concert. They are the same cowboy:

> John Grady came riding up behind Billy and swung his rope and heeled the yellow dog and quirted the horse on with the doubled rope and then dallied. The slack of Billy's catchrope hissed along the ground and stopped and the big yellow dog rose suddenly from the ground in headlong flight taut between the two ropes and the ropes resonated a single brief dull note and then the dog exploded . . .
> Damn, said Billy, I didn't know you was goin to do that.
> I didnt either.

Moreover, acting from the impulse of his sympathetic heart again, the next day John Grady awakens Billy to retrieve the dead dogs' pups, and despite Billy's protests that this samaritan's action is madness, they rescue the pups together. What McCarthy says of John Grady and his heroism he also says of Billy. What is true of the courtly hero is true of the tragic hero. And they both become the anti-hero, futilely acting in a degraded world—not only a world beneath them, but a world indifferent to them. Therein lies the deconstruction of the entire trilogy. Heroism, no matter its form, is irrelevant in a world consumed in materialism and the instruments of its own destruction. The two heroes say it best themselves in a quiet conversation alone on the range. John Grady says about his own impossible desires:

You cant tell anybody anything, bud. Hell, it's really just a
way of tellin yourself. And you cant even do that. You just try and
use your best judgment and that's about it.
    Yeah. Well. The world dont know nothin about your judgment.
    I know it. It's worse than that, even. It dont care.

Then, toward the end, as Billy carries John Grady's lifeless body in a mock
pieta through the streets, he passes a group of children, halted by a traffic
guard, on their way to school. McCarthy says:

This man and his burden passed on forever out of that nameless
crossroads and the woman stepped into the street and the
children followed and all continued on to their appointed places
which as some believe were chosen long ago even to the
beginning of the world.

So what is the answer to the question of this narrative, the question
McCarthy's characteristic philosopher recalls to mind in the epilogue of the
story: 'Where's the all-american cowboy at?'? He is dead. Or he has played,
at best, an extra's role in the drama of American life. The romantic hero has
passed. The tragic hero has become pathetic. In the twenty-first century, the
anti-hero has regressed into a second childhood. Who is the new hero, now
that these are all relegated to irrelevance? Who knows? *Cities of the Plain* and
the Border Trilogy end with 'an uncommon want': 'I want a hero' (Byron,
Don Juan, Canto the First). That is, I think, the curious meaning of the
Dedication and its curious placement at the book's closing:

The world grows cold
The heathen rage
The story's told
Turn the page.

MARK BUSBY

Into the Darkening Land, the World to Come: Cormac McCarthy's Border Crossings

Cormac McCarthy's Southwestern novels are tied together by the repetition of the powerful metaphor of border crossings. In the three novels of the Border Trilogy—*All the Pretty Horses, The Crossing,* and *Cities of the Plain*—McCarthy uses the border as a metaphor for a complex and oxymoronic melding of nihilism and optimism, good and evil, illusion and reality, and several similar contrasts. He also employs similar structural patterns to examine the complex intertwining of positive and negative forces to present ultimately a worldview that suggests a nihilistic optimism. While all three novels dramatize a dialectic struggle between hope and despair, each has a different perspective and emphasis, moving from *All the Pretty Horses'* stress on human responsibility to *The Crossing's* focus on responsibility to nature, whereupon the third novel, *Cities of the Plain*, combines the styles, themes, and characters of the first two novels. In *The Crossing* McCarthy particularly stresses storytelling's power to provide synthesis, but the entire trilogy demonstrates the power of stories.

McCarthy therefore draws from a powerful tradition—from Dostoyevsky, to Melville, to Twain, to Crane, to Faulkner and southern literature, to American Westerns—for his powerful works that at the center are about ontology and epistemology—being and knowing. He uses the border metaphor to create a complicated way of knowing the world that is

From *Myth, Legend, Dust: Critical Responses to Cormac McCarthy.* ©2000 by the Manchester University Press.

not simply black or white, good or evil, life or death, but is an oxymoronic melding, an ongoing dialectic between the forces of death and life, end and beginning, and other apparent dualities. Metaphors of play acting and dream are seemingly opposed by the 'real' of trees, rocks, rivers and emphasize the liminal state of humankind, the border living in a world of between: the Dueña Alfonsa tells John Grady Cole: 'the world is quite ruthless in selecting between the dream and the reality, even where we will not. Between the wish and the thing the world lies waiting.' And yet at the center is paradox. As the judge in *Blood Meridian* asserts, 'Your heart's desire is to be told some mystery. The mystery is that there is no mystery.'

McCarthy's world yields violence, struggle, and despair; but there are also powerful moments that enhance living: John Grady Cole riding on a flatbed truck with *campesinos* as he escapes his hellish experience in prison, understanding that 'after and for a long time to come he'd have reason to evoke the recollection of those smiles and to reflect upon the good will which provoked them for it had power to protect and to confer honor and to strengthen resolve and it had power to heal men and to bring them to safety long after all other resources were exhausted'; Billy Parham attempting to take the wolf home, a gypsy treating a stabbed horse in *The Crossing*, moments of intense friendship as between John Grady Cole and Rawlins in *Horses* or between John Grady and Billy Parham in *Cities of the Plain*. These are the moments that mesh with the violence, sadness and despair and that are part of the fabric of life.

McCarthy's genius is that he melds the most significant concerns of southern literature, the dominant American fiction of the first half of the century, with Western fiction with its roots deep in the traditional frontier myth and its emphasis on the border between the east/west frontier. McCarthy then swivels north/south and uses several of the major elements of the east/west frontier myth in a new way—creating a Southwestern fiction that synthesizes these concerns.

As Lewis Simpson makes clear in *Dispossessed Garden*, the twentieth-century southern literary consciousness has struggled with two opposing forces, the force of memory and history—the presentness of the past in southern life—and the historyless post-World War II alienated self. The first force necessarily concentrates on the redemptive (or corrosive) power of memory to merge (or subsume) the individual into the communal force of time. The South is a region of memory, forever wedded to the tragic history of slavery, where, as Faulkner said, the past is not passed. The second alienated consciousness focuses on the power of the individual to wrest the future from time and to forge its own future. This individualistic emphasis is also the traditional land of the Western writer who draws from frontier mythology.

In his survey of 'Southern Fiction' in *The Harvard Guide to Contemporary American Writing*, Simpson elaborated on his analysis of southern literature in *Dispossessed Garden*, and drawing from Allen Tate's 'The Profession of Letters in the South' as his source, Simpson mentioned the metaphor McCarthy turned to for his title in the second novel of the Border Trilogy:

> Bringing into focus the history, and the historical aftermath, of a slave society at once novel and anachronistic—a society which had attempted at the same time to become a modern nation-state and a replication of a patriarchical community, a major supplier of raw materials to the world industrial machine and a pastoral retreat from it—southern novelists of the 1920s and 1930s realized the possibilities of the South as a representation of the crossing of the ways. They created in the southern novel a compelling drama of self and history.

Perhaps McCarthy realized that as long as he wrote about the South, he would seem a pale reflection of Faulkner. As Flannery O'Connor once said about Faulkner's overpowering image in southern literature, 'Nobody wants his mule and wagon stalled on the same track the Dixie Limited is roaring down.' So when McCarthy left the South for Texas in 1976, he switched to the Tex-Mex Express and turned to another territory with a fertile history of crossing and one with a rich frontier history.

Traditional American frontier mythology refers to a cluster of images, values, and archetypes that grew out of the confrontation between the uncivilized and the civilized world, what Frederick Jackson Turner called the 'meeting point between savagery and civilization.' Civilization is associated with the East, with the past and Europe, with society—its institutions, laws, its demands for compromise and restriction, its cultural refinement and emphasis on manners, its industrial development, and its class distinctions. The wilderness that civilization confronts offers the possibility of individual freedom, where single individuals can test themselves against nature without the demands for social responsibility and compromise inherent in being part of a community.

McCarthy draws from these frontier dichotomies, particularly the emphasis on the Southwest as a land of freedom and opportunity, where individuals can demonstrate those values that the Southwestern Anglo myth reveres—courage, determination, ingenuity, loyalty, and others. But Southwestern frontier history and geography produce deep feelings of ambivalence. On one hand, the vastness of its areas seems to negate borders; on the other, the region's location on the edge of Southern and Western culture and along the long Rio Grande border with Mexico reinforces an awareness of borders. As Tom Pilkington pointed out in *My Blood's Country*, the Southwest is a land of borders: 'Men have always been fascinated by rims and borders, ends and beginnings, areas of transition where the known and the unknown merge. In the Southwest one feels something of this fascination, because one of the central, never-changing facts about the region, I believe, is that it is a borderland.'

The border, therefore, represents a line between such opposing forces as civilization/wilderness, individual/community, fate/free will, past/present, aggression/passivity, and numerous others central to the Southwestern legend. This awareness of borders grows in intensity in the contemporary Southwest as the schism between old and new tears more strongly at the human heart. Increasingly, contemporary Southwestern writers such as McCarthy examine the sharp division between the frontier myth that lives inside and the diminished outside natural world fraught with complexity, suffering, and violence but leavened with humor, compassion, and love. What McCarthy adds to the older frontier formula is his use of 'la frontera,' the North/South border between the American Southwest and Northern Mexico, as the boundary line between warring forces.

As Alan Riding makes clear in his important book *Distant Neighbors* (published in 1984 when McCarthy was writing his first novel to use Mexico), the country provides the perfect setting for books that use complex and troubling opposition as a basic part of their structure:

> Probably nowhere in the world do two countries as different as Mexico and the United States live side by side. As one crosses the border into Mexico from, say El Paso [McCarthy's home], the contrast is shocking—from wealth to poverty, from organization to improvisation, from artificial flavoring to pungent spices. But the physical differences are least important. Probably nowhere in the world do two neighbors understand each other so little. More than by levels of development, the two countries are separated by language, religion, race, philosophy and history. The United States is a nation barely two hundred years old and is lunging for the twenty-first century. Mexico is several thousand years old and is held back by its past.

If the American frontier hero pushes west into a historyless land, then when that figure turns south and crosses the border, he encounters a land with a strong and troubling past, for Mexico represents a country with a lengthy and distressing history, part of which involves a complicated story of dispossession of land first from the Aztecs and Mayans, then from the remaining *Indios*, and later from the church. Aztec history may have been especially important to draw McCarthy to Mexico because of the Aztecs' violent emphasis on human sacrifice, on the importance of blood in Aztec ritual sacrifices, and on the Aztec belief in the repetition of history. Believing that the sun needed blood to be reborn every morning, the Aztecs performed human sacrifices that allowed the victim's blood to seep into the earth to satisfy the sun. This history connects with and highlights the violence in McCarthy's border novels and may account for the repeated blood imagery and expressions such as 'the bloodred sun.' Human sacrifice returns forcefully in the epilogue of *Cities of the Plain* as the deathlike traveler tells Billy Parham a dream about a rock with 'the stains of blood from those who'd been slaughtered upon it to appease the gods.'

Aztec mythology may have provided other images and ideas. The canine imagery may have been suggested by the Aztec deity Xolotl, who was usually pictured with a human body, clawed hands and feet, and a large canine head. He combined the human and the wild and was pictured with both human and animal sets of ears. Another story that relates to McCarthy's novel concerns how Xolotl was charged by the gods to journey to the underworld to retrieve the bones from an earlier race of humans to use to begin a new one. On his way back, Xolotl dropped and fragmented the bones into many pieces. The gods then sprinkled the fragments with their blood to produce first a male then a female child. Billy Parham, of course, journeys south to retrieve the bones of his brother Boyd, whose twin sister supposedly died when Boyd was young. McCarthy is known for his wide and varied reading. Perhaps these aspects of Aztec myth helped suggest some of the canine (dog, wolf), journey, bone, twin imagery in a book that uses contrasts and Mexican history.

Another possible result of Aztec history concerns Mexico's emphasis on repetition. The Aztecs adapted a complicated Mayan calendar based on a fifty-two-year cycle, and the belief in the returning god Quetzalcoatl led them to accept Cortes as the reappearing god. As a result Mexican time is circular, quite in contrast with Anglo-European linear concepts of time. Riding explains:

> For Mexicans, neither birth nor death is seen to interrupt the continuity of life and neither is considered overly important. In songs, paintings and popular art, death is even mocked. On the Day of the Dead each November, Mexicans crowd the country's cemeteries, carrying flowers and even food and drink to the graves of their ancestors, much as the Aztecs did. Belief in

communion with the dead is widespread, not in a psychic or spiritualist sense or as a function of a Christian faith in the afterlife, but simply as an outgrowth of the knowledge that the past is not dead.

Just as the Civil War in the southern American writer's most important historical touchstone, the single historical event that reverberates throughout Mexican history and in McCarthy's border novels is the Mexican revolution, which began in 1910 when Francisco Indalecio Madero, then thirty-seven, led opposition to President Porfirio Díaz who had controlled the country since 1876 and had allowed white landowners to seize the lands of its six million Indians and eight million mestizos. Through the revolution the exploited peons wanted to retake the large land holdings and distribute farmland among the *campesinos*. Madero, in fact, becomes a character in *All the Pretty Horses*, as the Dueña Alfonsa recalls her attraction to Gustavo Madero.

McCarthy, therefore, combines Southern, Southwestern, and Mexican history into a rich fiction that uses older American elements such as the story of the young boy's initiation as the basis. Each McCarthy novel takes a representative young boy's initiatory experience through a border crossing and turns the experience upside down so that the expected initiation is thwarted and seemingly denied. But ironically, it is through the denied experience that a young man is initiated into a more profound understanding than the expected initiation could have offered. Each novel focuses on a complex series of opposing forces, but each novel provides a different emphasis. While all three deal with reality/illusion, individual/community, linearity/circularity, home/not home, dispossession/possession, life/death, and father/son, *All the Pretty Horses* highlights the opposing forces of fate/free will, cowardice/courage, restriction/freedom, class/classlessness, time/timelessness, reason/imagination, order/chaos, master/slave, home/not home, and justice/injustice. *The Crossing* focuses more on wild/tame, reality/illusion, good/evil, kindness/malice, restriction/freedom, change/stability, time/timelessness, god/godlessness. Although the Trilogy suggests that the world is an amalgam of forces, all three novels in different ways suggest that the resulting mixture—the world—is mediated by the power of storytelling to bring order to the chaos of forces in the world. The final novel in the Trilogy also emphasizes valuing the natural world.

All the Pretty Horses

McCarthy's sixth novel won the 1992 National Book Award and the 1992 National Book Critics Circle Award for fiction. Like his fifth novel, *Blood Meridian*, *All the Pretty Horses* uses the history, geography, and landscape, of the Southwest and the border as setting for the story, which leads to a profound examination of a series of oppositions, particularly the theme of the individual and the community and the theme of the opposition of illusion and reality sounded in the novel's opening paragraph. Repeated images of illusion occur as John Grady Cole walks in to view his grandfather's dead body and sees reflections in the pierglass, portraits on the wall, and a wax imprint of his thumb:

> The candleflame and the image of the candleflame caught in the pierglass twisted and righted when he entered the hall and again when he shut the door. He took off his hat and came slowly forward. The floorboards creaked under his boots. In his black suit he stood in the dark glass where the lilies leaned so palely from their waisted cut-glass vase. Along the cold hallway behind him hung the portraits of forebears only dimly known to him all framed in glass and dimly lit above the narrow wainscotting. He looked down at the guttered candlestub. He pressed his thumbprint in the warn wax pooled on the oak veneer.

As he looks at the lifeless body of his grandfather, he considers the finality of death—an unambiguous reality that will continue to impinge upon his consciousness throughout the novel, as the life/death opposition returns though the deaths a Jimmy Blevins, the cuchillero whom John Grady kills in self-defense in the prisión Castelar, John Grady's father, and then the last death, the death of Abuela, John Grady's substitute mother, at the novel's close.

The grandfather's death sets in motion another important opposition for possession/dispossession recurs throughout the novel, from the beginning section's emphasis on how the grandfather's death signals John Grady's dispossession and loss of land. As Gail Moore Morrison in '*All the Pretty Horses*: John Grady Cole's Expulsion from Paradise' makes clear, the grandfather's death

> portends the loss of the family ranch. And, although [John Grady] is technically a boy, only sixteen, he recognizes that he is 'like a man come to the end of something.' The lost of his

grandfather's line with its generations-deep commitment to the land, he is certainly as powerless to protect it against foreign encroachment—twentieth century technology and the oil interests to which his often absent actress mother sells it—as was the Comanche nation he envisions as he rides out along their ancient war trail under a 'bloodred and elliptic' sun 'under the reefs of bloodred cloud' after his grandfather's funeral, 'with the sun coppering his face and the red wind blowing out of the west.' He hears 'the low chant of their traveling song which the riders sang as they rode, nation and ghost of nation passing in a soft chorale across the mineral waste to darkness bearing lost to all history and all remembrance like a grail the sum of their secular and transitory and violent lives.' The comparison to the defeated and eradicated Comanche is made explicit by John Grady's divorced, dying father during their last horseback ride together.

Connections with the past become even stronger once John Grady crosses into Mexico with its lengthy and troubling history as I have said, party of which involves a complicated story of dispossession of land first from the Aztecs and Mayans, then from the remaining *Indios* and the church. The character most fully representing the past is the Dueña Alfonsa, the grandaunt of Alejandra, the daughter of the hacendado for whom John Grady goes to work in Mexico: 'The Dueña Alfonsa was both grandaunt and godmother to the girl and her life at the hacienda invested it with oldworld ties and with antiquity and tradition.' It is she who invests human scars with an existential reality connected to the power of the past: 'Scars have the strange power to remind us that our past is real. The events that cause them can never be forgotten, can they?'

The power of forces outside the individual's control becomes one of the most important aspects of Mexico and suggests to Tom Pilkington that the novel's major focus is on the contrast between free will and fate:

Which is the dominant agent—free will or fate? Perhaps there is no either-or answer. In her final—rather improbable—conversation with John Grady, Alfonsa argues for a kind of modified predestination. The conditions of the physical universe impose certain conditions on the individual, including total unpredictability. But life is a shimmering web, and every time a strand is struck by the assertion of will, the web vibrates with consequences for all. Actually Alfonsa uses the metaphor of puppets. If one looks behind the curtain at the puppet show, she says one finds puppets who control puppets who control puppets and on to infinity. There is, in other words, a vast interconnectedness of things, so that clear causal relationships are impossible to isolate.

As Pilkington makes clear, when John Grady and Rawlins ride into Mexico they reenact a clearly recognizable Western story: 'A wandering cowboy and his sidekick ride innocently into hostile territory. There ensue fights against insurmountable odds, the hero's romance with a lovely young senorita, chases on horseback through a harsh but beautiful landscape.' And John Grady is the distinctly recognizable American: 'He believes in individualism, free will, volition. He thinks that every man born on this planet is an Adam, free of memory and external constraint, able to shape his illimitable "self" in any way he chooses. He is shocked when Alejandra refuses to break all ties to go with him.'

Two other important elements from the Western American literary tradition are the captivity narrative and the youthful Adam who becomes a messianic figure following an initiation. John Grady's initiation through captivity and imprisonment recalls numerous other American heroes from Mary Rowlandson through James Fenimore Cooper's Natty Bumppo and captured females to Ralph Ellison's Invisible Man to Joseph Heller's Yossarian. After or during initiation many of these archetypal youthful heroes become Christlike figures, either messianic like Faulkner's Ike McCaslin, Ellison's nameless narrator, and Yossarian or martyred like Joe Christmas, Stephen Crane's Jim Conklin, or Steinbeck's Jim Casy. These last three figures' initials signal their symbolic status, and it is interesting to point out John Grady Cole's initials put him in their company. These Christlike figures in American literature, along with others such as Melville's Billy Budd and Ken Kesey's Randall Patrick McMurphy, introduce the theme of communal responsibility.

Certainly, John Grady's ultimate recognition of the limitation of self is one important aspect of the novel. Indeed the sharp contrast between the individual and community, between concern for self and concern for the other, is another one of the central conflicts. Faced with his grandfather's death, rejected by his girlfriend and his mother, supported weakly by an ineffectual father, John Grady replaces his broken family community with the comradeship of Lacey Rawlins, and this small community is broadened by chance when the irrepressible Jimmy Blevins joins them. Blevins forces John Grady to consider his responsibility for another, much to the pragmatic Rawlins' dismay. John Grady is initially led to these concerns when Blevins (pointing to another contrast—rationality/irrationality) crazily shucks his gun, horse, boots, and clothes out of his fear that he is fated to be struck by lightning ('I'm double bred for death by fire'). John Grady tells Rawlins: 'I dont believe I can leave him out there afoot.'

John Grady's strong feelings of responsibility for Blevins continue and expand after Blevins is executed in the woods by the captain. Haunted by his failure to act and only vaguely understanding his motives, John Grady makes a choice to pursue the captain in language that recalls probably the most famous moral decision in American literature, Huck Finn's famous conclusion, 'All right then, I'll go to hell', when he decides not to return Jim to slavery. Rejected by Alejandra, John Grady rides aimlessly until he reaches a crossroads. Sitting on his horse, he reads road signs and seeing the arrow to La Encantada, he 'looked toward the darkness in west. The hell with it, he said. I aint leavin my horse down there.' Unlike Huck's clear decision, John Grady's is murky and unformed, and he only vaguely understands why he sets off to repossess his horse from the captain.

Later he feels compelled to tell his story to the judge, saying 'The reason I wanted to kill him was because I stood there and let him walk that boy out in the trees and shoot him and I never said nothing.' But in McCarthy's world good and evil are often intertwined, and John Grady must seek out the judge after the hearing to tell him, 'I guess what I wanted to say first of all was that it kindly bothered me in the court what you said. It was like I was in the right about everthing and I dont feel that way.' Instead, he says, 'I dont feel justified.' Ultimately, then, John Grady Cole's border crossing has taken him into a world of complexity, ambiguity, and ambivalence—a mixture of good and evil, rationality and irrationality, fate and free will in a mestizo culture that is itself an amalgam. Nowhere is the complex mixture more apparent than in John Grady's dealings with the Dueña Alfonsa, whose statements and personal history are belied by her actions, Gail Morrison points out the mixture:

> Alfonsa is both a radical and a reactionary. On the one hand she rebels against the suppression of women and paternal authority, refusing marriage and rejecting a conventional marriage for her great-niece. She has espoused the reformist causes of the Maderos, in her seventeen-year-old idealism, although they run counter to the traditional interests of the landed aristocracy of which she and the Maderos are members and which seems to have managed to preserve its way of life. But she is sent safely out of the line of revolutionary fire to Europe where she is checkmated by being not only unable to rebel against her father but also unable to forgive him for her deportation. Her

frustration is reflected in her vision of the world as a 'puppet show.' And if she been in her youth a puppet, so now in her old age she becomes the puppeteer who pulls the strings of her great-niece's life. What is left her is to live vicariously through Alejandra, who 'is the only future' she contemplates, whose name echoes her own. Without scruple, she bends the girl to her will and changes her destiny by taking advantage of the opportunity to save John Grady's life.

Ironically, it is Alfonsa, the former idealist, who most fully challenges John Grady's idealism, telling him: 'In the end we all come to be cured of our sentiments. Those whom life does not cure death will. The world is quite ruthless in selecting between the dream and the reality, even where we will not. Between the wish and the thing the world lies waiting.'

For John Grady, the idealistic dream is represented by the world of horses, an ideal world of peace achieved in dreams:

That night he dreamt of horses . . . and in the dream he was among the horses running and in the dream he himself could run with the horses . . . and they ran he and the horses out along the high mesas where the ground resounded under their running hooves and they flowed and changed and ran and their manes and tails blew off of them like spume and there was nothing else at all in that high world and they moved all of them in a resonance that was like a music among them and they were none of them afraid horse nor colt nor mare and they ran in that resonance which is the world itself and which cannot be spoken but only praised.

After the experiences in prison and with Alejandra and Alfonsa, John Grady still dreams of horses, but the early dream's idealism is tempered by the disorder, death, and sadness now part of John Grady's knowledge:

In his sleep he could hear the horses stepping among the rocks and he could hear them drink from the shallow pools in the dark where the rocks lay smooth and rectilinear as the stones of ancient ruins and the water from their muzzles dripped and rang like water dripping in a well and in his sleep he dreamt of horses and the horses in his dream moved gravely among the tilted stones like horses come upon an antique site where some ordering of the world had failed and if anything had been written on the stones the weathers had taken it away again and the horses were wary and moved with great circumspection carrying in their blood as they did the recollection of this and other places where horses once had been and would be again. Finally what he saw in his dream was that the order in the horse's heart was more durable for it was written in a place where no rain could erase it.

Although John Grady's idealism is challenged and he now understands the sadness in the world,

He remembered Alejandra and the sadness he'd first seen in the slope of her shoulders which he'd presumed to understand and of which he knew nothing and he felt a loneliness he'd not known since he was a child and he felt wholly alien to the world although he loved it still. He thought that in the beauty of the world were hid a secret. He thought the world's heart beat at some terrible cost and that the world's pain and its beauty moved in a relationship of diverging equity and that in this headlong deficit the blood of multitudes might ultimately be exacted for the vision of a single flower.

This mixture of sadness and beauty is now part of John Grady's more intricate understanding of the world of responsibility to both humans and animals. On the way back to Texas he sees a wedding, a celebratory beginning that is tempered by the 'pale rider' as he passes. Very shortly after seeing the wedding's traditional ceremonial beginning, he attends the funeral of the woman who had worked for his family for fifty years:

he said goodbye to her in Spanish and then turned and put on his hat and turned his wet face to the wind and for a moment he held out his hands as if to steady himself or as if to bless the ground there or perhaps as if to slow the world that was rushing away and seemed to care nothing for the old or the young or rich or poor or dark or pale or he or she. Nothing for their struggles, nothing for their names. Nothing for the living or the dead.

When John Grady rides off into the sunset at the end of this novel, it is not the optimistic triumph of the traditional Western. It is instead a complex image of how the 'rider and horse passed on and their long shadows passed in tandem like the shadow of a single being. Passed and paled into the darkening land, the world to come.'

The Crossing

Crossing the border, of course, is the central image that connects the three novels, of the Border Trilogy. Indeed, in *The Crossing* McCarthy tells the same story he told previously in *All the Pretty Horses*, and in the second novel of the Trilogy, he tells the same story three different times. It is the story of Billy Parham's crossing from his New Mexico home into northern Mexico and his travels around the state of Chihuahua. The first time he takes a she-wolf he had trapped; the second he goes with his younger brother, Boyd, who meets and stays with an enigmatic Mexican girl; and the third time Billy returns in search of Boyd.

As Charles Bailey notes, these crossings are presented in a carefully structured novel: 'The novel's three crossing are divided into four artistic parts, each presenting a storyteller, an Ancient Mariner whom Billy serves as wedding guest. Bailey explains: 'Each narrates a different story, but each has the same message. And the message of the four storytellers (from McCarthy's perspective, the message of all storytellers) is, not incidentally, about time' (' "Doomed Enterprises" and Faith').

As in *All the Pretty Horses* McCarthy continues to explore contrasts such as diverging approaches to time symbolized by the cultures north and south of the border. In *Horses* McCarthy concentrates on more earth-bound concerns, particularly the individual's freedom to counter the demands of class, circumstance, the past, and particularly, human responsibility to others. *The Crossing* shifts the focus from the human to the natural world in the first part and to more metaphysical questions, especially the existence and purpose of God in a violent and inhumane world. Billy Parham's crossings into Mexico and encounters with numerous characters in quest for God recall Mexican dictator Porfirio Díaz's famous statement: 'Poor Mexico, so far from God, so close to the United States.'

As before though, the novel is concerned with the relationship between self and other, beginning initially when Boyd looks into the eyes of the Indian he and Billy discover lurking nearby:

> The indian squatting under a thin stand of carrizo cane and not even hidden and yet Boyd had not seen him. He was holding across his knees an old singleshot 32 rimfire rifle and he had been waiting in the dusk for something to come to water for him to kill. He looked into the eyes of the boy. The boy into his. Eyes so dark they seemed all pupil. Eyes in which the sun was setting. In which the child stood beside the sun. He had not known that you could see yourself in other's eyes nor see therein such things

as suns. He stood twinned in those dark wells with hair so pale, so thin and strange, the selfsame child. As if it were some cognate child to him that had been lost who now stood windowed away in another world where the red sun sank eternally. As if it were a maze where these orphans of his heart had miswandered in their journey in life and so arrived at last beyond the wall of that antique gaze from whence there could no way back forever.

In the Indian's eyes, Boyd finds himself twinned and intimations of worlds beyond, worlds of red suns and wandering orphans, in short the world of the novel to follow.

Similarly, when Billy looks into the eyes of the she-wolf he has made it his mission to befriend and care for, he also sees worlds beyond:

When the flames came up her eyes burned out there like gatelamps to another world. A world burning on the shore of an unknowable void. A world construed out of blood and blood's alcahest and blood in its core and in its integument because it was that nothing save blood had power to resonate against that void which threatened hourly to devour it. He wrapped himself in the blanket and watched her. When those eyes and the nation to which stood witness were gone at last with their dignity back into their origins there would perhaps be other fires and other witnesses and other worlds otherwise beheld. But they would not be this one.

The emphasis on the connections between the wild creatures of the world and the innocent, growing youth recalls the night John Grady Cole lies considering the stars, sensing that

In that false blue dawn the Pleiades seemed to be rising up into the darkness of the world and dragging all the stars away, the great diamond of Orion and Cepella and the signature of Cassiopeia all rising up through the phosphorous dark like a sea-net. He lay a long time listening to the others breathing in their sleep while he contemplated the wildness about him, the wildness within. (*All the Pretty Horses*)

These are the kinds of questions that return throughout *The Crossing*. What is the relationship between the self and the 'other,' particularly the wild and violent other such as the Indian, the wolf, and the numerous violent

human beings Billy and Boyd encounter on their border crossings? Often the
questions are answered by the many wandering *filósofos* the two meet. Along
the roads they travel, Billy and Boyd meet numerous characters—an Indian
shaman, old man in the ruined church, a blind revolutionary, a gypsy—men
and women who feel compelled to tell their stories to the innocent *güeritos*,
the blond Americans whose youth inspires the telling of stories meant to
guide them through the violence and suffering, the kindness and comfort in
the world.

On the first crossing, after the death of the wolf, Billy is heading north
and after stopping among Indians in the mountains, an old man, perhaps a
shaman 'dressed in odd and garish fashion,' speaks to him earnestly:

> He told the boy that although he was huerfano still he must cease
> h is wanderings and make for himself some place in the world
> because to wander in this way would become for him a passion
> and by this passion he would become estranged from men and so
> ultimately from himself. He said that the world could only be
> known as it existed in men's hearts. For while it seemed a place
> which contained men it was in reality a place contained within
> them and therefore to know it one must look there and come to
> know those hearts and to do this one must live with men and not
> simply pass among them. He said that while the huerfano might
> feel that he no longer belonged among men he must set this
> feeling aside for he contained within him a largeness of spirit
> which men could see and that men would wish to know him and
> that the world would need him even as he needed the world for
> they were one. Lastly he said that while this itself was a good
> think like all good things it was also a danger.

The old Indian is one of several mentors the wandering Billy meets,
each providing similar instructions about understanding a world of
seemingly irreconcilable forces, forever separate. Shortly after leaving the
old shaman, Billy chances upon an old man living in the ruins of an adobe
church destroyed by an earth-quake. As happens throughout this novel, the
old man tells Billy his story, explaining the terrors and joys of his life and his
reasons for his existence, as best as he understands them. He says that he had
come because of the devastation from the *terremoto*:

> I was seeking evidence of the hand of God in the world. I had
> come to believe that hand a wrathful one and I thought that men
> had not inquired sufficiently into miracles of destruction. Into

disasters of a certain magnitude. I thought there might be evidence that had been overlooked. I thought He would not trouble himself to wipe away every handprint. My desire to know was very strong. I thought it might even amuse Him to leave some clue . . . Something unforeseen. Something out of place. Something untrue or out of round. A track in the dirt. A fallen bauble. Not some cause. I can tell you that. Not some cause. Causes only multiply themselves. They lead to chaos. What I wanted was to know his mind. I could not believe He would destroy his own church without reason.

Ultimately the old man tells Billy that what he had learned was the 'corrido. The tale. And like all corridos it ultimately told one story only, for there is only one to tell.' He continues:

For this world also which seems to us a thing of stone and flower and blood is not a thing at all but is a tale. And all in it is a tale and each tale the sum of all lesser tales and yet these also are the selfsame tale and contain as well all else within them. So everything is necessary. Every least thing. This is the hard lesson. Nothing can be dispensed with. Nothing despised. Because the seams are hid from us, you see. The joinery. The way in which the world is made. We have no way to know what could be taken away. What omitted. We have no way to tell what might stand and what might fall. And those seams that are hid from use are of course in the tale itself and the tale has no abode or place of being except in the telling only and there it live and makes its home and therefore we can never be done with the telling. Of the telling there is no end. And whether in Caborca or in Huisiachepic or in whatever other place by whatever other name or by no name at all I say again all tales are one. Rightly heard all tales are one.

The old man's belief in the power of storytelling seems the closest statement of McCarthy's own aesthetics in all of his works, a defense of the charges against his tales of violence and blood, of his repetition. The old storyteller suggests why McCarthy headed for new territory when the old man remarks that the difficulty in stories is not creating unity out of diversity but of making many of the one,' since all stories are the same story. And the old man's emphasis on the power of stories to unify disparate elements suggests the reconciliation or amalgamation of contrasting forces that seems to be at work in these border novels. In fact the story is one of borders and contrasts. He tells of the man he calls 'the old anchorite,' a man doubly damned, having lost his parents and his child in the 1887 earthquake. After wandering the earth, he returns to the church of La Purísma Concepción de Nuestra Señora de Caborca where his parents had died and begins to challenge God and in turn test the beliefs of the local priest (who turns out to be the old storyteller himself). In his attempt to understand God, the old anchorite wants to '[a]ssess boundaries and metes. See that lines were drawn and respected.' Ultimately, he decided that God could only be known through those who witness his works and that God could have no witness:

> And he began to see in God a terrible tragedy. That the existence
> of the Deity lay imperiled for want of this simple thing. That for
> God there could be no witness. Nothing against which He
> terminated. Nothing by way of which his being could be
> announced to Him. Nothing to stand apart from and to say I am
> this and that is other. Where that is I am not. He could create
> everthing save that which would say him no.

This conclusion challenges the priest, who 'believed in a boundless God without center or circumference. By this very formlessness he'd sought to make God manageable. This was his colindancia. In his grandness he had ceded all terrain. And in this colindancia God had no say at all.'

The storyteller's tale is a paradox, for the old anchorite's firm brief against God, even unto his deathbed where he drives the priest away with stones, challenges the priest's faith in a boundless God. His faith shaken by the heretic's unbending opposition to God, the priest becomes a wanderer, searching, and, he suggests, finding God. For his final statement to Billy confirms the paradox of his tale: 'In the end we shall all of us be only what we have made of God,' and, of course, the stories about God such as the one he h ad just told Billy (and by extension the one McCarthy tells his readers).

Billy then returns to the United States to find that he is indeed, as the Indian shaman had told him, an orphan, his parents having been killed while he was gone. With his brother Boyd he then sets out on the second crossing, another possession/dispossession story, as he and Boyd cross determined to regain the family's horses, which they soon find and recover, only to be set upon and Boyd shot. Trying to escape in the night, Billy encounters the third major storyteller, whose tale continues the emphasis on the illusion/reality contrast along with the other contrasts of past/present, dark/light, chaos/order, and evil/good. The past returns through the story of an old revolutionary, violently blinded in his youth when the federales took him prisoner and a German captain with enormous hands named Wirtz bent as if to kiss him and suddenly leaned 'to suck each in turn the man's eyes from his head and spit them out again and leave them dangling by their cords wet and strange and wobbling on his cheeks.' This radically evil, grotesque act recalls Flannery O'Connor's statement about extremes:

> The novelist with Christian concerns will find in modern life distortions which are repugnant to him, and his problem will be to make these appear as distortions to an audience which is used to seeing them as natural; and he may well be forced to take ever more violent means to get his vision across to this hostile audience. When you can assume that your audience holds the same beliefs you do, you can relax a little and use more normal means of talking to it; when you have to assume that it does not, then you have to make your vision apparent by shock—to the hard of hearing you shout and for the almost blind you draw large and startling figures.

The blind man eventually draws similar conclusion about the existence of such excessive evil:

> He said that even the sepulturero would understand that every tale was a tale of dark and light and would perhaps not have it otherwise. Yet there was still a further order to the narrative and it was a thing of which men do not speak. He said the wicked know that if the ill they do be of sufficient horror men will not speak against it. That men have just enough stomach for small evils and only these will they oppose. He said that true evil has power to sober the smalldoer against his own deeds and in the contemplation of that evil he may even find the path of righteousness which has been foreign to his feet and may have no power but to go upon it. Even this man may be appalled at what is revealed to him and seek some order to stand against it. (*The Crossing*)

The existence of violent evil calls forth the opposite, the desire for forces to oppose it. In his one public interview McCarthy told Woodward:

> There's no such thing as life without bloodshed . . . I think the notion that the species can be improved in some way, that everyone could live in harmony, is a really dangerous idea. Those who are afflicted with this notion are the first ones to give up their souls, their freedom. Our desire that it be that way will enslave you and make your life vacuous.

Ultimately, the blindman goes beyond his conclusion about the power of evil and explains to Billy his conclusion about justice in the world when he tells Billy in Spanish:

> Lo que debemos entender, said the blind man, es que ultimamente todo es polvo. Todo lo que podemos tocar. Todo lo que podemos ver. En este tenemos las evidencia más profunda de la justicia, de la misericordia. En este vemos la bendición mas grande de Dios. [What we must understand, said the blind man, is that ultimately all is dust. All that we can touch. All that we can see. In this we have the most profound evidence of justice, of mercy. In this we see the greatest blessing of God.] (*The Crossing*)

This is another of many statements about the nature of reality—all is dust. But that the world is ultimately dust and to be interpreted by humans—and that is all he can know.

Several critics such as Edwin T. Arnold and Sven Birkirts have pointed out the combination of good and evil in McCarthy. Arnold labels him a 'mystic in the way his favorite writer Melville is a mystic, acknowledging and in fact honoring the majesty of the astounding and awful as well as of the simple and beautiful' ('The Mosaic of McCarthy's Fiction'); and Birkirts calls him a Gnostic:

> McCarthy has been, from the start, a writer with strong spiritual leanings. His orientation is Gnostic: he seems to view our endeavors here below as a violation of some original purity. But a sensibility so attuned to earthly beauty cannot be oblivious to the higher promptings of the soul. His intuitions are of the most primary sort, never even remotely doctrinaire. In the early books we heed his exacerbated awareness of violence and cruelty, of evil, without finding much place for the good. But now, in these most recent works, we meet up quite often with decency. There are venal killers, yes, but they are outnumbered by the poor who emerge from their dwellings to offer succor.

Indeed as Billy leaves the blindman, a woman rushes up and drops into his hand a small silver heart, saying it is 'Un milagro,' a good heath and healing charm for his wounded brother. When he answers that Boyd was not wounded in the heart, she waves him on. Ironically, when Billy returns to the States, discovers that World War II has begun, and tries to enlist, he is rejected because of a 'heart murmur.' After wandering, Billy with perhaps his heart aching for a reconnection with his brother, makes his final crossing into Mexico to search for Boyd, only to discover that Boyd has died, fighting against the establishment, and become a hero with corridos sung about his fame.

After Billy decides to dig up Boyd's bones and return then home (in a scene recalling Larry McMurtry's *Lonesome Dove* where Woodrow Call returns Gus McCrea's dead body to Texas for burial), Billy encounters his final major mentor/philosopher, a gypsy hauling the remains of an old airplane. McCarthy's description of the airplane suggests the connection between the plane and Boyd's bones:

> The airplane was little more than a skeleton with sunbleached shreds of lines the color of stewed rhubarb clinging to the steambent ashwood ribs and stays and inside you could see the wires and cables that ran aft to the rudder and elevators and the cracked and curled and sunblacked leather of the seats and in their tarnished nickel bezels the glass of instrument dials glaucous and clouded from the pumicing of the desert sands.

The connection between the plane and Boyd becomes clear when the gypsy tells the plane's story(ies). Like Boyd the plane has a twin, but the most important connection refers to storytelling: 'Con respecto al aeroplano, [the gypsy] said, hay tres historias.' (With respect to the airplane, he said, there are three histories.) He then tells how he and his band had been recruited by a grieving father to recover the plane and return it and how they worked in brutal conditions to bring it home. The truth of this story is challenged later when Billy encounters a horseman from Texas who tells that he engaged the gypsies to recover the plane. It is the stories that have life, as Billy has learned about Boyd. Although Billy believes he knows the truth about Boyd's life and death, now that Boyd has entered history, his story has a life and truth of its own in the corridos, just as the plane has three histories. Charles Bailey explains:

> There are the 'real' story (the rider's story) and the 'true' story (the gypsy's fiction); and the third story is 'la historia de las historias [his story of the stories],' the 'really true or the truly real' story, 'the one story,' God's story, at which the other two can only hint. For McCarthy, the 'real' story does not matter, for it has no witness; the 'true' story matters, the fiction, the one shaped by the witness/artist; and the 'true' story matters desperately because it implies the 'really true' story, which must

always lie beyond human power to know or to tell. (' "Doomed Enterprises" and Faith')

The only human history available, the gypsy says in Spanish, is the telling: 'Es que ultimadamente la verdad no puede quedar en ningun otro lugar sino en el habla [It is ultimately that the truth of it cannot be placed in any other place but in the speaking of it].' He explains:

> The past, he said, is always this argument between counterclaimants. Memories dim with age. There is not repository for our images. The loved ones who visit us in dreams are strangers. To even see aright is effort. We seek some witness but the world will not provide one. This is the third history. It is the history that each man makes alone out of what is left to him. Bits of wreckage. Some bones. The words of the dead. How make a world of this? How live in that world once made? (*The Crossing*)

Not only is the past an argument among counterclaimants, but McCarthy's world life itself is. Even Billy's encounter with the gypsies suggests the intertwining of good and evil in the world, for they come upon Billy shortly after he was attacked by bandits who spilled Boyd's shrouded bones and stabbed Billy's horse. In another counter act, the gypsies treat the horse's wound and help Billy return where he encounters an old, grotesque dog. In one of McCarthy's most affecting scenes of ambivalence, when Billy sees the 'arthritic and illjoined thing . . . wet and wretched and so scarred and broken that it might have been patched up out of parts of dogs by demented vivisectionists,' he first throws rocks and chases if off with a pipe, the dog howling '[a]s if some awful composite of grief had broke through from the preterite world.' But when Billy awakens the next day, he calls out for the dog, and when it does not come, he 'bowed his head and held his face in his hands and wept.' This powerfully compassionate scene ends the novel, and the last line denies differences as 'the godmade sun' rises 'for all and without distinction.'

As Alex Hunt demonstrates in 'Right and False Suns,' when Billy is awakened by a flash of 'white light of desert noon' that is 'no sun . . . and no dawn,' he is probably witnessing, the Trinity Test that occurred in Alamogordo, New Mexico, July 16, 1945. for both McCarthy and Leslie Silko, who uses the test at the climax of *Ceremony*, the dawning of the atomic age is the ultimate symbol for human alienation from nature. The novel begins with Billy Parham's compulsion to reintegrate with the natural world that the pregnant wolf represents and ends with the nuclear test. In between, the old man's emphasis on stories that connect all things carries much of McCarthy's argument.

All of this is told in night literary style, with lilting Faulknerian prose and memorable descriptions such as this one referring to the eyes of a drunk who challenges Billy in a bar: 'Like lead slag poured into borings to seal away something virulent or predacious.' Some readers may find the style heavy-handed, but every page McCarthy reveals a careful stylist, a writer who refuses to yield to the cliché, and whose language, characters, and plot simultaneously seem as new as afterbirth and as old as dust. *The Crossing*'s language steps constantly across the border as well, merging Spanish and English seamlessly. Throughout *The Crossing*, McCarthy returns to the complex intertwining of good and evil that appeared in the earlier border novel. These repeated stories continue to tell stories of good and evil, reinforcing McCarthy's acute awareness of the inextricable mixture of force with the border as the overriding metaphor and storytelling as the intermediary.

Cities of the Plain

Cities of the Plain combines many of the varied elements of the first two books in a powerful end of the millennium examination of human responsibility, desire, chance, folly, the changing natural world, and of the ineluctable human desire to make sense of things.

On the surface, the first books in the Trilogy seem quite similar: both are about youthful Southwestern boys who travel south of the border and undergo initiatory experiences involving houses, cattle, senoritas, and vaqueros. Despite these surface similarities, the two books are quite different. *All the Pretty Horses* is a spare, more traditional story of romance, imprisonment, and revenge, while *The Crossing* is dense, philosophical, often violent book filled with long stories that seem like parables, particularly the long opening section in which Billy Parham captures a wolf and then tries to return her and free her in Mexico.

For the first half, the concluding novel seems more like *All the Pretty Horses*, even though both John Grady Cole from *Horses* and Billy Parham from *The Crossing* appear, at first in a whorehouse in Juárez, where the older Billy takes John Grady Cole and introduces him to beautiful sixteen-year-old prostitute significantly named Magdalena. It is three years the end of *All the Pretty Horses*, the early 1950s, and Billy and John Grady work near El Paso for an aging West Texas/New Mexican rancher named Mac. The first half is filled with a crisp West Texas dialog that is so right in nuance and sound no one would know the writer spent his first forty-five years outside of Texas, much of it in his home state, Tennessee. But when McCarthy moved to El Paso in 1976, he began to listen and to capture the language and dialect so completely that the dialog resounds with authenticity (rendered, like McCarthy's major influence Faulkner, without quotation marks). Here, fore example, McCarthy dramatizes a horse auction as John Grady and his boss Mac examine a horse:

> A Fool and his money, said Mac. John Grady what's wrong
>   with that horse?
> Not a thing that I know of.
> I though you said it was some kind of a mongrel outcross. A
>   Martian horse or somethin.
> Horse might be a little coldblooded . . .
> I got five got five got five now, called the auctioneer . . .
> The horse was sold at seven hundred. Wolfenbarger never
>   bid. Oren glanced at Mac.
> Cute sumbuck, aint he? Mac said. (*Cities of the Plain*)

McCarthy's stylistic debt to William Faulkner has long been clear, and he echoes the Faulknerian language with the long sentences and heightened vocabulary in much of the last section of the novel, particularly in the epilogue. The stylistic debt in the first part is clearly to Ernest Hemingway with this almost pure Hemingway paragraph with its straightforward description and 'there is/there are' statements:

> Eduardo stood at the rear door smoking one of his thin cigars and looking out at the rain. There was a sheetiron warehouse behind the building and there was nothing much there to see except the rain and the black pools of water standing in the alley where the rain fell and soft light from the yellow bulb screwed into the fixture over the back door. The air was cool. The smoke drifted in the light. A young girl who limped on a withered leg passed carrying a great armload of soiled linen down the hall. After a while he closed the door and walked back up the hallway to his office.

And Hemingway may have influenced McCarthy's use of the contrasting elements suggested by the title: the plains versus the mountains. As Carlos Baker made clear in his seminal study of *A Farewell to Arms*,

Hemingway used the mountains to represent the high, appealing country far from the war below on the plains. Similarly, McCarthy's high country here is the refuge from much of the corruption of the cities of the plain. In the mountain John Grady renovates the Cedar Springs cabin that he hopes will be the wedding grotto to which he can escape. But as in much of McCarthy, the dichotomies are often set up and collapsed. It is the mountains where the feral dogs are slaughtered and pups saved.

The realistic often humorous dialog lulls the reader into a seeming light-toned book, another initiatory story with Billy playing the realistic foil to the romantic John Grady as he purses Magdalena. But as the walks down the street with the foreshadowing name of *Calle de Noche Triste*, the street of the sad night, it soon becomes clear that the last novel in the trilogy is, like of other ones, a tragicomic examination of the twists and turns along life's journey.

In several ways, *Cities of the Plain* returns to, and in some cases, comes closer to resolving themes and issues that appeared in the previous novels. *Like All the Pretty Horses*, it presents the conflict between realism and romance, but where the previous novel left the issue in limbo after John Grady Cole loses his Alejandra but recovers his houses, *Cities of the Plain* offers several characters and events who come down squarely on the side of romance. Again and again, characters endorse the notion that one should follow his or her heart. 'I think you ought to follow your heart, the old man said. That's all I ever thought about anything.' And later: 'I only know that every act which has not heart will be found out in the end. Every gesture.' 'A man is always right to pursue the thing he loves.' Later John Grady catches a ride with a man who has been married for sixty years. And hovering behind the novel is the story of the love affair between Mr. Johnson's daughter and the current story of John Grady's relentless and tragic pursuit of the epileptic whore Magdalena.

Her biblical name connects with John Grady Cole's initials. Like numerous previous characters in American literature, his initials signify the youthful Adams who become messianic figures following an initiation. In *All the Pretty Horses* John Grady Cole's awareness of responsibility for others is played out in his relationship with Blevins, for whom he demonstrates concern throughout. In *Cities of the Plain* the theme of human responsibility takes several forms, through Billy's concern for John Grady, and primarily through Cole's almost inexplicable connection with Magdalena. John seems drawn to her simplicity and helplessness, never acknowledging either her life as a whore or her epilepsy.

Ultimately, then, John Grady Cole's border crossings take him into a world of complexity, ambiguity, and ambivalence—a mixture of good and evil, rationality and irrationality, fare and free will in a mestizo culture that is itself an amalgam. Ambiguity prevails at the end of *All the Pretty Horses*, continues in *The Crossing*, but *Cities of the Plain*, except for the inchoate epilog, leaves the indeterminate and takes stands on such issues as human responsibility for others, for the value of love, and for the landscape.

The powerful theme of responsibility is doubled in *Cities of the Plain*, for John Grady shoulders the responsibility for Magdalena's welfare and sacrifices himself to his vision. Billy Parham's feelings of responsibility for John Grady mirror Cole's. And these two figures bring together the various themes of the earlier books.

Cities of the Plain continues McCarthy's emphasis on the changing landscape of the Southwest. Again McCarthy dramatizes the negative results that are the effect of human alienation from the natural world. In *Cities of the Plain* a subtle background motif concerns the end of things, especially the changing natural landscape. The title, for example, is an allusion to Sodom and Gomorrah, which was the title of one Marcel Proust's volumes of *Remembrance of Things Past*. McCarthy presents the following dialogue between John Grady Cole and an again cowboy. With gentle nostalgia, the old cowboy recalls the older natural world:

Mr. Johnson . . . flipped the butt of his cigarette out across the yard in a slow red arc.

Aint nothin to burn out there. I remember when you could have grassfires in this country.

. . . There's hard lessons in this world.

What's the hardest?

I dont know. Maybe it's just that when things are gone they're gone. They aint comin back.

Yessir.

They sat. After a while the old man said: The day after my fiftieth birthday in March of nineteen and seventeen I rode into the old headquarters at the Wilde well and there was six dead wolves hangin on the fence. I rode along the fence and ran my hand along em. I looked at their eyes. A government trapper had brought em in the night before. They's been killed with poison baits. Strychnine. Whatever. Up in the Sacramentos. A week later he brought in four more. I aint heard a wolf in this country since. I suppose that's a good thing. They can be hell on stock. But I guess I was always what you might call superstitious. I know I damn sure wasnt religious. And it had always seemed to me that somethin can live and die but that the kind of thing that they were was always there. I didnt know you could poison that. I aint heard a wolf howl in thirty odd years. I dont know where you'd go to hear one. There may not be any such a place. (*Cities of the Plain*)

Like other Texas writers, McCarthy approaches the natural world through an ironic double vision. He suggests that humans derive value from working the harsh landscape but adds the notion that the disappearance of that harsh landscape is being accomplished by the acts of the same people who begin to understand the value of the disappearing world—the cattlemen who destroy the wolves, the people who cause the overgrazing that diminishes the grass. It was a good old world, the one that is disappearing, and it was good because it allowed us to work in it, and that work led us to destroy it. This emphasis on caring for wolves, of course, ties the last novel to the long beginning story in *The Crossing*. Similarly, the episode concerning the killing of the feral dogs that ironically leads to John Grady's concern for the pups points to this double nature of the human relationship with the natural world that must lead to caring for that world lest it disappear.

And in the Epilogue and Dedication to *Cities of the Plain*, McCarthy draws together the various themes of the Trilogy. With John Grady's death, Billy decides to return to his home territory of De Baca County, New Mexico. The Epilogue begins: 'He left three days later, he and the dog,' again returning to the theme of responsibility to the natural world that the Trilogy's emphasis on horses, wolves, and dogs has stressed throughout. Billy responds to the 'pup shivering and whining until he took it up in the bow of the saddle with him.' Then he and Mac make their goodbyes, and Billy says, 'I should of looked after him better' to which Mac responds, 'We all should of.' Thus the Epilogue begins by combining the themes of the responsibility to the natural and human worlds that McCarthy stressed in various ways throughout the Trilogy with crossing borders as its central metaphor.

The Epilogue then returns to the power of storyteller, one of the dominant themes in *The Crossing*, when the aging Billy in 2002 encounters the deathlike traveler under the highway bridge and shares his meager food with him. As before in McCarthy's telling of another story of human journeys, it becomes clear that we are all actually on the same journey told again and again in different but always similar ways in which deep questions about the process and the telling are often explored. As before, those questions are traced by this strange minor figure who becomes an interlocutor for Billy and by extension for the readers. This figure ushers in the millennium and recounts a dream about a dream within a dream. As Edwin Arnold notes, the Epilogue is about 'the role of the artist, or the dreamer, or the creator, and his responsibilities to the subjects of his dreams'

('First Thoughts').

McCarthy reemphasizes the theme of human responsibility again at the end when the old Billy lives with a family near Portales and helps their children care for a colt. When Billy awakes from an uneasy dream about Boyd, the mother, named Betty, sits comforting him with her hand on his shoulder. When Billy tries to tell her that he is unworthy of her concern and that he is not who she thinks, she tells him emphatically, 'I know who you are.' She also states clearly that she also knows why she cares for him. Such is the stuff that dreams and the novels of Cormac McCarthy are made of, and *Cities of the Plain* is the product of the vision of perhaps America's most important writer at century's end.

It is a world that grows warm and cold, a world with both love for children and the old and heathens who rage, as the concluding Dedication stresses. The seeming oppositions exist in the stories told in the Border Trilogy, stories of raging love and other oxymoronic border crossings. And as we turn the final page, we wait for the next story to give shape to the world to come.

YOOJIN GRACE KIM

"Then They All Move on Again": Knowledge and the Individual in Judge Holden's Doctrine of War

> This is the nature of war, whose stake is at once the game and the authority and the justification. Seen so, war is the truest form of divination. It is the testing of one's will and the will of another within that larger will which because it binds them is therefore forced to select. War is the ultimate game because war is at last a forcing of the unity of existence. War is god.[1]

For McCarthy's Judge Holden, war orders the world and the men in it. He places absolute faith in violence, commanding others to do the same, unironically, by the sword. Merciless and brutal, the judge does not tolerate difference—not in men, in creation, or even in himself. Although he does not acknowledge it, the judge's stance is essentially insecure, for his "metaphysics of violence"[2] does not sustain evaluation, but only brute force. His god is a greedy one who must be constantly appeased with blood, but who offers no redemption or transcendence in return. Thus, there is little, if any, saving grace in an entire continent of gore-drenched landscapes in *Blood Meridian*. Yet even in this unholy terrain, the mad order of the judge does not go wholly unchallenged, and it is the rough drawl of the young orphan recruit that answers his rhetoric with impassive, if silent, rebuttal. Certainly, "the

---

From a paper Yale University (December 1999): pp. 1–23. ©1999 by Yoogin Grace Kim.

169

kid" represents no revolutionary or even consciously dissenting force. But as surely as the judge stalks and murders him, the heretic of war, the kid reveals a character of rare individuality among the cast of Judge Holden's universalized warriors, unwittingly threatening the necessary unity of the judge's doctrine. In the end, the kid's refusal to kill the unarmed judge acts as his ultimate betrayal of the laws of war, for it fails to uphold the integrity of pure violence crucial to that religion. It is in the face of this heresy that the judge's original paternal intentions for the kid become terribly unhinged. In this essay, I will argue that the crucial break between Judge Holden and the kid emerges from the tension between the universal and the individual, or in other words, the known and unknown; and that his attempted paternity over the kid reflects an effort to assert his own imagined divinity by eliminating the unknown—in this case, the unknown origins of the apparently parentless kid. Finally, I will discuss the implications of reading "the idiot" as the substitute son-figure to the judge following the noncompliance of the kid.

This desert upon which so many have been broken is vast and calls for largeness of heart but it is also ultimately empty. It is hard, it is barren. Its very nature is stone (330). In *Blood Meridian*, the judge haunts us for the same reason that McCarthy's desert haunts its travelers. Both are "ultimately empty" of spirituality even as they appear supernaturally transcendent of ordinary humanity—they are inscrutable, deadly, awesome. The judge's rhetoric resonates in the desert, yet it opens countless holes that can only be filled by a never-ending stream of blood. And the desert responds with the necessary sacrifices, the true "ceremonies" of blood. Samuel Chamberlain describes this violence in *My Confession*, a personal narrative of the bloody westward procession of Glanton and his troops. As it remains the only documentation of the historical Judge Holden, McCarthy closely followed Chamberlain's narrative in his characterization of the judge's physical and intellectual powers. An unexpected trait appears in Chamberlain's writing, however, that does not explicitly appear in the novel: "[Holden was] with all an arrant coward. Not but that he possessed enough courage to fight Indians and Mexicans or anyone where he had the advantage in strength, skill and weapons, but where the combat would be equal, he would avoid it if possible."[3] Clearly, the judge's desire for violence derives from the pleasure he gains from dominating over a weaker other, thus his god of war closely involves a god of sadism as well.

In *Blood Meridian*, violence does not discriminate by any means of human classification. Assassins and victims alike are white, black, Indian, or Mexican, and the blood of men, women, children and the elderly mingle in the barely broken ground of the new American West. Even the central cast of killers joins a diverse mix of Southern whites, Delaware Indians, a

Hispanic, and an African American. Here, as Judge Holden believes, war unites all. Robert L. Jarrett takes it farther; he writes "*death* unites all," (my italics) and to a large extent, he is right. Inevitable death meets each man, either in war or in refusal of war, as in the case of Grannyrat, the Mexican War veteran whose desertion Glanton punishes with swift execution. And if we accept the judge's more abstract standards of treason, in the case of the kid as well. But in the end, the judge's vision of the universal is more accurate than that of the critic, for while war pervades the very fabric of the novel, death does not defeat all of McCarthy's characters. The judge prevails to dance his triumphant dance of death, paradoxically, a dance that can only be danced alive.

The judge is a priest of war, whose faith relies on universal truth in violence and death. Yet the narrative portrays the judge not only as a priest, but also as a divine being in his own right. Referring to McCarthy's description of the judge as a "great ponderous djinn" (96) and a "sootysouled rascal" (124), Edwin T. Arnold asserts: "Judge Holden is clearly satanic." Vereen M. Bell perceives the same, although his association of the judge with Satan is less religious and more existential and nihilistic: "If the judge is a failed priest, he may as well be Satan; but if he is Satan, he may as well be God also, for in this context [of the judge's metaphysic] the two are not conceived as inversions of one another." This rhetoric, which undermines the ordinary opposition of God and Satan, may very well describe the novel's ambiguity concerning the traditional figure of the divine, yet Bell's interpretation of the judge as a "failed" priest of a "false religion" gives only a summary reduction of the judge's complex and terrifying presence. In light of the novel's conclusion, in which the judge claims triumph, one must not dismiss his visions of order merely as a false religion. The judge's religion of war and his obsession for knowledge inspires others' awe as well as his own belief in elevation to the divine, and according to the expriest, the troop follows Holden "like disciples of a new faith" even shortly after their meeting with him in the desert (130).

Unlike Faulkner's Darl in *As I Lay Dying*, the judge's knowledge is not necessarily supernatural or innate. Instead, his knowledge, which he believes accords him power over the world, results from a deliberate gathering of information and details: "[I]n the evening he would dress expertly the colorful birds he'd shot, rubbing the skins with gunpowder and stuffing them with balls of dried grass and packing them away in his wallets. He pressed the leaves of trees and plants into his book and he stalked tiptoe the mountain butterflies with his shirt outheld in both hands, speaking to them in a low whisper, no curious study himself. Toadvine sat watching him...and he asked him what was his purpose in all this.... (198)

> Whatever exists, he said. Whatever in creation exists without my knowledge exists without my consent.... These anonymous creatures, he said, may seem little or nothing in the world. Yet the smallest crumb can devour us. Any smallest thing beneath yon rock out of men's knowing.... (198) But that man who sets himself the task of singling out the thread of order from the tapestry will by the decision alone have taken charge of the world and it is only by such taking charge that he will effect a way to dictate the terms of his own fate. (199)

For the judge, the process and achievement of knowledge parallels the attainment of divinity. He believes that by knowing the universe, he owns it. Inversely, anything he does not know represents a threat to his lordship. Thus the judge cannot but harbor an acute paranoia of the unknown, for despite his superhuman competence and erudition, the judge is not omniscient. And unlike Yahweh God or even the pagan god Prometheus, the judge never claims himself a creative force. Instead, he believes as Jarrett states that "[m]an instead must impose his will on the natural world and other men—first through his knowledge of nature...and finally through violence..."Although he is no creator, the judge commands a terrible order by acts of senseless violence, which become his own special mode of creation. In one instance of especial cold-blooded murder, the judge adopts an Apache child and endears him to the group only to scalp him three days later. Thus, the judge's "thread of order" weaves in and out of the human skulls he bloodies and binds the pages of his books. As Steven Shaviro argues, the judge does not distinguish between acts of war and writing. Just as the skins of newly discovered animals record the judge's increasing knowledge, the flesh of each of his victims yields another tally of blood to underscore his doctrine of universal violence, war, and death.

Significantly, the character that emerges in stubborn individuality against Judge Holden's pursuit of universality remains the most anonymous throughout the novel. Unlike the judge, who one unimpressed reviewer dubs "The Man Who Never Shuts Up," the kid has no spokesman. Without clear origins, distinct characteristics, or even a name, the kid's anonymity appears essential. His individuality, however, is not as easily perceived, for on the surface, the kid does not seem to differ from the general troop in any way. Despite the judge's final accusations of "clemency," the boy is not a lesser participant in the constant warfare throughout the journey. In fact, as he fires round after round upon the pursuing Yumas, the kid's mass murder appears so matter-of-fact that the expriest, his fellow scalphunter and spiritual guardian, expresses a hint of regret for the kid's deadly skill even in his admiration: "Aye, you're a cool one, he whispered. But it's cunning work all the same and wouldn't it take the heart out of ye" (280). Besides the judge, Tobin the expriest is the only one in the group who preserves a genuine concern for the boy's body and soul, but unlike the judge, Tobin expresses true remorse for the boy's heartlessness in sin.

Yet, despite his apparent prowess in "the ultimate game," the kid appears in only a few of the novel's ceaseless scenes of violence, essentially disappearing from the narrative after his recruitment into Glanton's murderous gang. If, according to the judge's metaphysic, violence and war are universal, the kid's narrative absence from communal scenes of violence represents a refusal of participation and significant break from this universe. Yet this is no conscious separation by the boy, whose perceived individuality is not necessarily inherent to his being. In the novel's opening paragraphs, McCarthy fixes the boy's identity to man's communal history: "All history present in that visage, the child the father of the man" (3). In a strange adaptation of the original Wordsworthian verse, McCarthy implies that all of history has produced the kid, whose existence extends, and even engenders anew, the history of man. However, the kid ends this succession, leaving home at the age of fourteen, never to return to it in any form. Just a year later, the author describes an altered consciousness: "Only now is the child finally divested of all that he has been. His origins are become remote as is his destiny and not again in all the world's turning will there be terrains so wild and barbarous to try whether the stuff of creation may be shaped to man's will or whether his own heart is not another kind of clay" (4-5). Clearly, the kid rejects "history," his origins and "all that he has been" as he wanders upon the land to challenge creation by his own will. Like the judge who wars against the unknown to claim the universe from its intolerable mysteries, the kid throws himself into wild creation to test his own unconquered Self.

Accordingly, the novel's few descriptions of the kid's acts of violence are instances of his *individual* attacks against distinct persons. His first brawl of the novel begins when a drunk man, later introduced as Toadvine, orders him out of his way. The kid answers with a swift kick in the jaw. A second, more vicious, scene begins with a similar non-reason when the barman legitimately refuses the kid a drink.

> The kid crouched lightly with the bottles and feinted and then broke the right one over the man's head. Blood and liquor sprayed and the man's knees buckled and his eyes rolled. ... he backhanded the second bottle across the barman's skull and crammed the jagged remnant into his eye as he went down. (25)

Although as senseless and willful as a routine Indian scalping, the violence of
the kid in this case differs from that of Glanton's men in their mass acts of
war. The intensity of violence is largely unchanged, yet the difference is
simply that this incident is *not* a routine Indian scalping. Instead, McCarthy
presents distinct characters and grievances, however insubstantial, which
account for the violence aside from its own sake. No such accounting exists
for Granton and his men, whose apparent motives of money and Indian
hatred do not ring quite true. The band sportingly adds Mexican scalps to
their collections in territories with too few Indians and values money only
temporarily to buy drink and women in frontier towns.

Even as a new member of Granton's troop, the kid does not shift from
his instinct for the individual. He asks: "What kind of indians was them?,"
demanding identity and subjectivity for the Indian victims (56). Not
surprisingly, his companion, Sproule, does not know and most probably does
not care. After experiencing the "death hilarious, … a hell more horrible yet
than the brimstone land of christian reckoning" of the Comanche attack, it
is indeed remarkable that the kid should care either. Yet he alone does not
abandon the implicit individuality of either victims or assassins in the
terrifying affair, for even the author seems to paint a continuity of time and
space of universal war in his description of the Comanche's charging
company:

> A legion of horribles, hundreds in number, half naked or clad in
> costumes attic or biblical or wardrobed out of a fevered dream
> with the skins of animals and silk finery and pieces of uniform
> still tracked with the blood of prior owners, coats of slain
> dragoons, frogged and braided cavalry jackets, one in a stovepipe
> hat and one with an umbrella and one in white stockings and a
> bloodstained weddingveil and some in headgear of cranefeathers
> or rawhide helmets that bore the horns of bull or buffalo and one
> in a pigeontailed coat worn backwards and otherwise naked and
> one in the armor of a spanish conquistador, the breastplate and
> pauldrons deeply dented with old blows of mace or sabre done in
> another country by men whose very bones were dust… (52)

The author's detailed descriptions of the warriors' varied dress seem to
highlight their individuality, but in fact this description produces the
opposite effect. Principally a "legion," the Comanche fighters are, by
definition, a unit. Among their thousands, the Comanches' dress represents
a chaotic conglomerate of the human condition—rich and poor, divine and
mundane, present and past. Some warriors dress in the "silk finery" of the

bourgeoisie—one in a stovepipe hat, another in a "pigeontailed coat." Others make do in animal skins, or more appropriately, in a mixture of both. "Biblical" "costumes" and even a weddingveil add to the mix, but both are defiled images of the church. Here, the word "costume" highlights the sense of mocked reality, as does the bloodied weddingveil—now a raped sacrament. Fantastically, nothing of the silk finery or the wedding attire, bloodied or not, is appropriate for the battlefield. More fitting, then, are the cavalry jackets, spanish armors and horned helmets. Yet even these outfits of war are foreign to the American West. They belong to the Old World and another time of dragoons, vikings, and Roman legions. As purposeful anachronisms and relics of the judge's god, the absurd outfits of the Comanches prove the divine continuity of war. In this mutual massacre, the Comanches drench the fabric of the already bloodied uniforms with their own freshly drawn blood, and make new dents in their armor beside the "old blows...by men whose very bones were dust." For this war is all wars, the first war and the last ever to be. Killers of the present repeat the same blood rituals and the same violence of killers past, who are separated by time and space but reunited by war.

Necessarily, the kid upsets this continuity, for he is a warrior only of the present. His utter incapacity to realize figurative representations manifests in his refusal to universalize destruction, extending to a rejection of the universality of creation as well. Early in the novel, the kid encounters a hermit who asks, "God made his world, but he didn't make it to suit everbody, did he?" Revealing an astonishing self-determination, the boy answers: "I don't believe he much had me in mind" (19). Here, the kid implies that God's creation does not suit him, and further, that divine creation is an imperfect universality since it does not take him into account. To modify the judge's own words "a false book is no book at all," an imperfect universality is no universality at all (141). Yet despite his perception of failed order, the kid holds no hostility against the universal divine, either creative or destructive. Neither does he preach his doctrine, as does the judge. The judge's philosophy boasts copious documentation, as it must for his order to hold, yet the kid needs no such high rhetoric or scholarship to sustain his free will.

The judge selects the kid to be his disciple and adopted son precisely because he is the most individualistic and resistant, and thus inscrutable, character among the men of the troop. The judge, who despises even the freedom of birds as personally insulting, cannot bear the kid's difference from the group (199). As Bell points out, "everything in his view is predicated on there being 'no mystery' ... He seems to fear that there is indeed a mystery and that its being would deny his own." To the judge, the kid remains a mystery, what Shaviro calls "a blankness," but the kid does not mirror the judge's intrigue—a severe breach in the judge's order, where he alone must find enjoyment in baffling others by such statements as "the only mystery is that there is no mystery" (252). But unlike the others—Brown, Toadvine, Webster, even Tobin—the kid dismisses the mystery, not only of the world, but also of the judge. He rejects Holden's religion, instinctively recognizing that there is no divinity without mystery. In reply to the expriest's invitation to study the judge's numerous talents, the kid flatly declines: "I done studied him" (122). The kid implies that he knows the judge and is not impressed. The crucial problem is that the judge does not know him.

The judge's final rejection of the kid hinges on two events: the kid's hesitancy and ultimate refusal to kill the judge while he appears naked and defenseless in the desert and the judge's subsequent belief that he now knows the kid, if only as traitor and not a son. First, the kid's refusal of violence asserts both himself and the judge as distinct individuals removed from the universal battleground, and represents a critical transgression against the judge's god, war, which Arnold calls a "collective enterprise." Arnold adds: "For the kid to restrict the group's common ethos of murder by his own individual consciousness is a betrayal of history, the gang, and their 'communal soul.'" Here, Arnold brings to light the decisive conflict between the individuality of the kid and the judge's imagined community of killers. As a killer, the kid is a "free agent," killing freely but not universally. His perverse failure to shoot the judge breaks from the norm of easy violence, which the judge cannot forgive. Even as each unknown creature threatens the judge's consciousness, the slightest perceived hesitation in battle represents a treachery to the judge, for whom the distinction between the individual and communal warrior is decisive. In his inmost mind, the judge fears the notion of the individual, which he associates with the hidden and unknown, while he approves the idea of the community, which implies a shared area of knowledge.

Bell interprets the kid's nonviolence to the judge as an "inability to kill." Arnold attributes it to a failure to "take a stand." Neither are entirely accurate critiques, for the text clearly shows that the kid does indeed take a stand and that he is, at least physically, a very able killer. Three times the kid rejects the expriest's murderous exhortations, at first even physically, ("the expriest clung to his arm whispering…the kid pulled away" 285) and at least three times the kid, whom the expriest boasts is "a deadeye," allows the judge to pass within his gunsights unharmed. Why does the kid allow the judge to live? Fundamentally, the kid's failure to kill represents a failure in knowledge. As I alluded earlier, the kid cannot realize anything beyond what is literal;

essentially, he does not kill the judge because he cannot grasp the reality of the judge's threat. The kid feels a concrete transgression against him when a drunk orders him to move out of his way; similarly, when a barman refuses him a drink, the kid sees a very real problem. In such cases, the kid moves to assault as if by reflex. However, the judge—naked, unarmed, and accompanied only by a slobbering fool—presents absolutely no clear and present danger to the kid, and he will not shoot. Thus, Shaviro's description of the kid's "eerie affectlessness" is at least half correct; for while the kid is fully affected by literal reality, the figurative realm has no place in his consciousness, producing the "blankness" that becomes his fatal flaw.

The judge's most serious grudge against the kid is that he is "no assassin...and no partisan either" (299). He further accuses the kid: "There's a flawed place in the fabric of your heart. Do you think I could not know? You alone were mutinous. You alone reserved in your soul some corner of clemency for the heathen" (299). Here, critics have focused on the judge's condemnation of the kid's supposed "repudiation of the gang through his disavowal of its violence..." While I agree that the judge blames the kid for perceived acts of mercy in their journey, I am more convinced that this passage reflects the stirring of a greater outrage in the inmost depths of the judge's consciousness. Greater than betrayal, greater than treachery, the kid's greatest sin against his potential father figure is his inscrutability, which the judge must conquer before he feels empowered over the kid. Significantly, the judge asks the kid, "Do you think I could not know?" Throughout the novel, in speaking much and asking little, the judge emphasizes the rhetorical strength of his questions, which he also carefully words. Here, he does not ask, do you think I *would* not know. His question is specifically that of capacity. "Do you think I *could* not know?" (both italics mine) The judge views the boy's acts of clemency as a defiance of his ability to know. Twenty-eight years later, the question still burns in the judge: "Was it always your idea, he said, that if you did not speak you would not be recognized? ... I recognized you when I first saw you..." (328). Even when his triumph over the kid is imminent, the judge's obsession with "knowing" and "recognizing" the kid still remains of ultimate importance.

In contrast to the judge, the kid knows almost nothing. Illiterate and schooled only in violence, the kid, according to one critic, seems detached from "an inner life...[which] he does not appear to have." Yet, I believe that the narrative does not wholly eliminate the kid's spirituality. In a rare moment of tenderness, McCarthy writes: "The child's face is curiously untouched behind the scars, the eyes oddly innocent" (4). In light of the implicit opposition of the judge and the kid, the author seems to align knowledge with the irreverent combination of evil and the divine, and ignorance with comparative innocence. Thus, Tobin, significantly an expriest who "has put by the robes of his craft," always knows more than the kid, although far less than the judge (250). Tobin's knowledge only fuels his fear of the judge, a consternation that proves sound in the end, for the judge, in his warfare against the unknown, takes no prisoners. As in the case of the birds and plants that he collects in his ledgers, the judge's record of knowledge exists only by an act of death. In other words, whatever the judge incorporates into his knowledge, he destroys. Earlier, I stated that the judge's special mode of creation is violence. Similarly, his understanding of creation always just precedes its destruction. In one symbolic instance, the judge discovers and traces ancient rock etchings into his book, then scratches out all but one of the walls of art after he finishes with his documentation. On an earlier occasion, the judge studies and sketches the footpiece of a valuable antique suit of armor, but casts the metal into the fire after he completes his sketch.

> ...he seemed much satisfied with the world, as if his counsel had been sought at its creation. A Tennessean named Webster had been watching him and heasked the judge what he aimed to do with those notes and sketches and the judge smiled and said that it was his intention to expunge them from the memory of man. (140)

By capturing representations of creatures and objects into his book and then destroying the original, the judge believes that he is the sole owner of that creation, or that he is essentially the creator himself. He finds power not in the actual knowledge of the universe, or even in the process of gaining that knowledge. Instead, Holden empowers himself against the unknown by the symbolic and actual destruction of all things that enter into his realm of knowledge. In his extreme extension of that logic, the judge's desire to "expunge" all creation "from the memory of man" reflects not only his destructive force but also his longed for creative force. It is the judge's special secret that the more he gains in knowledge, the less the world has to know, for if he finally becomes omniscient, the judge will have destroyed the world.

For the judge, the order of war must prevail, even if that order commands his own death. According to the judge's system, the kid should have killed him, or at least attempted to kill him, for death is universal and violence "the ultimate extension of the individual's will on the opposition of nature and other men." Frustratingly for the judge, his will becomes superfluous in the kid's unresponsiveness, and in their final meeting almost three decades later, the judge returns to this moment as "[t]hat feeling in the breast that evokes a child's memory of loneliness such as when the others have gone and only the game is left with its solitary participant. A solitary game, without opponent" (329). Only a slight figuration of the judge's literal truth, this metaphor recalls the judge's belief of war as a game and underscores his fundamental need for violence and opposition, without which he must endure the "loneliness" of a child without playmates. The kid's nonviolence in this case denies the judge's claim to the ultimate game and immortality, which both rely on the integrity of his god: "If war is not holy man is nothing but antic clay" (307). The judge believes that if war is holy and universal, then he, as the ultimate warrior, is immortal. Paradoxically, he is willing to martyr himself for that faith, for he believes that he is already dead, only mortal "antic clay," without his faith in the divinity of war.

Steven Shaviro notes that "[o]rphanhood is taken for granted in *Blood Meridian*." Like the new American West, the kid, whose "origins are become remote as is his destiny," little values the establishment of ties to the past (4). He remains firmly grounded in the here and now, maintaining disinterest in the judge's approaches for alliance. And when the judge visits him for the second last time, the problem still hinges on the conflict of knowledge: "Don't you know that I'd have loved you like a son? ... You came forward to take part in a work. But you were a witness against yourself. You sat in judgement on your own deeds. ... Hear me, man. I spoke in the desert for you and you only and you turned a deaf ear to me" (306-307). Like their blood that is literally strange to the other, there flows no succession of knowledge from the judge to the kid. Ultimately, whether the judge could have loved the kid, whether his words could have stirred the boy's soul, remains unimportant. Only the kid's recognition of the judge's knowledge and his voice in the desert, has relevance, for the judge continues to rely on knowledge of the *other* and not self for his immortality. The kid's *self*-witness and *self*-judgement, according to the judge, are abominations against his order that require atonement by blood. Although the judge initially desires to adopt the kid as his son, he abandons this plan for that of violence after he feels that he has found the distasteful inner depths of the boy's "good heart." With apparent satisfaction of having solved the problem of the kid's anonymity, Holden seems to withdraw his interest in the kid. Still, the kid remains outside of the judge's knowledge and will, and thus he is not without the judge's destructive intentions.

Judge Holden's belief that he has gained knowledge of the kid should have dissolved the mystery surrounding the young soldier. That it does not seems to recall the judge's own words: "the only mystery is that there is no mystery." Holden intends to confuse the gang by stating that the lack of mystery is a mystery itself, yet the greatest impact of this explanation falls squarely on his own shoulders. The judge cannot tolerate mystery; the mystery of a non-mystery utterly collapses his own system of knowledge.

The judge's hatred of the other, emerging from the legacy of Faulkner's Addie, compels him to know the other and remove his/her alien status. As Bell remarks: "When Judge Holden and what he embodies prevail in history... what is not known and not knowable must become extinct." Yet the judge makes no such demands of the idiot, who, despite his utter alienation from the world's normal order, successfully fills the role denied by the kid. Admittedly, the idiot, who at least has a name and a kin brother, seems less anonymous than the kid, whose name remains only the pronoun 'he' throughout the novel. Still, the idiot is as inscrutable as any unknown beast and even more silent than the kid, traits that normally arouse the judge's violence. Yet the idiot survives as the only nonviolent figure in the book that the judge does not destroy. The judge implicitly understands that the idiot is, by nature, unknowable, not only to him, but to the world, and a peculiar similitude emerges between him and the idiot. For the idiot, who is beyond normal human understanding, beyond even the understanding of violence itself, emanates a perverse sense of the divine that aligns effortlessly with the strange eminence of the judge. Like the judge, who appears immortal, "descended from another world," the idiot resists ordinary human narratives and needs. His brother explains: "He was left to me. Mama died. There was nobody to take him to raise. They shipped him to me... Just put him in a box and shipped him. Took five weeks. Didn't bother him a bit. I opened up the box and there he set. ... Big as life. Never hurt him a bit. I had him a hair suit made but he ate it" (238). In this bizarre tale, the brother traces the idiot's origin to a shipping box. In it, the idiot transcends the mundane deprivations of human necessities for five weeks and emerges from this extraordinary "birth" a superhuman being.

Unlike all the other characters of *Blood Meridian*, who can barely account for even one origin, the idiot sustains a second birth narrative. This time, however, the idiot appears fully human and needs a Savior to "deliver" him from a drowning death. Ironically, it is the judge who saves, for once in unironic benevolence; and unlike the rescue of the Apache boy, the idiot's salvation remains unviolated.

> [The judge] stepped into the river and seized up the drowning idiot, snatching it aloft by he heels like a great midwife and slapping it on the back to let the water out. A birth scene or a baptism or some ritual not yet inaugurated into any canon. He twisted the water from its hair and he gathered the naked and

sobbing fool into his arms and carried it up into the camp and restored it among its fellows. (259)

Although McCarthy leaves the final image of the judge cradling the idiot as a mother carries her babe, the true lasting impression of the passage remains that of a savage and monstrous rebirth. Despite appearances, the judge is no gentle Savior. He "seizes," "snatches," and "twists" the body of the fool and gathers it into his arms. This gesture repeats in the narrative half a lifetime later, when the judge performs an uncanny reversal of this restoration. He kills the kid by smothering him as he "gathers him in his arms against his immense and terrible flesh." Here, the "him" refers to the now-grown kid, the prodigal son who refused the father-figure in the desert. Thus the terrible order of the judge remains intact in his treatment of the three potential son-figures—the kid, the Apache boy, and the fool—all of whom receive some aspect of his universal violence. With the same embrace, the judge restores life to the fool and kills the kid. And, after twenty-eight years, the kid becomes the extended version of the Apache boy whom the judge rescues only to kill later. In the case of the kid, the judge suspends his violence not for three days but for three decades, yet his perverse desire for a universal death has no ultimate variation from his senseless murder of the Indian child so long ago.

Like the one rock painting that the judge leaves to represent the whole, the idiot remains as the symbolic figure of the sons he destroyed. Significantly, the idiot lives because the judge accepts him as unknowable, and fortunately for the fool, the judge only kills after his knowledge of the victim is made complete. However, the kid's dreams prophesy that his name is already entered into the judge's ledgerbook, which only awaits the actual sample or likeness of the man to close the account of the kid forever. Yet the judge allows an inordinate lapse of time to pass before opening the account of the kid again. In the meantime, the kid, now man, seems to undergo a change once more such that he exhibits true "clemency for the heathen." Finding an elderly survivor in the otherwise desolate scene of a massacre, the kid extends a sincere rescue effort, only to find that he is talking to a corpse. Unlike the judge, who appears as a Savior by his unholy resurrection of the fool, the kid, receives no such blessing. Although critics blame the utter frustration of the kid for the anticlimactic and anticathartic nature of its conclusion, I disagree and say that only the kid's defeat is entirely consistent with himself and the novel. From the first pages of *Blood Meridian*, the kid resists immortality, preferring the reality of mortality instead. It is the judge who aspires to immortality, thus the judge who prevails. Shaviro protests: "But there is no purgation or release in this recognition, no curative discharge of fear or pity." Yet despite the violence and the bloodshed, McCarthy's novel elicits very little fear or pity, either in the readers or the characters themselves. The novel thus closes quietly in epilogue: "Then they all move on again"(337). In this final sentence that recalls continuity, movement and repetition, there is purgation and release, for while the judge says he will never die, he is not the only one left alive.

Yet the judge reveals the crucial failure of his claim to divinity in his refusal, indeed destruction, of all potential successors or heirs. To accept an heir, to allow one to survive him, would appear at least an implicit acceptance of his own mortality, which the judge will not grant, except in the most extreme case of martyrdom. Despite the apparent cowardice of the historical Judge Holden, McCarthy's Holden does not fear injury or death in the physical sense. Instead his fear of mortality is deeply, though irrationally, philosophical such that he is willing to die a martyr for the cult of war rather than face its failure as an universal force of creation and destruction both. Thus, Holden's religion remains rather gnostic in nature: maintaining his extreme self-possession, his almost solipcistic certainty of his own metaphysics, the judge boasts he will never die. For as far as we are made to know and as far as he is willing to know, the judge is the sole priest of his faith. He alone knows, he alone survives. Yet, even in his triumph the judge cannot escape his own mortality, which hunts him like a desert lizard and haunts him even in his dance. Thus the judge sacrifices the kid on, and for, the altar of his own immortality. The universe, in his mind, cannot sustain them both, and the knowledge of this difference that remains unconquered even in death takes the judge in a frenzied desperation that is revealed only in the doubletime of his feet to the hideous goading of the fiddlers. Indeed, the kid's murder performs only temporary appeasement for Holden's War, while the procession of bone collectors gathers increasing numbers and fiery sequence. The kid—the son, the heir, the enemy—is dead, but for the killer, there is no joy in victory, indeed no true victory, at all. For a greater challenger approaches—a man with fire and implement of steel—perfectly silent, unknown.

Notes

[1]Blood Meridian, 249.

[2]Vereen M. Bell, *The Achievement of Cormac McCarthy*: "The Metaphysics of Violence" (Baton Rouge: Louisiana State University Press, 1988), pp. 116–135.

[3]Chamberlain, Samuel E. *My Confession*. 1956. Lincoln: University of Nebraska Press, 1987. p271–272.

Chronology

1933	Born in Providence, Rhode Island, the third of six children, to Charles Joseph and Gladys McGrail McCarthy.
1951-52	Attends the University of Tennessee as a liberal arts major.
1953-57	Serves in the U.S. Air Force.
1957-60	Returns to the University of Tennessee.
1961	Marries a fellow student, Lee Holleman, with whom he has a son; divorces later.
1965	*The Orchard Keeper* is published.
1966	Marries Anne DeLisle in England.
1968	*Outer Dark* is published.
1973	*Child of God* is published.
1976	Separates from wife; divorces later. Moves to El Paso, Texas.
1977	*The Gardener's Son*, a screenplay, premieres on public television.
1979	*Suttree* is published.
1985	*Blood Meridian, or The Evening Redness in the West* is published.
1992	*All the Pretty Horses* is published; wins National Book Award for fiction.
1994	*The Stonemason*, a play, is published. *The Crossing* is published.
1998	*Cities of the Plain* is published.

Contributors

HAROLD BLOOM is Sterling Professor of the Humanities at Yale University and Henry W. and Albert A. Berg Professor of English at the New York University Graduate School. He is the author of over 20 books, including *Shelly's Mythmaking* (1959), *The Visionary Company* (1961), *Blake's Apocalypse* (1963), *Yeats* (1970), *A Map of Misreading* (1975), *Kabbalah and Criticism* (1975), *Agon: Toward a Theory of Revisionism* (1982), *The American Religion* (1992), *The Western Canon* (1994), and *Omens of Millennium: The Gnosis of Angels, Dreams, and Resurrection* (1996). *The Anxiety of Influence* (1973) sets forth Professor Bloom's provocative theory of the literary relationships between the great writers and their predecessors. His most recent books include *Shakespeare: The Invention of the Human*, a 1998 National Book Award finalist, and *How to Read and Why*, which was published in 2000. In 1999, Professor Bloom received the prestigious American Academy of Arts and Letters Gold Medal for Criticism.

EDWIN T. ARNOLD is Professor of English at Appalachian State University. He is the co-editor of *Perspectives on Cormac McCarthy*, as well as other literary titles.

VEREEN BELL teaches English at Vanderbilt University. He is the author of *Robert Lowell: Nihilist as Hero.*

MARK BUSBY is Director of the Center for the Study of the Southwest and Professor of English at Southwest Texas State University. He is coeditor (with Dick Heaberlin) of *Southwestern American Literature* and since fall 1996, *Texas Books in Review*

LEO DAUGHERTY has taught literature and linguistics at The Evergreen State College, where he has also been the director of the Center for the Study of Science and Human Values.

JOHN M. GRAMMER teaches English at the University of the South. He is the author of *Pastoral & Politics in the Old South*.

WADE HALL has been a professor of English at Bellarmine College. He is the author of articles, reviews, and books on southern literature.

YOOJIN GRACE KIM has been a literature major at Yale University.

DIANNE C. LUCE has been a Professor of English at Midlands Technical College, Columbia, S.C., where she has chaired the department. She is the co-editor of *Perspectives on Cormac McCarthy* and has written other works on southern writers.

BARCLEY OWENS has taught composition and American literature at Big Bend Community College. He also writes short fiction.

TIM PARRISH teaches English at Southern Connecticut State University. He is the author of a book of short stories.

SARA L. SPURGEON has been a Ph.D. student at the University of Arizona in Tucson. She is the co-author of the nonfiction study *Writing the Southwest*.

Bibliography

Aldridge, John W. "Cormac McCarthy's Bizarre Genius," *Atlantic Monthly* 274 (1994): p. 89.

Arnold, Edwin T. "Blood and Grace: The Fiction of Cormac McCarthy," *Commonweal* 121, no. 19 (November 4, 1994): pp. 11-12, 14, 16.

———. "Cormac McCarthy's *The Stonemason*: The Unmaking of a Play," *Southern Quarterly* 33, nos. 2-3 (Winter-Spring 1995): pp. 117-29.

———. "Naming, Knowing and Nothingness: McCarthy's Moral Parables," *Southern Quarterly* 30, no. 4 (Summer 1992): pp. 31-50.

Arnold, Edwin T., and Luce, Dianne C., eds. *Perspectives on Cormac McCarthy*. Jackson: University Press of Mississippi, 1993.

Bartlett, Andrew. "From Voyeurism to Archaeology: Cormac McCarthy's *Child of God*," *Southern Literary Journal* 24, no. 1 (Fall 1991): pp 3-15.

Bell, Vereen M. *The Achievement of Cormac McCarthy*. Baton Rouge: Louisiana State University Press, 1988.

———. "The Ambiguous Nihilism of Cormac McCarthy," *Southern Literary Journal* 15 (1983): pp. 31-41.

Berry, K. Wesley. "The Lay of the Land in Cormac McCarthy's *The Orchard Keeper* and *Child of God*," *Southern Quarterly* 38, no. 4 (Summer 2000): pp. 61-77.

Bingham, Arthur. "Syntactic Complexity and Iconicity in Cormac McCarthy's *Blood Meridian*," *Language and Literature* 20 (1995): pp. 19-33.

Campbell, Neil. "'Beyond Reckoning': Cormac McCarthy's Version of the West in *Blood Meridian or the Evening Redness in the West*," *Critique: Studies in Contemporary Fiction* 39, no. 1 (Fall 1997): pp. 55-64.

Cawelti, John G. "Cormac McCarthy: Restless Seekers." In *Southern Writers at Century's End*. Jeffrey J. Folks and James H. Justus, eds. Lexington: University Press of Kentucky, 1997, pp. 164-76.

Cheuse, Alan. "A Note on Landscape in *All The Pretty Horses*," *Southern Quarterly* 30, no. 4 (Summer 1992): pp. 140-42.

Cole, Kevin L. "McCarthy's *The Crossing*," *Explicator* 55, no. 2 (Winter 1997): pp. 112-14.

Ditsky, John. "Further Into Darkness: The Novels of Cormac McCarthy," *Hollins Critic* (April 18, 1981): pp. 1-11.

Dougherty, William H. "Crossing," *Verbatim* 21, no. 4 (Spring 1995): pp. 5-7.

Hada, Kenneth. "McCarthy's *The Crossing*," *Explicator* 58, no. 1 (Fall 1999): pp. 57-60.

Hall, Wade, and Rick Wallach, eds. *Sacred Violence: A Reader's Companion to Cormac McCarthy*. El Paso: Texas Western, 1995.

Holloway, David. "Modernism, Nature, and Utopia: Another Look at 'Optical Democracy' in Cormac McCarthy's Western Quartet," *Southern Quarterly* 38, no. 3 (Spring 2000): pp. 186-205.

———. *Proceedings of the First European Conference on Cormac McCarthy*. Miami, FL: Cormac McCarthy Society, 1999.

Hunt, Alex. "McCarthy's *The Crossing*," *Explicator* 56, no. 3 (Spring 1998): pp. 158-60.

Hunt, Alexander. "'Strange Equality': A Reading of McCarthy's *Blood Meridian*." In *The Image of the American West in Literature, the Media, and Society*, Will Wright and Steven Kaplan, eds. Pueblo, CO: Society for the Interdisciplinary Study of Social Imagery, 1996, pp. 237-40.

Jarrett, Robert L. *Cormac McCarthy*. New York: Twayne, 1997.

Longley, John Lewis, Jr. "*Suttree* and the Metaphysics of Death," *Southern Literary Journal* 17 (Spring 1985): p. 79-90.

Luce, Dianne C. "Cormac McCarthy: A Bibliography," *Southern Quarterly* 30, no. 4 (Summer 1992): pp. 143-51.

———. "Cormac McCarthy's First Screenplay: 'The Gardener's Son,'" *Southern Quarterly* 30, no. 4 (Summer 1992): pp. 51-71 .

———. "On the Trail of History in McCarthy's *Blood Meridian*," *Mississippi Quarterly* 49 (1996): pp. 843-49.

———. "The Vanishing World of Cormac McCarthy's Border Trilogy," *Southern Quarterly* 38, no. 3 (Spring 2000): pp. 121-46.

MacDonald, Andrew, and MacDonald, Gina. "Heroism and Romance in *All the Pretty Horses*," *Creative Screenwriting* 7, no. 6 (November-December 2000): pp. 44-46.

Masters, Joshua J. 'Witness to the Uttermost Edge of the World': Judge Holden's Textual Enterprise in Cormac McCarthy's *Blood Meridian*," *Critique* 40, no. 1 (Fall 1998): pp. 25-37.

Mills, Jerry Leath. "Cormac McCarthy (1933-   )." In Flora, Joseph M., and Robert Bain, eds. *Contemporary Fiction Writers of the South: A Bio-Bibliographical Sourcebook.* Westport, CT: Greenwood, 1993, pp. 286-94.

Owens, Barcley. *Cormac McCarthy's Western Novels.* Tucson: University of Arizona Press, 2000.

Phillips, Dana. "History and the Ugly Facts of Cormac McCarthy's *Blood Meridian*," *American Literature* 68, no. 2 (June 1996): pp. 433-60.

Pilkington, Tom. "Fate and Free Will on the American Frontier: Cormac McCarthy's Western Fiction," *Western American Literature* 27, no. 4 (February 1993): pp. 311-22.

Pitts, Jonathan. "Writing On: *Blood Meridian* as Devisionary Western," *Western American Literature* 33, no. 1 (Spring 1998): pp. 7-25.

Pughe, Thomas. "Revision and Vision: Cormac McCarthy's *Blood Meridian*," *Revue Française d'Etudes Américaines* 17, no. 62 (November 1994): pp. 371-82.

Ragan, David Paul. "Values and Structure in *The Orchard Keeper*," *Southern Quarterly* 30, no. 4 (Summer 1992): pp. 10-18.

Schafer, William J. "Cormac McCarthy: The Hard Wages of Original Sin," *Appalachian Journal* 4 (Winter 1977): pp. 105-19.

Schopen, Bernard. "'They Rode On': *Blood Meridian* and the Art of Narrative," *Western American Literature* 30, no. 2 (Summer 1995): pp. 179-94.

Sepich, John Emil. "A 'Bloody Dark Pastryman': Cormac McCarthy's Recipe for Gunpowder and Historical Fiction in *Blood Meridian*," *Mississippi Quarterly* 46, no. 4 (Fall 1993): pp. 547-63.

———. "The Dance of History in Cormac McCarthy's *Blood Meridian*," *Southern Literary Journal* 24, no. 1 (Fall 1991): pp. 16-31.

———. "'What Kind of Indians Was Them?' Some Historical Sources in Cormac McCarthy's *Blood Meridian*," *Southern Quarterly* 30, no. 4 (Summer 1992): pp. 93-110.

Shaviro, Steven. "'The Very Life of the Darkness': A Reading of *Blood Meridian*," *Southern Quarterly* 30, no. 4 (Summer 1992): pp. 111-21.

Shaw, Patrick W. "The Kid's Fate, the Judge's Guilt: Ramifications of Closure in Cormac McCarthy's *Blood Meridian*," *Southern Literary Journal* 30, no. 1 (Fall 1997): pp. 102-19.

Shelton, Frank W. "*Suttree* and Suicide," *Southern Quarterly* 29, no.1 (Fall 1990): pp. 71-83.

Softing, Inger Anne. "Desert Pandemonium: Cormac McCarthy's Apocalyptic 'Western' in *Blood Meridian*," *American Studies in Scandinavia* 31, no. 2 (1999): pp. 13-30.

Spencer, William C. "Evil Incarnate in *Blood Meridian*: Cormac McCarthy's Seductive Judge," *Publications of the Mississippi Philological Association* (1995): pp. 100-105.

———. "On the Range of Styles in *All the Pretty Horses*," *Publications of the Mississippi Philological Association* (2000): pp. 55-61.

Sullivan, Nell. "Boys Will Be Boys and Girls Will Be Gone: The Circuit of Male Desire in Cormac McCarthy's Border Trilogy," *Southern Quarterly* 38, no. 3 (Spring 2000): pp. 167-85.

Sullivan, Walter. "Model Citizens and Marginal Cases: Heroes of the Day," *Sewanee Review* 87 (April 1979): pp. 337-44.

———. "'Where Have All the Flowers Gone?' Part II: the Novel in the Gnostic Twilight," *Sewanee Review* 78 (October 1970): pp. 654-64.

———. "Worlds Past and Future: A Christian and Several from the South," *Sewanee Review* 73 (Autumn 1965): pp. 719-26.

Snyder, Phillip A. "Cowboy Codes in Cormac McCarthy's Border Trilogy," *Southern Quarterly* 38, no. 3 (Spring 2000): pp. 147-66.

Twomey, Jay. "Tempting the Child: the Lyrical Madness of Cormac McCarthy's *Blood Meridian*," 37, nos. 3-4 (Spring-Summer 1999): pp. 255-65.

Wallace, Garry. "Meeting McCarthy," *Southern Quarterly* 30, no. 4 (Summer 1992): pp. 134-39.

Wallach, Rick. "From Beowulf to *Blood Meridian*: Cormac McCarthy's Demystification of the Martial Code," *Southern Quarterly* 36, no. 4 (Summer 1998): pp. 113-20.

———. *Myth, Legend, Dust: Critical Responses to Cormac McCarthy*, New York: St. Martin's Press, 2000.

Wegner, John. "Whose Story Is It? History and Fiction in Cormac McCarthy's *All the Pretty Horses*," *Southern Quarterly* 36, no. 2 (Winter 1998): pp. 103-110.

Winchell, Mark Royden. "Inner Dark: Or, the Place of Cormac McCarthy," *Southern Review* 26, no. 2 (Spring 1990): pp. 293-309.

Witek, Terri. "'He's Hell When He's Well': Cormac McCarthy's Rhyming Dictions," *Shenandoah* 41 (Fall 1991): pp. 51-66.

———. "Reeds and Hides: Cormac McCarthy's Domestic Spaces," *Southern Review* 30 (1994): pp. 136-42.

Woodson, Linda Townley. "'The Lighted Display Case': A Nietzschean Reading of Cormac McCarthy's Border Fiction," *Southern Quarterly* 38, no. 4 (Summer 2000): pp. 48-60.

Woodward, Richard B. "Cormac McCarthy's Venomous Fiction," *New York Times Magazine* (April 19, 1992): pp. 28-31+.

Young, Thomas D., Jr. "The Imprisonment of Sensibility: *Suttree*," *Southern Quarterly* 30, no. 4 (Summer 1992): pp. 72-92.

Acknowledgments

"Cormac McCarthy: *Blood Meridian*," by Harold Bloom. From *How to Read and Why*. ©2000 by Harold Bloom. Reprinted by permission.

"A Thing Against Which Time Will Not Prevail: Pastoral and History in Cormac McCarthy's South," by John M. Grammer. From *The Southern Quarterly* 30, no. 4 (Summer 1992): 19-30. ©1992 by the University of Southern Mississippi. Reprinted by permission.

"Gravers False and True: *Blood Meridian* as Gnostic Tragedy," by Leo Daugherty. From *The Southern Quarterly* 30, no. 4 (Summer 1992): 122-33. ©1992 by the University of Southern Mississippi. Reprinted by permission.

"Between the Wish and the Thing the World Lies Waiting," by Vereen Bell. From *The Southern Review* 28, no. 4 (October 1992): 920-27. ©1992 by Louisiana State University. Reprinted by permission.

"The Mosaic of McCarthy's Fiction," by Edwin T. Arnold. From *Sacred Violence: A Reader's Companion to Cormac McCarthy*. ©1995 by Texas Western Press. Reprinted by permission.

"The Human Comedy of Cormac McCarthy," by Wade Hall. From *Sacred Violence: A Reader's Companion to Cormac McCarthy*. ©1995 by Texas Western Press. Reprinted by permission.

"The Killer Wears the Halo: Cormac McCarthy, Flannery O'Connor, and the American Religion," by Tim Parrish. From *Sacred Violence: A Reader's*

Companion to Cormac McCarthy. ©1995 by Texas Western Press. Reprinted by permission.

"'Pledged in Blood': Truth and Redemption in Cormac McCarthy's *All the Pretty Horses,*" by Sara L. Spurgeon. From *Western American Literature* 34, no. 1 (Spring 1999): pp. 25-43. ©1999 by the Western Literature Association. Reprinted by permission.

"Thematic Motifs in *Cities of the Plain,*" by Barcley Owens. From *Cormac McCarthy's Western Novels.* ©2000 by the Arizona Board of Regents. Reprinted by permission.

"'They Aint the Thing': Artifact and Hallucinated Recollection in Cormac McCarthy's Early Frame-Works," by Dianne C. Luce. From *Myth, Legend, Dust: Critical Responses to Cormac McCarthy.* ©2000 by the Manchester University Press. Reprinted by permission.

"The Last Stage of the Hero's Evolution: Cormac McCarthy's *Cities of the Plain,*" by Charles Bailey. From *Myth, Legend, Dust: Critical Responses to Cormac McCarthy.* ©2000 by the Manchester University Press. Reprinted by permission.

"Into the Darkening Land, the World to Come: Cormac McCarthy's Border Crossings," by Mark Busby. From *Myth, Legend, Dust: Critical Responses to Cormac McCarthy.* ©2000 by the Manchester University Press. Reprinted by permission.

"'Then They All Move on Again': Knowledge and the Individual in Judge Holden's Doctrine of War," by Yoojin Grace Kim. Paper, Yale University (December 1999): pp. 1-23. Reprinted by permission.

Index